Bittermelons and Mimosas

A Philippine Memoir

Nieves Catahan Villamin

PORTLAND • OREGON
INKWATERPRESS.COM

Copyright © 2012 by Nieves Catahan Villamin

Edited by: Susie Borrero and Ann Schafer
Foreword by: Margie Talaugon

Cover and interior design by Masha Shubin

Floral Background © Misha. BigStockPhoto.com

All rights reserved. No part of this book may be reproduced or transmitted in any form or by any means whatsoever, including photocopying, recording or by any information storage and retrieval system, without written permission from the publisher and/or author. Contact Inkwater Press at 6750 SW Franklin Street, Suite A, Portland, OR 97223-2542. 503.968.6777

www.inkwaterpress.com

ISBN-13 978-1-59299-602-5
ISBN-10 1-59299-602-7

LCCN: 2011929730

Publisher: Inkwater Press

Printed in the U.S.A.
All paper is acid free and meets all ANSI standards for archival quality paper.

3 5 7 9 10 8 6 4 2

Praise

❧ NIEVES VILLAMIN'S BOOK is an indispensable reference for anyone interested in Philippine history, customs, and superstitions.

As a child in the Philippines, Nieves' life was a challenge – back-breaking fieldwork, a father who often wasn't there, and dirt-poor living conditions. Yet, this little girl found things to be thankful for such as the singing of the workers while they toiled under blistering sun. Her childlike sense of hope will inspire young readers and make them grateful for living conditions in America.

Full of historical data, the memoir also describes in detail a sort of magical thinking that ruled the Philippine people; plus, it celebrates foods, traditions, and rituals that will interest all.

How she and her young husband escaped to America and found "a land of opportunity" will amuse, impress, and inspire all-age readers. I enjoyed reading this memoir; in fact, I read it three times. You are sure to enjoy it, too.

BECKY WHITE
Author, *Double Luck* and *Betsy Ross*

❧ NIEVES VILLAMIN TAKES us on an unforgettable journey. Her stories are powerful. The writing is heartfelt. This book is part history, part cultural document, and part testimonial to the power of the human spirit.

DAVE CONGALTON
Clear Channel Radio

❧ FLEDGLING AUTHOR NIEVES Villamin has created a graphic memoir of life in the Philippines in the 1960s. It's the tale of a young girl who grows up with a special connection to the Sumacab barrio and the Pampanga River, and who struggles to get the one thing most important to her – an education. Then, in the midst of the Marcos regime, she and her husband Danny flee to the United States, leaving behind their daughter until they can get settled. They escape for a life of freedom, knowing it will be hard but full of hope, and eventually they're able to bring their family back together. Because, in Villamin's own words, "Among Filipinos, everyone is a relation – be it by blood or by acquaintance. We take care of one another in good and bad times."

Villamin's natural writing style and her keen storytelling ability create a tapestry of the close-knit community of Sumacab, with relatives, neighbors, and other assorted characters, each with their own personalities. Her anecdotes are rich with detail, and she turns mundane into memorable with lively vignettes.

It's a fascinating look at life short on luxuries but long on compassion, joy, and family. For a glimpse into this world, just pick up *Bittermelons and Mimosas* and start reading.

JANET MUSICK
Senior Editor, Tigress Press, LLC

FACING INSURMOUNTABLE CHALLENGES, the writer embraces life with vigor, courage, and passion, as it is art itself. Nieves produced a literary gem that is rich in culture of the natives of her birthplace. Though she may have lived in America for more than 35 years, her heart continues to beat for the people she left behind. This is a must read for anyone who wants to transcend the beauty and tradition of another culture. Historically, the Filipinos have been under numerous oppressors and saviors that any attempt to understand its unique culture would be a challenge to anyone not familiar with it. But once it's met, you will find yourself with a priceless possession of a friend who would give everything for a lasting friendship. Anything.

PURA DUMANDAN
President, Cabanatuan City Association
of Los Angeles 2007–2009

NIEVES' STORY REMINDS us that despite our perceived cultural and individual differences and the divergent ways in which we navigate through life, certain experiences are universal and guaranteed:

we will all know the joys of love, the sorrows of death and loss, and the apprehension and excitement of the change, uncertainty, and new beginnings that ultimately prove to be life's only constant. It is through reading stories like *Bittermelons and Mimosas* that cultural gaps are narrowed and we come to understand and celebrate each other for what makes us unique in addition to what makes us simply human.

BRYN SMITH
Assistant Coordinator, Cal Poly
Multi Cultural Center
Cal Poly State University,
San Luis Obispo, California

NIEVES VILLAMIN IS in every sense a true humanitarian and a "point of light" in this troubled world. Her book, *Bittermelons and Mimosas*, is an inspiration to us all. She traveled a difficult journey and has become a true global citizen dedicated to a better world. Hopefully all who read her book will change into more loving persons, who will, in turn, make their small piece of life better for those around them. For those who come to the USA seeking a more rewarding life, *Bittermelons and Mimosas* will provide guidance and perspective to a challenging adaptation to a new culture and way of life. She brought America a strong heart and sturdy back which had improved the country for native born and immigrant Americans, even her humor provides an in depth understanding of life, adjustment and overall zest for small happiness and sorrow. Her joy in living is expressed throughout her book and brings a gentle smile to all her readers. Her story-telling format makes the book fun to read even during the difficult passages. She provides a role model for immigrants and paves the way for enriching the American society.

BARBARA R. ANDRE
Associate Director, International
Education and Programs
California Polytechnic State University
San Luis Obispo, California

Dedication

To my parents Margarito and Marcela Catahan
who gave me life. I miss you very much.

and to

My husband Danny; and children, Edna and Elaine;
I love you with all my heart.

and to

My granddaughter Isabelle,
the girl whose smile glows lovelier and brighter
than the moon and stars combined
with every passing day.
You are my most precious, my joy, and my love.

and in memory of

Satchmo and Mocchi,
our beloved pets who gave us tremendous joys.

Table of Contents

Praise iii
Dedication vii
Acknowledgments xi
Foreword xv
Introduction xvii
Chapter 1: 8,000 Miles Away From Home 1
Chapter 2: Heroes and Lost Souls 20
Chapter 3: Country First 49
Chapter 4: The Young Ones 63
Chapter 5: Missing Coins in the Year of the Bounty 78
Chapter 6: Farmers in the Dell 90
Chapter 7: A Year of *"Halo-Halo"* Blessings 115
Chapter 8: Beautiful Dreamers 130
Chapter 9: Breaking Away 150
Chapter 10: Almost There 163
Chapter 11: A Wilted Mimosa Bloomed 170
Chapter 12: The Charlatan, the Macho, and the Prince 183
Chapter 13: The *Sukob* Fears 202
Chapter 14: Because We Have Each Other 211
Chapter 15: Postcards From the United States 224
Chapter 16: The *Sukob* Years 256
Chapter 17: The Rest of the 20th Century 260
Chapter 18: Sinners or Saints 266
Chapter 19: Breaking the Cycle 271
A Letter From My Father 283
Chapter 20: Epilogue 290
A Reflection on Historical Contexts and Themes in *Villamin's*
  Bittermelons and Mimosas 302
The Pilipino Cultural Exchange (PCE) 307
Bibliography – Suggested Books and Reading Materials 336
About the Author 338

Acknowledgments

I extend my eternal gratitude and appreciation to the following:

To my father, who, through our exchanges of letters and hours of conversation during my visits, had recounted to me: the unbelievable tales of woe about his farmer lineage which helped define his idealism and passionate traits; the challenges of being a father to a large and growing family while fighting for a cause during and after the war. To my mother who, during my father's absences, wore her pants better than most men in our neighborhood did. I miss you both so much.

To Dr. Marcelino D. Catahan, my Kuya Lino, my brother and my keeper, and our family's Moses. I thank you for your invaluable contribution through research, and for reliving and sharing your juvenile experiences while growing up in Sumacab. I would not have been able to put together this book without your massive input. I owe you a lot for what I have accomplished professionally.

To Sanse Conchita Catahan Lestones, the toughest foot soldier in my father's battalion and my mother's right arm. You worked harder than any man to help feed and clothe eleven children for many years. Thank you for providing me with details of our family's struggles especially during our father's incarceration for being a Huk member. I was there but I was too young to remember all.

To my sister, Amelia Catahan Reyes. Parts of your body may have been broken from the accident that killed our oldest sister, but your spirit remained whole. You were an inspiration during one of our family's most trying periods. To my little sister Beth Catahan Sarmiento, our Bunso (youngest), who as years passed became the token eldest. Thanks a million for all your sacrifices to make our parents comfortable during the last days of their lives. To Gertrude, my sister with

Nieves Catahan Villamin

the purest of all hearts, and the one I treasure the most. You filled my place the first time I left Sumacab so I could pursue a higher education in Manila. To my other brother, Diko Unti, for continuing our father's legacy with the same passion that endeared him to our barriomates. I appreciate all your efforts. And I love you all.

To our HUK days councilman Andres Quimzom, Sr., and Second Teniente del Barrio Basilio Catahan of Sumacab, Cabanatuan City, Uncles Gorio and Pedro, and their families. Tatang's children got a new lease on life when you sought my father's early release from prison and helped feed his family. Thankfully you had the power to do it. Like my father, you were all true patriots. I can see you all in heaven, having an animated discussion about the HUKs, our unsung heroes.

To my favorite elementary school teacher Mr. Patricio Navarro. That one afternoon in the fifth grade when you picked me to lead the Pledge of Allegiance for our daily morning flag ceremonies became a turning point in my juvenile years. I wish I were able to tell you in person that your trust had laid out the foundation for my aspirations of a better life beyond Sumacab.

To all my Sumacab barriomates, dead and alive, thank you for the memories!

To Bert Pajar. You were the first step on the ladder of success I was determined to climb, as I clutched my dreams close to my heart with fervor and resolve. Your friendship, first with my brother, then with me, is a treasure I will always cherish.

To Chairman Demetrio Quirino, Jr., and Dr. Teresita U. Quirino, I can't thank you enough for all the opportunities you gave most of your deserving students, me included. You turned my dream into hope and hope sprung eternal. Since then, I have looked up to both of you with much regard and awe.

To Rita and Jimmy Yalung. I have yet to meet another newlywed couple that would give up two weeks of their honeymoon so they could share their home with total strangers. You demonstrated Filipino hospitality in its purest form: friendly, trusting, and selfless. For that, my family is forever grateful.

To Atty. Ruperto Sampoleo, Cal Poly San Luis Obispo, CA's Dr. Barbara Andre and Dr. Taufik, first my mentors, then my friends. The Pilipino Cultural Exchange Club (PCE) was very fortunate to have you as advocates during my club advisory days. I applaud your courage in taking part in PCE's Philippine educational and cultural explorations. Both you and the students motivated me greatly to transform my memoirs into print.

To Mayor Jay Vergara of Cabanatuan City. Many thanks for hosting Cal Poly PCE's cultural/educational program over the past few years. I so admire your commitment to better the lives of the residents in our beautiful city.

To Pura Dumandan, you are a wise woman. I valued your score of suggestions and our volley of ideas during the few past months. You were a great listener and a communicator as well. I am privileged to have you as a friend because you share my passion in writing.

To all members of my cheering squad: Jun and Cynthia Gonzalez, Roger and Lydia Marcelo, Gerry and Marina Perez, Lito and Vangie Aquilizan, Drs. Art and Anna Onglao, Nestor and Yvonne Arguilla, Donna Brown, Jorge Jacinto, James Steitz, Mary Jane Puett, for your bighearted WOWs – it was great to have all of you on my team.

And to Becky White and Ann Schafer: My everlasting gratefulness goes to both of you for resuscitating my book and giving it a new life. I appreciate the fact that I did not have to break my bamboo bank to obtain your professional advice.

Last but not least I give my greatest appreciation to TIP's "Hawkeye" Dean Severino (Boy) Pader, who did an excellent job in proofreading my manuscript. Your "third eye" did the trick.

Foreword

To the first Filipino immigrants, the price of leaving their homeland was beyond their expectations. Their memories of growing up with family and the warmth of their culture and traditions that bound them together were things they would always remember for the rest of their lives. My father, Serapio (Apiong) Cabatuan, like many of our *manongs* (elder brothers/relatives), could never return home. Until he married my mother, he had lived a life of desperation in California and Alaska. The promises of equality, education, and freedom never came to be. At the turn of the 20th century, Filipinos were already considered "nationals" of the United States. A campaign to recruit the new work force to America – via Hawaii – was successful.

Like the farmer tenants in the Philippines, the *manongs* had no rights. Worse, they lived in an all-male society of their own, segregated from the larger population, unlike the society from which they were uprooted. As monolingual residents – in their different dialects – only a very few became educated in the American language. They served as the agricultural and domestic workers in America. Laws were used against them – to the extent that any other nationality that chose to marry a Filipino was threatened to lose their citizenship as an American. My mother Margaret Lopez was fortunate to arrive in the United States with her family in 1924. Grandpa Lopez was a cement finisher, who was contracted and sponsored to work in America by an American cement company. Mom was educated in

Margie Talaugon with her husband Joe.

xv

Nieves Catahan Villamin

Stockton, California. At home, they observed Filipino customs and traditions; it was punctuated with Grandpa Lopez's Hispanic ways, particularly his style of enforcing discipline. He always reminded his family that he was to be respected and his word was law.

I was born in America and so were my four siblings. As Filipino-Americans, we grew up hearing our parents speak Filipino, seeing them comfort themselves following the Filipino ways, and listening to their stories that had anywise transmitted to us Filipino culture. My father became a naturalized citizen after World War II but never was Americanized. My husband Joe and I feel our children, grandchildren, and great-grandchildren will benefit from our Filipino culture and traditions.

Nieves Villamin has given a poignant description of her family and the strength of family in celebrating their culture and traditions, through adversity and the struggles in life. Her memoir is an absolute narrative of family, tradition, and culture. It bolsters the creed that says that one's homeland will always be in the heart and never lost in memory.

A memoir well worth reading.

MARGIE TALAUGON
Co-founder of the Guadalupe
Cultural Arts and Education Center

Introduction

When I was growing up, life in the barrio lane was like a narrow road that ended where it began and led to nowhere. My ancestors lived and died as tenant farmers. Their simple lives were devoid of material things, but very fulfilled because their family units were strong. When the western culture along with modern inventions pervaded their simple lives, it offered the younger generations changes and opportunities beyond their imaginations. Migration to other places or countries became the norm – thus unsettling the once stable family unit. Separation was bitter at first, but the payback later was sweet. Bitter at first like the taste of a bittermelon. The bittermelon, or the *ampalaya*, is one of my favorite Asian vegetables, even though its taste measures up to its name; the bitter taste goes all the way down to the seeds. When cooked with the right ingredients, however, it becomes a magnificent dish. When you are fortunate enough to have an icy mimosa drink to follow, the meal becomes an Epicurean delight.

Thus was my childhood – fraught with difficult periods of adversity and pain, and times when the future loomed bleakly before me. But the prevalence of love and affection from my family and friends had helped me understand early on that love for one's country transcends all boundaries, and often it could cause untold hardships to a growing family. I had an absentee father who chose to serve the HUKBALAHAP movement and helped spread the doctrine of "country first before family" for many years when I was growing up. The HUKs in the beginning were economic freedom fighters that had waged war against their landlords for a better share of the fruits of the land they farmed. And when bigger battles were fought, whether they were the American or Japanese invaders, they hungered for freedom more than ever. Many families like ours suffered immeasurably during those hard times.

Nieves Catahan Villamin

Farmers – perhaps because of their longing for economic freedom – had a tunnel vision about their children being apparent foot soldiers that would march with their parents' legacies even after they, themselves, were long gone. More foot soldiers were always better, so they thought.

I left Sumacab many years ago, but Sumacab never left me. If I moved back to Sumacab tomorrow, I would feel as if I had never left. I would breathe the same cool, early morning air and swelter in the midday heat with the people I loved. I would catch up on family gossip – as we gathered in front of a neighbor's small variety store – and join the women in a "washing soiled clothes marathon" in the river during the summer days. In my younger days, I abhorred living this kind of life. I was a dreamer; the one whom they labeled "Ebeng Mapangarap" or "Ebeng The Dreamer." The one who was willing to do anything to avoid being a farmer's daughter for the rest of her life. Yet now that I am in my "golden years" and away from my childhood home, I have come to understand and appreciate my life in Sumacab. Maybe it has something to do with the way people in Sumacab bonded to survive the difficult days, especially when harvest was scant and hunger lay in wait, and neither private help nor government aid was anywhere in sight.

In adulthood, I traveled half the world to a foreign land and settled thereat to change the life I despised in my youth. And so it was in my adulthood when the mimosa drink chased away the aftertaste of bittermelon. This is the time of joy and contentment, when all seemed well with the world engulfing me. Bitter and sweet both words describe the childhood memories I shall forever cherish.

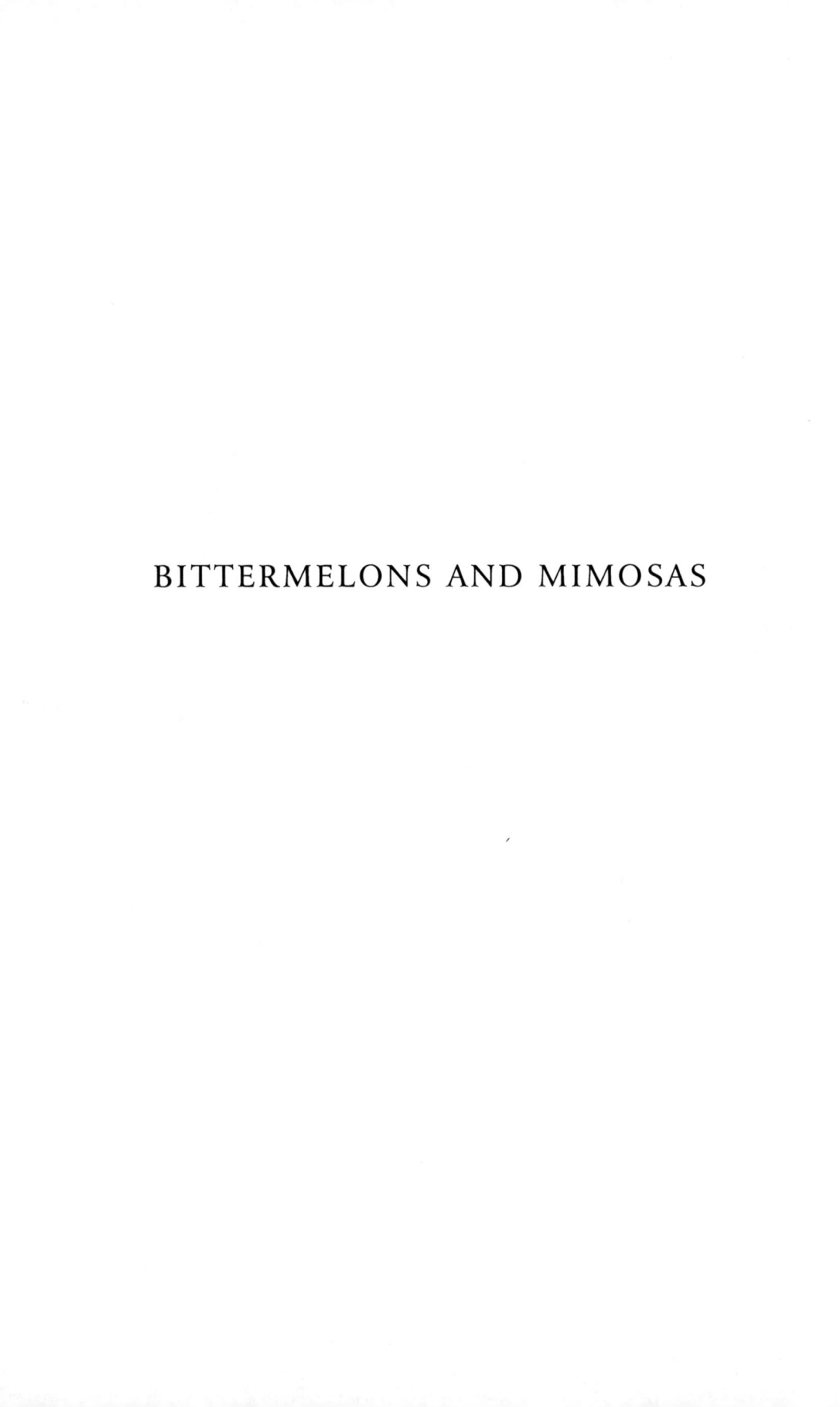

BITTERMELONS AND MIMOSAS

Chapter One

8,000 Miles Away From Home

The only wealth I have had
in my youth were my parents.
Sans a mother or a father,
life would have been unbearable.

Anonymous

I knew it was almost six o'clock in the morning because Satchmo, the whiter-than-snow Persian Himalayan alarm clock with matching ears and paws of gold, was on top of our bed, already harassing Master Danny. Anxiously purring as if he could sense an ominous morning.

"Satchmo, no, stop kissing me! I need some more sleep." Danny's voice sounded annoyed yet almost pleading lovingly at the cat.

It was our daughter Elaine who gave Satchmo his name. She said the cat reminded her of an Ella Fitzgerald quote: "If you don't know Satchmo, you don't know love."

And it wasn't hard to fall in love with Satchmo. Danny and Satchmo had become instant buddies the minute Satchmo set foot in our living room a few days before. Satchmo would meow and Danny would respond to him; Danny would call and Satchmo would readily come to him, purring and whirling around Danny's legs. But this morning was different. Master Danny hadn't gone to bed until almost 12 o'clock the previous night, having made a ten-hour marathon trip to the Bay area to deliver a job. I wondered – would Satchmo turn his new master into an enemy? Teasing a sleep-deprived Danny would

1

be Satchmo's undoing. And from the looks of it, nothing would get Danny out of bed – not even an earthquake like the 1989 San Francisco temblor that rearranged parts of the San Francisco Bay Bridge into a stack of pancakes.

So how could Satchmo's kisses do otherwise? Satchmo was not about to argue. He was a very smart cat. During the week we had been taking care of Satchmo for our daughter, he had learned that when Master Danny says "NO," you didn't get anything if you kept on insisting.

"Meow, meow." He jumped over to my side of the bed and purred into my right ear. I made the mistake of tapping his head gently. His purr got louder. Like the sucker I was, I held him closer to me.

"What do you need anyway?" I talked to him as if he were the son we never had.

He was kissing me now. "Meow, meow, what do you mean what do I need?" Satchmo lifted his head like a child (sometimes I think he thought he was) and meowed in my face. He was getting annoyed. I felt his whiskers tickling my cheek.

"Meow, food, woman, food." Satchmo's meow got louder. "You made me eat leftovers last night. Master Danny always makes sure my bowl is filled with fresh chow." The cat was taking out his frustrations on me.

It was my turn to get annoyed. "Don't you yell at me! I was just trying to be nice to you. Go harass your Master Danny, instead of me." I pulled up my blanket and covered my head.

Satchmo was about to hop back on Danny's side when the phone rang. The ringing startled him. He leaped out of bed and stalked off in disgust. Experience has taught me that phone calls coming through before the crack of dawn are long distance calls – mostly for emergencies. My mind raced through possible scenarios as I reached above the headboard and grabbed the receiver, almost dropping it on Danny's head. My hands were unsteady.

"Hello. Hello." It was my sister Beth on the other end.

"What's happening?" I asked.

"Kaka (title of respect for a fifth older sister), Tatang (Tagalog

Bittermelons and Mimosas

word for father) is in the hospital. I've already made calls to our other sisters."

Though she was miles away, I could hear the anxiety in Beth's voice. I rose out of bed and reached up to turn on the headboard lights. I sat on top of the mattress and prepared myself for a serious and lengthy conversation.

"How sick is he?" My words almost choked me. I felt as if I might pass out. I could sense the worst about my father's health.

"Very. The prostate cancer is back. It's stage four already." A nurse, Beth understood the gravity of our father's illness. "Come immediately if you want to talk to him while he is still coherent."

Danny was fully awake when I said goodbye to Beth. As I put down the receiver, he said, "I think you should go ASAP." He got up to follow Satchmo, who, upon hearing his master's footsteps, hurried to the kitchen and waited there beside his empty bowl, looking proud of himself. In just a few days, he had already trained his master to be out of bed at six o'clock every morning. Not fully awake, Danny would turn on the coffeepot in the kitchen then fill the cat's bowl with fresh chow.

I didn't think twice about visiting my father. I booked a flight as soon as Japan Airlines opened its lines for reservations. Airlines go out of their way to accommodate passengers with medical emergencies or deaths in the family, so I didn't have any problem booking an immediate flight to Manila.

After the 16-hour flight that seemed longer than eternity, Japan Airlines taxied down the tarmac. On my way out of the airport building, I passed by a currency exchange bank. The neon clock on its wall told me the time was almost 12 midnight. Outside the M-Z section, where most relatives waited for emerging passengers with last names starting with those letters, Beth and her two friends welcomed me warmly. And so did the weather; it was pleasant, not humid, and uncommon at that time of year. After a few exchanges of hugs and sobs, we were on our way to Cabanatuan.

Manila has always been a special city for me. All the time, it is livelier than New York, even if the Frank Sinatra song says that this U.S. city never sleeps. ("New York, New York" is a popular song among Karaoke enthusiasts. I once tried singing it and when I reached the high notes, I croaked like a frog. I sang my heart out, but the machine only gave me a 49 score, or "Keep Trying.") As we drove along Roxas Boulevard in Manila, we passed by one of my favorite places, the Aristocrat Restaurant. In my previous visits, we always stopped by the Aristocrat and savored my favorite dishes that I missed so much. Not this time, however. It didn't matter that there was no fried chicken and spaghetti for Beth and her friends, and no *halo-halo* (my favorite mixed dessert of sweetened fruits ice, and milk) for me. Tatang was all that we could think of.

Tatang was awake when we arrived at the hospital at 3:00 A.M. He gestured me his blessings and we briefly exchanged greetings. Then, he pointed to the sofa at the foot of his hospital bed and told me to get some rest. "You had a long flight. I know that you are very tired." I lay down and tried to rest, but I couldn't. I was wired up to my bones because I was looking at the ghost of a once handsome man whose wisdom guided the Catahan clan through its many transformations. My heart went out to him as he moaned incessantly. The pain whipping his body made him fidgety and angry. I watched him toss and turn, unable to sleep that night and the many nights that followed.

My sisters Ammie and Conchita arrived from Canada a couple of days later. Tatang's children, some coming from the other side of the world, surrounded his hospital bed. We thought he would be happy and pleased to see us, but his face showed despondency. His eyes were searching for somebody else's face! Worse than a love-starved teenager, Tatang was looking for his ladylove, who had walked out in the middle of an argument with Beth two days ago.

"Please find her and bring her back to me. It is important that I talk to her for the last time." His voice begged for mercy and compassion. His eyes pleaded for forgiveness and understanding from all the people surrounding his hospital bed, mostly his children.

"We did, Tatang, but she refused to see you," Romeo, his confidant and one of his older grandsons, managed to answer.

I looked at Romeo. I could see he hated himself for failing to

༺ Bittermelons and Mimosas ༻

grant his grandfather his last wish. We looked at each other, and then shook our heads in disbelief. Tatang looked like a child wailing for milk. Oh, how we hated this woman! She had transformed our gallant hero into a cowardly soldier. We couldn't believe this was happening to Tatang. We were angry with her as we felt Tatang's emotional grief become more intense than his physical pains. My anger toward this woman melted away when the memory of my mother on her deathbed nine years ago flashed through my mind. Tears sprang to my eyes as I remembered Inang or mother gasping for her breath, asking for Tatang's missing face, hoping to touch and caress it one last time before she closed her eyes for eternity. Tears of sadness for Inang and compassion for Tatang flowed freely down my cheeks. Choking with emotion, I turned toward the door of his hospital room.

"I'll be right back," I told them, as I left the room to regain my composure. I remembered the chapel at the far end of the building and decided to visit it. I sat in solitude for maybe an hour. I tried to shake off the heart-wrenching scene in Tatang's room and tried to reflect on our happy times as a family, when we were growing up in Sumacab. Although time had taken its toll, these pictures remained very vivid in my memory.

ONCE UPON A TIME, my parents were young, healthy, and wealthy in love and respect for each other. My father's wisdom and heroism and my mother's ancillary demeanor and love of life endeared them to our barriomates. As most Filipino farmers did, my parents saw their children as apparent foot soldiers of the land that would march with their legacies even after they were long gone. More kids were always better, so they thought. Sario, my cousin Pining's husband, always welcomed a new baby with remarks of so much hope, "One of you will make our family rich and proud someday, and I will be

৩৬ Nieves Catahan Villamin ৩৩

there to enjoy it." It was bound to happen because of the changing global economy. Much later, two of his children gained employment overseas and regularly began sending home financial assistance. Sario retired from farming and lived his dream of becoming a *pensionado*, or a retiree receiving a monthly pension.

My father never became a *pensionado* because he loved farming too much. But as it happened, he was grinning ear-to-ear each time a Catahan left Sumacab. We were the first ones in our barrio to try our luck abroad. My mother's brood of two boys and nine girls, I used to think, was the size of an army platoon. We shared everything – food, fieldwork, and fistfights with neighbors, and, occasionally, a bottle of Royal Tru-Orange soft drink during the December cold spell. Our comfort food, *bahog-tubig* or hot rice stirred with water and salt, or occasionally with milk instead of water, was the dish of choice during hard times. None of us children complained about my mother's vending my father's catch of wild quails and fish, no matter how badly we salivated over them, roasted. We understood that our

Taken in 1973 a few months after we immigrated to the United States. My daughter Edna sat between my parents. Eleven of the children pictured above have immigrated to Canada.

Bittermelons and Mimosas

parents had to provide for our basic necessities. We felt blessed even during the roughest of times because we knew our parents and the older siblings would create ways to feed us.

We always found something to laugh about, even the silliest of things. Like that time when Gertrude refused for the first time our mother's command to fetch a bucket of drinking water from an artesian well approximately a mile distance from our house. "Carrying a big bucket filled with water on my head on a dirt road is hard. The weight on my head puts pressure on my back – thus making me fart like a horse." (What? You are always farting because you eat like a horse! I couldn't verbalize my thought. I knew how Gertrude was, once she blew her top.) Then she continued, "I could end up having *almoranas* or hemorrhoids either from farting or carrying the weight. And that would be so awful!"

Gertrude was adamant to be not a *kariton* anymore. We laughed so hard at her argument that our bladders exploded to our mother's disgust. We had been had, but we understood. Gertrude is special! Whatever Gertrude wants, Gertrude gets. I stopped laughing when my mother told me that fetching drinking water was my job now.

Heartaches came aplenty too. Some never left us, no matter how hard we tried to brush them off. Like the time when my sister let go of the big bundle of clothes she was going to wash at the river. With it was my first-ever, stylish, green gingham cotton jumper overflowing with lace and ruffles. I was happy she didn't drown, but I cried a river until my eyes had no more tears to shed. In sickness and in health, in hunger and in feast, in bitterness and in sweetness, we were always together. We were a family.

Uncle Pepe, a close relative and my brother Lino's mentor, was the first in our barrio to break the chain of a farmer's thankless life. He was one of four children from a family whose parents were born privileged. Uncle Pepe's father inherited the small piece of land they farmed. Sans a landlord their rice granary overflowed with *palay* after every harvest. It also helped that his wife was earning good wages as she was the only midwife in our barrio for many years until other women, upon discovering how profitable such a vocation could be, decided to train to become midwives, too. Uncle Pepe's family was not only prudent; they were also more hardworking than most. Thus Uncle Pepe was a farmer during the day and a scholar in the evening. I am sure it was a hard feat for him, but he wanted more out of his life. He didn't abandon farming even when he became a teacher. Only then, he had hired hands. Soon his family lived comfortably, basking in the respect and admiration of their barriomates, us included. It became a joke that the whiffing aroma of food cooking from Uncle Pepe's kitchen was the condiment that made *bahog-tubig* an enjoyable supper for most families around his neighborhood.

Having witnessed all made me even more determined to pursue my studies. So I finished college, entered a reputable profession, married a very hardworking man, and started a family. As icing on the cake, we immigrated to the United States. Our hard work and sacrifices here rewarded us with a life much, much better than Uncle Pepe's.

But the void I felt after I left Sumacab stayed with me. I continued to yearn for the place where I grew up. Sumacab, "my home," is the place where my heart has always belonged. If I moved back to Sumacab tomorrow, I know that when I got back home, it would feel as if I had never left. I would breathe the same Sumacab northeast cooler wind that brings forth rain, my nose getting stuffy because of the cool early mornings and midday heat. I would catch up on family gossip wondering who had become pregnant outside of wedlock, which had a mistress, or who was the henpecked husband as I warmed myself in front of the morning bonfire. In my younger days, I had abhorred living this kind of life.

And now that I am in my "golden years" and away from home, I have come to understand and appreciate my life in Sumacab. Maybe it has something to do with the way people in Sumacab bonded to survive the difficult days, especially when harvest was scant and hunger laid in wait, while private help or government aid was nowhere in sight.

Bittermelons and Mimosas

SUMACAB IS A BARRIO of Cabanatuan, a city in Nueva Ecija province. Cabanatuan City, now considered the commercial, industrial, and educational hub of the province, became highly urbanized under the stewardship of visionary Mayor Julius Vergara, 1998–2007; 2010 to date. The city is the site of the historical "Plaza Lucero" and the Cathedral, where General Antonio Luna was ambushed on his way to Palanan. During World War II, the occupying Japanese built Cabanatuan Prison Camp, where many American soldiers were imprisoned, some of whom had been forced to endure the infamous "Bataan Death March." In January 1945, the U.S. Army and guerillas rescued the prisoners in what became known as the Raid at Cabanatuan. Cabanatuan was also the epicenter of a massive earthquake at roughly 3 P.M. on July 16, 1990. The earthquake leveled some buildings, including the Christian College of the Philippines (formerly Liwag Colleges, my high school alma mater) in the midst of class time. At 7.7 on the Richter scale, it killed 1,653 people.

Sumacab, my barrio, lies between a wide creek where schools of indigenous fishes once shared the cloudy waters occasionally with mosquitoes and leeches, and a river roaring with spirit like my 38-month-old granddaughter Isabelle. Sumacab's thousands of hectares of rice fields and farmlands were the hearth and home of my barriomates. Sumacab is where I was born.

The creek links the main barrio to its fertile rice fields. When I was younger, the backwoods that surrounded the creek was a hotbed for tall bamboos, wild shrubberies and flowering plants. Most of these plants were our sources of food, shelter, and medicine. The bamboo trees that bowed to the storms, only to lift their heads with elegance after the calm, became the posts and beams of my brother Diko Unti's (Diko is a title of respect for the second older brother) house that my father built for him and his new wife. Wild bushes, which grew aplenty along the creek side, occasionally sheltered snakes during an over-100-degree summer's day. During the Yule season, the taller wild shrubs were our token Christmas trees and later were used as firewood that cooked our daily meals. Cousin Casio cut two mature bamboo poles, tied them together with rattan and attached

Nieves Catahan Villamin

a bamboo handrail to make a bridge connecting the barrio to the rice fields. For many years, we used this bridge to reach our rice fields, which grew a variety of rice. Toward harvest time, rice stalks would grow past the shoulders of *Kalakian*, our *carabao* (domesticated water buffalo). Each stem was laden with golden grains. Each grain, I thought, was heavier than a gold nugget. A couple of rice varieties made Sumacab famous in the rice market. When cooked, Sumacab's whiter-than-pearls rice let out a flavorful smell that is as sweet as my grandbaby Isa's breath.

The river was the gateway to farmlands where top grade vegetables were produced during summer. Fat string beans hung from vines twisted around bamboo posts. Japanese eggplants of a beautiful lavender color and fist-sized plump red tomatoes dangled loosely on their stems, in groups, and brought a twinkle to my mother's eyes every summer. The taller than my father's knee oblong watermelons of pink or crimson red and the rounder than a dinner plate turnips which crack from freshness once pulled from their beds were all the best cooling aids during the hot summers. The same farm also grew the fat fodder grass vines my mother and I gathered and sold to horse owners during the summer months. Trees, such as acacia or monkey pod, *kamatsile* or Madras thorn fruit, *sampalok* or Tamarind, and *santol* or Sandoricum koetjape completed the landscape. The majestic trees provided the shepherd shade from the fierce midday sunlight. The exotic fruits they bore delighted children all summer long also.

Sumacab had one road – a dirt road that was bumpy and rough. It was muddy after a rain deluge and dusty in summer. During the dry season, the dirt road was our Sumacab desert, the rutted sections transformed into sand dunes. On weekends, Uncle Duardo's passenger jeepney loaded with locals dashed recklessly to catch a cockfight at the fiesta in a nearby barrio, sending dust flying into the air. Enjoying their mini roller coaster ride, passengers roared with amused laughter that rose above the dust.

I believe my barrio folks were among the happiest people on earth. They always found something to laugh about in spite of their arduous lives. On clear mornings, I watched as hawks spiraled up into

Bittermelons and Mimosas

the bright sky. I fancied them as small airplanes, although the only airplane I had seen was in pictures. And wafting through the breeze was the fragrance of my favorite blooms of white ginger lily, lady of the night, and jasmine. My friends and I gathered the flowers and pressed their pristine white petals between the pages of our books so we could enjoy their fragrance longer.

A wild plant I remember vividly is the *makahiya*, a mimosa variety that thrives freely on the Philippine landscape. If the pink flowers and dainty leaves that fold upon human touch don't make an impact on you, the thorns that sting like a bee if you're not paying attention might. A legend says the plant personifies a jilted Sumacab maiden. She died grieving over a failed romance and is transformed into a *makahiya*. Like the jilted maiden who closed her heart forever, the *makahiya* recoils when touched.

At the end of a day, the radiant Sumacab sun dipped into the thick forest. The dazzling sight of the full moon, which glittered like a golden *bilao* (a circular shallow basket-tray made of split bamboo), buoyed the romantic nature of Diko Unti and his male friends. Dressed in their neatly ironed gabardine pants and white oxford shirts, they cruised down the dirt road for an evening visit with their sweethearts. Sometimes, they serenaded visiting women friends.

A few hours later, like an alarm clock, Conrado, the barrio milkman, whom our nursing *carabao* we called Dumalaga loved to hate, made his rounds. Up on their perches, the roosters crowed, "Tik – ti – laok." On their bicycles, the hot bun peddlers called out. "Hot buns, buy hot buns." It never ceased to amaze me that the Sumacab sun lit up the sky with a smile repeatedly to welcome the backbreaking day ahead.

During the rainy days, we bathed under the rain in spite of our mothers' admonitions of pneumonia and other respiratory sicknesses. We played the Sumacab children's version of soccer – instead of balls, we would strike out water with our feet outside the potholes like a golfer teeing his golf balls. The one who jerked the water out of the hole the furthest would be the winner. The prize was a ride on the loser's back from Uncle Gorio's front yard to the big acacia tree bordering our house. However, when the rainfall continued for days, our cheers turned into fears. We knew the Pampanga River and the yellow brook would soon overflow and drown our crops.

May and June were my favorite months. I loved the feel of the calming breeze on late afternoons as much as I dreaded the sight of the blue skies quickly turning gray. I knew a downpour would follow the rumbling thunder. It would be so sudden that sister-in-law Lucing would not have enough time to collect her laundry drying on clotheslines before the first droplet fell. Still, I knew that the all-night stream of raindrops gave the earth the respite it longed for all through summer. Soon flora spread out to cover every inch of the ground. I have always been a dreamer. As a young girl, I looked at our countryside as if it was a canvas on which God had spilled the greenest of paint, especially during the month of June.

I don't know how Sumacab got its name. Once, I asked my father about it. He drummed up something as stunning as the story about the Yamashita treasure hunt. (I remember that, when I was 12 years old, Kuya Lino [Kuya is a title of respect for the oldest brother] joined him and Uncles Turing and Ensong in the treasure hunt.)

But Kuya Lino, our own Professor Higgins, had another story about the origin of Sumacab's name. Sitting in my father's rocking chair with a lit cigarette hanging from his mouth, Kuya Lino told us this version:

"The name originated from the old Tagalog word *sakab*, which means to slip in between two obstacles. The barrio is sandwiched between two natural barriers: the Pampanga River to the west and the creek to the east. The infix -um could have been added into the word *sakab* as years went on, making it Sumacab."

I don't know if he was right or not, but Kuya Lino had studied many things and his explanation made a lot of sense.

Sumacab taught me about hard work and appreciation of the land and streams that supplied the basic nourishments so I could grow up healthy and strong. It taught me respect for the other species that cohabited with us – even the birds that chose to live in our roof when they had a palatial birdhouse close to our well.

Bittermelons and Mimosas

A RIVER NAMED PAMPANGA ran through Sumacab's heartland. Because of its geographical location, the river was once a battleground where two opposing political ideologies were fought over with guns through the darkest of hours. Many times, Pampanga's pebbles safeguarded the fallen lying in solitude by the shoreline. In loneliness, Pampanga wept. Then as the morning light shone forth Pampanga rejoiced. Inspired like a chameleon, Pampanga River transformed itself into a huge swimming pool, or a giant washtub, or a colossal fishpond. Each was its own haven where the barrio people rid their bad memories of the night before.

I don't think my barriomates enjoyed the river's conflicting personalities and remember them with fondness like I did. My river-friend, Pampanga, I am sure now was ruled by the zodiac sign Gemini because she exhibited great mood swings, dependent upon who her companion was. The sun made her happy, and when it visited, Pampanga was our best friend. But when thunderstorms raged in winter, Pampanga became a formidable foe.

Pampanga provided for her friends in summer, Sumacab's liveliest time of the year. On days of over one-hundred-degree temperature, Aunt Juana, with her arthritic hands and with her face half-submerged in the clear water, caught shrimp bedded down in the rocks. Aunt Felisa cast her fishing pole for freshwater fish we called *ayungin* or small carp. Men and their teenage sons cast their nets to trap mudfish or catfish. The river abounded with these species then. Mothers washed soiled clothes along the sandy bank of the river, their children helping them. As they scrubbed away, knowing they were being spied upon, the maidens stole glances at their suitors swimming nearby in a fence-it position. Just a few feet away where the *carabaos* soaked leisurely, my mother and I washed the *zacate* grass we had gathered early in the morning. And the farmers cleansed their newly harvested turnips and other vegetables inside their *karitons* (carts pulled by a *carabao* for transportation of goods), to obtain better selling prices from the local or Manila market vendors. Pampanga was never alone all day long.

During the monsoon months of August to December, nature's darker side dropped an onslaught of rainstorms that filled the basin parts of the mountain's rugged top in rapid succession. Overflows from the basins cascaded down taking dried bushes and tree stumps along the way. The soup-like mixture of liquefied soil and dried wood splinters settled close to Pampanga's banks and at length became breeding grounds for lilies and other water plants. As the cloudbursts let loose more rainfall, the water in the river rose ever higher. Sensing the damage that loomed ahead, my friend, the river, would start to brood. If the rain didn't stop, Pampanga would overflow and crops and lives would be in danger.

Sometimes nature relented and the sun appeared and we were able to breathe a sigh of relief. On those days, I ran to the riverbank to watch the rising water. I saw gusts of wind chase the raindrops away and create bigger waves in the process. With booms and whistles, the strong currents rocked the water hyacinth beds like puppets on strings. Firmly attached to their floating beds like Siamese twins joined at their hips, the water hyacinths moved about with grace and beauty like the ballerina figurine I first saw dancing atop a music box.

Once in a while, geese or chickens rode on the beds. I imagine they did it either for fun or adventure. When clumps got close to the bank, birds often flew down on them, perhaps in search of food. As the water hyacinths swam with the currents farther and farther from shore, the birds flew back to the trees and bushes lining the riverbank to escape the danger from the wild water. These interactions made my heart throb faster than the drumbeats from a marching band during an Independence Day parade in the city.

The river was a lifeline for our family during the monsoon rains. As the gateway to the farmlands, our neighbor farmers were dependent upon my father's *banca* or small boat for transport when it swelled. Transporting crops across a swollen river in exchange for a portion of the crops was one of the many ways he supplemented his income.

My father built his carved *banca* out of a big *molave* tree he had

ᛊᛇᏮ Bittermelons and Mimosas Ꮾᛊᛇ

single-handedly chopped down in the forest. The *banca* was approximately 20 feet long and three feet wide. A bamboo outrigger extending from its right side increased its stability. He braved the river many times while transporting farm produce. With mixed feelings of fear and astonishment, I watched him row back and forth across the surging water. I witnessed his countless skillful maneuvers as he steered the boat away from the paths of moving objects. Had my father not been adept in paddling, the wooden *banca* would have collided with them, causing the load to roll over and my father to drown.

Whenever I remember these things, I am awed and saddened at the same time that so few people in my neighborhood took the opportunity to appreciate such sights.

～ Nieves Catahan Villamin ～

Planting rice until the set of sun.

My nieces trailing and picking-up after Kalakian during the yams' harvest.

Award-winning artist Don Dumandan's canvas interpretation of a woman planting rice.

Bittermelons and Mimosas

Ate Cirila and her grandson giving her a bath in the river.

Danny and I sat on the banca my father carved from a big *mulawin* tree.

Nieves Catahan Villamin

A summer laundry marathon at the bank of Pampanga River.

A way of passing time by the Sumacab folks when I was growing up. L-R: Niece Mariett F. Abaya; my sister Mila, who died in February 1989; Niece Emily F. Baylon. Before immigrating to Canada in 1976, my sister Ammie helped Mariett secure her first job at the Manila City Hall. A CPA, Mariett is currently the Head of Accounting of the same division where she started as a clerk. Emily immigrated to Canada in late 1989 through my sister Ammie's petition as her nanny. She had since gotten married and had several children of her own.

◈◇ Bittermelons and Mimosas ◇◈

Standing back L-R: Beth, Andoy, and Ammie. My parents posed with some grandchildren.

Taken after my mother's death in 1993. Standing L-R: Ammie, Beth, Huling, me, and Gertrude. Sitting L-R: Diko Unti, Ditse Clarita, Sanse Conchita, and Kuya Lino.

Chapter Two

Heroes and Lost Souls

In the land of my birth,
men are born with courage.
The women are like gems
both prides of my motherland.

Anonymous

"Why was I given a name that is more common as a family name among Filipinos?" I asked my father one August evening as our family gathered around separating corn ears from their cobs using a hand-crafted tool we called *gadgaran*. The kernels would be sun-dried for a couple of days, and then milled at a grain mill in the city. Milled corn, "the poor man's rice," was a staple part of our diet when I was growing up.

"You were born on Thursday, July 5, 1945, the day after General Douglas MacArthur announced that the Philippines had been completely liberated. Thursday is *Huwebes* in Filipino," my father started to explain.

"And *Huwebes* rhymes with Nieves, so that's why you gave me that name?"

"Something like that." He nodded his head and pointed his lips toward (a common Filipino way of pointing instead of the finger) my mother. "Your mother and I were trying to honor the significance of that day. Naming you Nieves was the closest thing we could do." I should have known. Ever since I was a little girl, I had realized my father was very patriotic.

After World War II, American influence pervaded the Filipino culture. Soon, being bilingual meant proficiency in Spanish and English, not in the local language. The Americans campaigned for education for all, not just the elite, as it was during the Spanish regime. The Catholic religion still played a major role in our everyday lives. In our schools, most classroom walls displayed posters of the praying Virgin Mary, with the catch phrase underneath, "The Family that Prays Together, Stays Together." That motto reflected Filipino culture and what it was all about.

Family. Among Filipinos, everyone is a relation be it by blood or by acquaintance. We take care of one another in good and bad times. So it was true with the Sumacab folks. We were one big family. We learned about God, family values, love and compassion, and friendship and respect through the examples of our elders and neighbors. In spite of their limited education, the elders in my barrio knew the excesses and evils of the modern world would corrupt the young minds and eventually alter our traditions. How they lived their everyday lives carved lasting impressions on those of us fortunate enough to grow up in their shadows. The lessons I learned from them prepared me well in my search for a better life beyond Sumacab.

Come along and meet some of the very important Sumacab people that influenced me in one way or another.

I WAS ONLY FIVE years old. But I remember the ghost-dark midnights and the noises of startled chickens flying from their coop after being roused by blasts of gunfire. My mother was yanking us from our beds to hide in the *lungaw* or dugout underneath our house to shield us from stray bullets coming from shooting on the riverbank.

"Get up, get up! Conchita, Marcelino, help me move all the children." The shots were meant for HUKBALAHAP (refers to HUKbo ng Bayan Laban sa Hapon or People's Anti-Japanese army) members being chased like wild animals by the Philippine Constabulary and civilian guards as they crossed the river on their way back to their mountain hideout after brief visits with their families in the lowlands. As the gunshots were getting louder, we knew it was just a matter of time. Casualties, more likely HUKs, were bound to surface at the riverbank. They were outnumbered and outweaponed.

But even in the heartland of doom and gloom, hope grew and love bloomed. As it happened with my sister and an underground fighter named Pascual. Older sister Clarita and Pascual's romance was an open secret in our neighborhood that was peopled almost entirely by HUK members and their sympathizers. Among the handful of suitors my sister had, she chose Pascual. He was perfect husband material and the embodiment of an ideal Filipino youth: respectable, principled, handsome, and hardworking. As a couple, they epitomized Maria Clara and Crisostomo Ibarra, the lead characters from *Noli Me Tangere*, a novel written by Dr. Jose Rizal, our national hero. My sister's natural beauty and inner strength had supported Pascual's political affiliation, which like Ibarra, brought him more than his share of enemies. Because Pascual was living mostly on borrowed time, my sister treasured the rare moments when Pascual visited. They neither held hands nor kissed. Only an exchange of longing stares across the room conveyed their feelings. They understood each other perfectly well. One evening during the December harvest after Pascual had proposed, his parents did *pamanhikan*, the Filipino tradition of asking the bride's hand in marriage. They brought along poultry, fruits, rice grains, and some silverware as gifts to my parents. They didn't have to try harder.

Our family favored Pascual because he had once saved my father's life. It happened one night when a raid by the civilian guards caught the visiting HUKs by surprise. As bullets ran after them, my father in his haste stumbled on a pile of dirt. He fell on the ground and sprained his ankle. Pascual carried him on his back to safety. Our

Bittermelons and Mimosas

families agreed upon a traditional wedding. Pascual's parents promised to shoulder the wedding expenses and build the couple a small house once the country's peace-and-order situation got better. Both families looked forward to the nuptials with much hope and prayers.

On a cold morning in March 1951, bullet-ridden bodies of HUKs resting inside a *kariton* were brought to their families in Sumacab. One of them was Pascual's, Clarita's beloved boyfriend. She was so grief-stricken that she withdrew from everybody and went on a hunger strike. We thought she would lose her mind. However, former suitors took notice and courted her again. In time, my sister's wound healed and she fell in love again and married another HUK, named Islao. She was not destined to be an old maid.

That was the first time I learned about fate. If it weren't meant to be, then it would never be.

I REMEMBER THE MANY July Saturday mornings when I was in high school. On Saturday mornings, one could stay in bed a bit longer – but not during planting season. I wanted to sleep some more because it was still dark outside. But Aunt Didang, our labor contractor, and Sumacab's Julia Child, would awaken everybody, her voice sounding like the 12 o'clock noon siren in the city.

"Let's go before the sun breaks out. We have to walk at least seven miles today," she announced as she passed by our houses.

Heat didn't bother me as much as the downpours. On mornings after an all-night rain, I dreaded getting up. I knew we had to cross two waist-deep creeks where my friends swore snakes and leeches shared domain.

"Yes, the snake that bit one of Sergio's legs swam out of that stream. And he never made it to the hospital alive." Ofelia told the story as if she were there when the tragedy happened.

Snakes and leeches. They were the rice planters' deadliest worries long before the outbreaks of dengue fever and the Nile virus. No matter how afraid I was of snakes and leeches, I didn't want to upset Aunt Didang with a no-show. She was like my patron. She was sympathetic to the point of being indulgent to younger and amateurish rice planters like me. Aunt Didang knew that fieldwork was one of the few ways we could earn the school allowances our parents were unable to provide us regularly. She made sure that all rice planters, young and experienced alike, were paid the same. She believed in education and understood our aspirations for a better life out of Sumacab.

Aunt Didang was also a chef de cuisine. After the planting season, she traded her big wide-brimmed native hat made of wooden split bamboo, rattan, or palm leaves for an apron, which she donned as she shared her culinary expertise with our community. Long before Julia Child graced the television in the United States, Aunt Didang was creating 12-course meals from a 150-pound pig. She was the culinary expert who did not open a recipe book. I doubt if she ever knew what a cookbook was. She created a palette of fabulous meals craved by people, even those who lived across the far corners of my province.

I still remember a fiesta day in August 1956 when Nana Didang cooked for the mayor of San Leonardo, a town about an hour's drive from Sumacab, and the place where my baptismal godparents lived. Nana Didang asked four of my cousins and me to assist. As a bonus, she said I could visit with my godfather, who was a close friend of hers. (I missed that opportunity because we became occupied as soon as we got there.)

At almost nine o'clock in the evening on fiesta day, many cooking pots were already empty, but not the mayor's house. The stream of guests gushed from all parts of town. I heard Marci and Pina talking in whispers as they handed us more dirty plates to wash, "If the flow of guests doesn't ease up, we will go home on empty stomachs." The helpers were tired and hungry, most especially us dishwashers who, unlike the cooks and servers, had limited access to the food.

As Marci and Pina turned their backs, I felt the throes of hunger thrusting me into the kitchen. I was unstoppable. However, before I could fill my plate, the growls of a vicious lion watching over the food made me loosen the grip on the scoop of *menudo* (a dish of pork and liver in tomato sauce) I held in my hand.

"Here, have this instead." Salud, one of the cooks, was nice enough to hand me a plate of rice topped with sautéed bittermelon.

Bittermelons and Mimosas

"Oh, thank you," I said, and then I noticed that there was no pork meat in it. I knew that we had put some generous cuts of meat in the dish. "But where's the pork?" My fondness for pork dishes had often been the butt of jokes by my siblings because I always suffered from indigestion after my once-a-year binge during our fiesta celebration.

"I took them all out," Salud said.

"What?" I was ready to attack her because I thought she had put aside the pork for herself.

"Because we might end up serving that pork and bittermelon dish if the flow of guests doesn't stop. Just eat. Don't complain." I could see she was agitated.

Helpers fed themselves only after all the guests were served. She was just being nice to me because I was the youngest in our group. After that, bittermelon became one of my favorite vegetables. Its taste reminded me of comfort, and I savor the sweetness, not the bitter taste that many Asians could not tolerate.

Aunt Didang taught me about hard work, and that woman could do what they called a man's work. Seeing her toiling everyday to better her life reinforced my belief that a college education would be the only way I could save myself from living such an unrequited and thankless life in the fields.

AUNT ELENA WAS NOT a blood relative, but over the years she became an unofficial member of most families in Sumacab, including ours. As a letter courier for the HUK organization during her underground days (she was a HUK Amazon), she was brave and articulate, beautiful and charming. She was also endowed with a majestic figure that men only saw in women featured in magazines. The envy of most of the ladies and the fantasy of all the men, her attributes could have brought her success had she pursued a career on the silver screen, which according to our neighbors she dreamt of when she was younger.

But as a dutiful daughter would, she cast aside her own ambitions to fulfill her parents' wishes in a pre-arranged marriage to a local farmer. In those days, an arranged marriage was all too common, and the bride-to-be almost always had no say in the matter. Aunt Elena's husband, although he inherited a small farmland, came nowhere near to being what she deserved for a life partner because he was ugly and lazy, her exact opposite. In those days, a piece of land was as good as gold and enough reward for a sacrifice in the name of love. Aunt Elena had no choice but to stay married. Divorce was not an option in our resolutely Catholic nation. Being married would have to be a till-death-do-us-part commitment. However, she managed to be the best wife to her husband and the best mother to her children.

Aunt Elena was also the village ophthalmologist, our own version of the "Medicine Woman." She shared her knowledge about herbal medications that she learned during her HUK days with the barrio folks. When I first had my eyes examined in the United States, my ophthalmologist found a couple of bruises around the retina of my left eye. The discolored spots were from bamboo splinters that accidentally hit my eye when I was gathering firewood back in Sumacab. Aunt Elena painstakingly took out all the splinters, using one of her daughter's sharpest and tiniest embroidery needles. Her delicate hands guided by her ingenuity, and the sap of the vines of a wild rattan plant Tatang gathered from the forest for eye drops, prevented me from being blind for life. The woman with the face and body of an uncrowned beauty queen, and the brains and hands of a future medical surgeon became a prisoner of her own marriage.

When not devoting time to her family, Aunt Elena was helping her dear friend Aunt Didang cook. She strived to be in a happy place always, and by doing so managed to bring out the best in people. She got them together to participate during holiday feasts, and helped families of the sick and the bereaved when death visited a family in our barrio, perhaps a self-therapy for her own unhappiness.

It was during that volunteerism that, in the village, she met a bachelor with whom she fell in love. Their romance was Sumacab's version of Shakespeare's Romeo and Juliet. Rumors had it that her lover, a handsome, poor, and educated local, remained a bachelor, and took their love affair to his grave. Until death his heart belonged to Aunt Elena. As the story went, Aunt Elena's heart belonged to him as well. Everybody knew that when Aunt Elena was dying, she called out his name and not her husband's. That was why we in Sumacab were certain that Aunt Elena was looking forward to her death – to free herself of the bondage of a loveless marriage.

Aunt Elena's life gave me the wisdom to prevent a loveless marriage for myself in later years. A marriage dictated by tradition, I thought, was akin to being in prison while awaiting the death sentence.

THREE OF MY BARRIOMATES (The Jolly, the Eccentric, and the Healer) personified Sumacab's seasonal changes, which I looked forward to every year because of the adventure each cycle brought to me. I see Jolly Purok's happy face when new growth abounded in Sumacab's fields and fresh air was everywhere. An ever cheerful and optimistic man, I compare him to a fallow tree that grew sturdy and fruitful, the tree that never blames Mother Nature for its misfortunes. Eccentric Agaton's fiery temper and rigid looks were enough to wilt a wildflower from its stem, yet the watermelon vines that roamed happily on his farm received only tender care. He and his watermelons, which were the best of Sumacab, remind me of summer. When the gentle wind began to blow, it brought back memories of Cousin Casio, our barrio's healer. Cousin Casio spoke like a preacher and healed the sick with wit and a touch of flair. He was a holy man to many of us.

During my junior and senior years in high school, Jolly Purok drove us home from school on his *karetela* (two-wheeled cart-like horse-drawn passenger-and-freight vehicle), narrating stories about his many adventures as a youngster in Sumacab. "He, he, he, oh yes, during my days I was called *bantay-salakay* (a guardian who assaults or steals from what he is asked to watch). I lost my best friend, but I gained the best wife a man could ever have." We giggled with him as he related how he was at first his best friend's messenger of love notes to the girl who later became his wife. (He was the only messenger I knew who didn't get shot.) And we shared his anger as he told us how he saw Japanese soldiers kill one of his guerrilla neighbors. He was hiding behind the bushes and the darkness of the night hid him well. "I witnessed Miguel, my next door neighbor, shot to death by two Japanese soldiers because a MAKAPILI (pro Japanese groups) ratted on him. God, I would have killed that spy if I knew who exactly he was." Each trip with Jolly Purok was a 45-minute educational journey, unlike anything we were learning in school. Sometimes, we exchanged local gossip. I still remember the greatest story he told us about a May-December marriage that happened in our neighborhood where he was a witness. An open secret to older folks but out of respect to the couple involved, it wasn't a story to be spread around. The tale was laden with improper virtues and parents were afraid the young ones would emulate them had they been made aware of it. Luisa, a self-taught seamstress and the sole breadwinner of an orphaned family of five (her parents were executed by the Japanese soldiers), now in her late thirties, was desperate to have a child before she became barren. She was attracted to Kulas, a dream bachelor (hardworking, healthy, and handsome) but 10 years her junior. Luisa's pining for Kulas seemed like it would stay unspoken because Kulas was already betrothed to Ana, one of the most beautiful women in the barrio, who was every man's dream wife. But cougar Luisa was determined to make the young man the father of her future child. So she did the unthinkable at that time. One midnight Luisa climbed through the window and helped herself into Kulas's bedroom. Pressing a pair of scissors at his neck, Luisa coerced the younger Kulas to make love to her. Nothing was honorable about the incident, except Kulas. Amidst Ana's tears and objections from relatives he married Luisa, to save her honor. Having lost no virtue, Ana traded up and married a doctor and moved to another village far away from Sumacab. Kulas in time learned to love Luisa, who became an astute businesswoman and treated Kulas like a king. Their marriage bore fruit, a son who grew up to be one of the most respected leaders in our barrio.

Jolly Purok had a daughter named Remy who didn't live long enough to appreciate and enjoy her father the way we did. One

Bittermelons and Mimosas

moonlit night, young Remy and her other friends were taking a break from the game of tag and blocking when a cobra bit her right heel. Washed by a recent flood into our neighborhood, the poisonous snake had taken sanctuary inside a hole at the foot of a century-old acacia tree. This tree was in our playground. Remy rested her back against the tree, her feet near the hole, making them a good target for the snake. In those days, quack doctors not medical doctors treated snakebites. Because the tea blend of special herbs and spices was not an antidote for snakebites, its venom killed Remy. Had it happened today, there would be antidote to save Remy. I am sure that Jolly Purok was shattered by the terrible loss of his beloved daughter. But he did not inflict his pain on everyone. He continued to smile and tell wonderful stories as he took us home from school.

Unlike Jolly Purok who was well liked by many of us, Eccentric Agaton was considered the oddball in Sumacab. He was atypical Filipino – unfriendly and acrimonious and stingy. As good as he was while tending to his watermelons, Eccentric Agaton was a grouch to children. Try asking for one of his watermelons and you'd have him snarling at you, and making you regret you ever asked him. He'd tell you, "If you want to eat watermelon, why don't you plant it yourself, just as I do?" People thought him rude and insensitive. But when I think about it now, I realize that Agaton was just living out the precept of reaping what you sow. One has to plant his own watermelon seeds to be able to eat a watermelon.

After harvest, farmers often left overripe watermelons for children to seed or birds to feed on. Like pumpkin seeds, roasted watermelon seeds are a popular snack among Filipinos, so it was not unusual for the children to gather around a farm while harvest was going on. One afternoon, my sisters Mila and Ammie and their friends Fely, Gaupo, and Lety assembled at a farm adjacent to Eccentric Agaton's and waited patiently for the last watermelon to be cut from the vine. After Carling, one of the merchants, had loaded the last watermelon in his *kariton*, the children proceeded to seed the leftover harvest, which, by then, was already swarming with birds. Eccentric Agaton saw the children. He saw them as thieves, not food hunters. He headed toward them, brandishing a sharp machete like a rebel and shouting, "You thieves, don't let me catch you! I will fillet all of you like bamboo slats for flooring." Eccentric Agaton might have been bluffing just to frighten them away. But he did scare off the children. They dropped their baskets and escaped toward the river, stumbling a few times along the way, and swam to safety. Ammie, who was the littlest among the group, swam like she had never done before, and in doing so, almost drowned, had Gaupo not taken her arm. All made it safely away from Agaton to the other side of the river.

The children did not talk about the incident for years. They knew that if they had told their parents, their parents would have chewed out Eccentric Agaton. This would have resulted in clashes similar to those Agaton had had with other families which had almost resulted in bloodbaths.

The opposite of Eccentric Agaton, Healer Casio, who is my first cousin and neighbor, was a giver. In spite of his farming duties and providing for his family, he always managed time for the sick and needy. Cousin Casio was also Sumacab's *albularyo*, or faith healer. He would treat those who came to him with their stomach aches, high fevers, high blood pressure, cysts, colds, sprained ankles, arthritis, and many other ailments, with his marbles and special herbs.

This is the story he told me when I asked him about his gift of healing: He was pasturing his *carabao* at a nearby field one day when an icy cold whirlwind embraced them and tried to sweep both of them off the ground. Cousin Casio could see the heat waves rising into the air as the temperature that day was in the high 90s, yet he felt very cold. His body felt as if he had been inside an ice factory for hours. Trembling, he reached into one of his pockets for a smoke to calm his nerves. No cigarettes there, so he tried the other one. His fingers closed in on some marbles. "Did you put some marbles inside my pocket this morning?" Cousin Casio asked his children as soon as he got home. "What marbles?" his children asked back.

It became apparent to him that the marbles had magically appeared inside his pocket. How else could he explain the sudden chill on a hot summer day? That night, a man dressed like one of

꧁ Bittermelons and Mimosas ꧂

Jesus' apostles appeared in his dream and told him the marbles had powers. God wanted him to use the marbles to heal the sick and spread the Faith to the people he met. The newly anointed faith healer humbly accepted his mission. "Casio is working too hard. Missing his meals has made him delirious. Bad air has addled his brain." My barrio neighbors made fun of him instead of appreciating his gift. Cousin Casio learned to wear a Teflon skin to ward off our neighbors' insensitive remarks. His heart was bigger than his bony frame and 5'2" height. He gave up his formal education so he could work full-time doing God's work, which, of course, was his lifetime assignment. He refused any form of payment for his healing services even though it often took him away from his farming duties. Do I believe the story of the marbles and his mysterious powers from God? Who am I to judge? I haven't worn his shoes yet to be able to feel how they fit. Others in Sumacab have ridiculed him. I see him as a very special person who has bettered the lives of those he meets. If that is not a gift from God, I don't know what is.

These people taught me how life should be lived. Jolly Purok showed me that life is what you make of it. You ride with the tide and go with the flow. A life of happiness or misery. You make your choice. Cousin Casio taught me about faith and the ability to care unconditionally. And, as Eccentric Agaton had said, if I want to eat watermelon, I should plant my own. I am proud to say that I did just that.

***

THERE WERE TWO "KINGS" that reigned in Sumacab during after the war. Old Menes (the Duplo King), and Uncle Basilio (the Arakyo King). They were the best of friends. I remember them trading barbs and wits during wakes and fiestas, and entertaining politicians during election time. Because both had good communication skills, according to some, they could sell stale fish, had they wanted to, and our barriomates would buy them without hesitation. (Thank God they didn't try!) The stage was never too small for them because they respected each other's talents.

Old Menes was a widower with grown children; yet he lived alone in a big house close to the school. The villagers never saw Old Menes work to earn a living, yet his lifestyle was very comfortable compared to others. And they had an explanation for this: "Tanda Menes dug up a pot of gold from his backyard, which was also home to 'little people,' who were his friends." That was the story that went around the neighborhood. While Uncle Basilio donned the title of an Arakyo king, Old Menes was Sumacab's Duplo (a game in verse held during a wake) king. Both were pioneers of *balagtasan* (a debate where participants reason and argue in verse) in our barrio.

As a young child, I loved watching Duplo even though the traditional socio-religious play was associated with death. I was captivated by the extemporaneous display of mental adeptness of the participants, and the exchange of dialogues in the poetic Tagalog language. It was staged after the nightly prayers of the religious women during the third and ninth night of the wake to comfort the bereaved. Duplo was unique because the arguments discussed legal provisions of the Penal Code in Greek and Roman philosophies. The jousting was spontaneous – both educational and entertaining.

The last time I saw Old Menes engaged in Duplo was at Grandpa Ciriaco's wake in November 1957. That night, the monsoon rain was at its heaviest because of a strong typhoon. The inclement weather, however, did not diminish the crowd's excitement at an opportunity to get a dose of Old Menes' Duplo prowess. Some spectators wore *salakot*, and the others huddled under umbrellas as they watched him and Feliciano engage in an extemporaneous exchange of verses under a makeshift stage.

Thirty years younger than Old Menes, Feliciano was a poet on the rise. (I had a huge crush on him until my late teens. One day I discovered he was *namamangka sa dalawang ilog*, or rowing his boat in two rivers simultaneously. He was courting me and one of my girlfriends in chorus.)

Bittermelons and Mimosas

Mesmerized by the flamboyance and wit displayed by both performers, the audience was oblivious of the rising water. The play ended around midnight, just about the time the water rushed through the streets. The villagers scampered back to their homes to save their belongings from being washed away by floodwaters. Old Menes hurried to save his firewood and tools, which were under a shed in his backyard. It was already very dark. The old man's poor eyesight could only help him so much. As he went farther back into his yard, the water got deeper. Old Menes lost his balance, fell down, and drowned, taking with him the secrets of his pot of gold. When the water subsided the following morning, the neighbors found his lifeless body cradled by the wild bushes that were once the refuge of his "little friends." Perhaps they had tried to save him albeit unsuccessfully; otherwise, his body would have been washed into Manila Bay.

Duplo, which I enjoyed watching, has been long gone in Sumacab. Gone, too, is the traditional nine-day novena. Nowadays, as in many places in modern society, the Duplo and the nine-day novena that were held during wakes and helped comfort the bereaved have been replaced by high-stake card games and mahjong sessions.

UNCLE BASILIO, THE ARAKYO King, was the true artist among the Catahan Brothers. He was my father's older brother. We nicknamed him "Bondat" because he was fat and waddled like a baby seal. We best remember him for pioneering the Arakyo tradition in the late 1950s. He was a man of many talents, different pursuits, and he possessed great communication skills. He would have looked like a highly decorated Christmas tree had he dressed for all his roles at one time. He was a politician, director, scriptwriter, poet, and a natural actor who danced and sang and memorized and delivered the Arakyo lines fluently. He wrote the Arakyo script in rhymes, basing it on history books, the Bible, and the Araquio of Alua, San Isidro, Nueva Ecija (1880). His passion for the Arakyo was sometimes eclipsed by his impatience, which was as short as his five-foot-four height. He often yelled at the slightest mistakes during practice, shaming his barriomates. His passion that we mistook as temper was so volatile that, as a joke among themselves, people wore hats all the time during rehearsals so they would not feel the heat emanating from his head. Of course, they knew that they had to do well during the practice performances so Uncle Basilio would stay cool-headed. Our barriomates would invariably overlook and forgive his shortcomings; they loved him because of his many talents.

Arakyo was almost quenched during its initial stage. One February day, Grandpa Dencio made a simple suggestion about a particular scene. This did not dwell well with Uncle Basilio. They argued heatedly until Uncle Basilio exclaimed, "Cousin Dencio, if you think you know more than I do, then go ahead and teach them."

Uncle Basilio was furious because he thought he was being criticized. He gathered the script and stormed out of the rehearsal. Upon arriving home, Uncle Basilio went into the kitchen and threw the script inside the clay stove. He lit a match and ignited the pile of papers. "Let's see what you can do now." His words thundered, as if he were Moses when he was calling for God to part the Red Sea in the movie *The Ten Commandments*.

Aunt Maria, his wife, was preparing supper when the burst of flames began consuming the dry, saltine-thin paper. Afraid the fire might shoot farther up and burn the kitchen ceiling made of cogon grass, Aunt Maria rushed to pour water on the burning script. The water poured on the burning paper sizzled like chicken pieces being deep fried in very hot oil. The sound jolted Uncle Basilio to his senses. He was speechless, overwhelmed, and unable to lift a finger to stop Aunt Maria as she picked up the remains of the burnt script. Aunt Maria delivered the few pages she had rescued to my father for safekeeping.

Uncle Basilio suffered from terrible headaches soon after. There were nights when he howled like a mad dog until the wee hours of the morning. Many believed he was being punished because he disrespected a holy tradition. He self-medicated by taking a popular over-the-counter pain reliever pill called Cortal tablets. First he took them as directed and later by the handful because the pain would recur. Each time was stronger than before. The heap of pills relieved his headaches. But taking so many at one time perhaps made him experience a high sensation, and probably caused his occasional

Bittermelons and Mimosas

unexplained behavior. On days when he felt better, he walked around the neighborhood with a big cigar in his mouth, like the Pied Piper playing his flute. Children followed him, yelling, "Captain Cortal," comparing him to Captain Barbel, one of the *komiks* characters of writer Mars Ravelo. He returned the affection by teasing and playing with them. However, in the end, taking too much Cortal damaged his liver. He died in 1958, a few days after the third Arakyo production. The barrio religious women interpreted his headaches and early death as punishment for his nearly burning all the pages of the Arakyo manuscript.

My father took on the task of leading the Arakyo until the late 1980s. When he turned 75, he passed the baton to Brother Unti, the younger of my two brothers, who has continued the Arakyo tradition up to the present. Although my family pushed forward this admirable community tradition, none of the nine daughters took part in the stage play. My older brother Lino did. My barriomates and I agreed that he was the best, the most handsome, and the most graceful King Constantine the Sumacab Arakyo ever had.

The Arakyo performers were amateurs whose dedication to their art matched those of their parents. Plums picked by the Arakyo seniors, they were the best looking and most talented locals, with ages ranging from a starry-eyed 16 to a worldly 46. A few of the participants were college students who, like my Kuya Lino, pursued a life beyond Arakyo and achieved success in their chosen careers. Like their predecessors, they hoped to learn self-confidence and grace from public appearances. The rest of the casts were farmers, hoping to attract the attention of potential spouses. Come the first Saturday night in February every year, rehearsals were held without fail. Parents watched their children with pride as they acted and danced their parts in preparation for the real show.

The Arakyo performers were not the only local talents. There also was the *bombo*, the local band. The four members were self-taught musicians who loved the musical tradition with as deep-rooted a faith as in the Catholic religion. Cousin Bining, our gregarious harmonica man, harmonized finer notes than John Lennon did in his popular song "I Should Have Known Better." Had my barriomates seen the "Ray Charles shoulder swing" in one of those old Pepsi commercials, I am sure they would agree that Cousin Bining's moves were comparable, if not better. Uncle Gorio, the drummer boy, played his instrument with ease because he was six feet tall! Cousin Matias tirelessly banged the big drum that almost eclipsed his scrawny 5'2" height during practice nights, often putting the Energizer bunny to shame. A frisky and Saltine-thin Boying clapped the *pompiyang* or cymbals. (One clapper of the cymbals was so badly deformed that no amount of copper surgery could restore it to its former glory. I have promised to replace the cymbals but haven't done so because other things took precedence.) The harmony of this "wannabe band" supported the Arakyo performers during their many nights of practice. However, during the actual theatrical production, the performers in multihued costumes marched and danced to the music of a professional and full ensemble band. The night of the performance of the Arakyo is an event the whole barrio looks forward to every year.

The 21st century brought major changes to Arakyo's presentation as production costs escalated in tandem with the rising prices of goods and commodities. Therefore, it became necessary to increase the number of sponsors. In spite of the financial burden (sometimes it required the sale of a whole harvest to bankroll the celebration), I never heard of anybody turning down a sponsorship, except possibly in a life-or-death situation. Legend has it that one reluctant sponsor was cursed and became ill. But unlike Uncle Basilio, the sponsor got his health back after fulfilling the Arakyo responsibility he had reneged on.

IN SOME PLACES AROUND the world, children are told that a stork delivers newborn babies. In our world, Aunt Senang, my father's oldest sister, was the baby-bearing stork. A self-taught and gifted local midwife, Aunt Senang was the poor woman's gynecologist. She delivered babies and taught Sumacab mothers about infant care. Sumacab's newborns saw the golden rays of sunlight through the slits of their parents' bamboo floor while dangling upside-down from Aunt Senang's capable hands. Today's babies, who are born in the

Bittermelons and Mimosas

hospital, open their eyes to a doctor's green scrub suit and the room's white walls.

The birth of a child was always like a stage production where everybody had a part to play. The older children huddled together in one corner of the house and quietly watched Aunt Senang clean the new baby.

The father was busy carrying out Aunt Senang's instructions that were like a litany: "Celso, have you prepared the hot pad? And the *balut* (fertilized duck egg), is it already cooked? Also, make sure the *sarsaparilla* (root beer) is at room temperature. Cold *sarsaparilla* can give your wife stomach cramps. She needs her energy back. She will breastfeed the baby soon."

"Everything has been prepared, Aunt. I'll bring them over," replied Celso, his smile warmer than the hot pad on the wooden tray he was carrying.

It was understandable. After four girls, his wife Adela had given birth to their first boy. The hot pad was a small cotton flour sack filled with hot ashes from guava firewood that had cooked the previous meal. Adela sat on the hot pad to fight off infection and boost blood circulation in her tired body. The *balut* and sarsaparilla helped her gain the strength lost from the strenuous labor of giving birth.

Most parents of bygone days chose their child's name after a biblical character or after a person they both admired. Using great care, the parents chose a couple to be given the honor of being the child's godparents. They needed a couple who they felt could assume parental roles if the inevitable happened. The newborn baby went through a pseudo-religious rite called the *pagbubuhos*, a ritual similar to the baptism done by Saint John the Baptist during biblical times. Done before the sacrament of baptism and soon after birth by a token priest or a respected elder of the community such as my father, this was to ensure the sanctification of the baby's soul and entry into Christendom should death come before a formal christening. The church baptismal rites could follow a few months or even years later, giving the parents time to prepare for the expenses for the formal ceremony, especially if the baby was the firstborn. Celso and Adela named their son John because he was born in June around the feast day of Saint John the Baptist.

"What kind of a name is that?" I asked my friend Sonya many years later when she requested my husband and me, along with four other couples, to be the godparents of her third child, Tyna. "Tyna" was an anagram for "Naty," a common Filipino first name. But spelled in a new way, the name sounded unique and sophisticated. And Sonya did not even blush when teased by others, "How much profit did you make?" With five sets of godparents, it was not surprising for Tyna's parents to make money off the baptismal ceremony.

The godparents of yesteryear took their roles seriously. They were truly the child's second parents, helping in every way they could in the upbringing of their godchild. People nowadays rarely take an interest in their godchild's well-being and don't perform their roles as godparents, perhaps because they are chosen only because of their position in society or how they can help out the family. Their role, sadly, ends at the ceremony. As a result, their godchildren hardly remember them.

RUPING, MY MOTHER'S SPECIAL friend, was the only enemy she had in all her life. Ruping was a blood relative and neighbor who lived across our street. A *sari-sari* or variety store owner, she was quite popular because she extended credit to most neighbors year round. And so, in deference to Inang, we avoided her like a plague for over 20 years. Like most farmers, the money to buy our basic needs such as salt, vinegar, and oil came mostly from the fruits of the soil. Silver coins reached my parents' calloused hands only after every harvest.

However, crops or none, my mother always made sure our debts were paid as promised. "Words make people – not the clothes they wear or the food they eat." I still remember her words. I know she was trying to teach us the value of commitment and responsibility at a very young age. And now I know that it was one of her ways of making us feel blessed, not deprived. I still can picture the quails and fish my father brought home after he had gone hunting and fishing for days with his HUK comrades. My mother peddled them in town so we could be debt-free until the next harvest. I wanted so badly to roast one for my supper. But I had to content myself by imagining I was feasting on one as I smelled the aroma of a roasting quail from the neighbors' kitchen at supper.

The animosity between Inang and Ruping started one harvest season after Inang questioned Ruping about our grocery credit list. I remember my mother's feverish face and tightly clenched fists as she walked back toward our house.

"We are not cheaters. We will starve but not cheat!" She was screaming, which she seldom did, and we tried to calm her. But Inang dashed past us and went straight to the kitchen. She took the *tabo* (water dipper) sitting at the foot of a big water jar and Tatang's sharp bolo latched on a holster hanging on the wall and headed towards her *alkansiya* that kept our emergency money. The *alkansiya* was actually the upper section of one of the bamboo posts that connected the frame of our kitchen walls. We watched in horror as her bolo traced the curve and slashed open the face of the post. Out dropped coin after coin into the big *tabo* she held. Counting the silver pesos, Inang grabbed a handful and went back to pay Ruping.

"Here, bitch. My children said they didn't do it. And I believe them."

"Yes, but they made the purchases when you were away," Ruping insisted.

"I know my children. They would not do that without my permission," Inang retorted.

This time, the discussion grew so intense and heated that concerned neighbors gathered around the store. My father came and defused the fistfight that was about to start. Inang started her own *sari-sari* store later that week to spite Ruping. She was too angry to care that her business might hurt Ruping's. All communications between them stopped. We Catahan children were encouraged to perpetuate the rift.

GRANDMA SEPA WAS ONE of the many migrants I looked forward to seeing in Sumacab year-round. She was a traveling saleswoman that hailed from Penaranda, a revivalist town that boasts cultural patriotism and music prowess. Every year in May, tourists flock to see *Arakyo*, their flagship theatrical production with roots grounded deeply as far back as 1898, accompanied by an award-winning brass band, one of the country's best. While men plowed Penaranda's rich soil that was a hotbed for many specialty crops, the most popular of which was the *ikmo* (pepper leaves) plant. Housewives labored in the kitchen and prepared native desserts. Penaranda was named after its founder, a Spanish engineer named Jose Maria Penaranda. His great-great-grandson Oscar wasa retired professor and award-winning author and poet (whose writing style was likened to that of N.V.M. Gonzales and Carlos Bulosan) whom I would have the pleasureof meeting here in the United States in 2007.

Grandma Sepa was the female Donald Trump of her generation. Like Donald, Grandma Sepa had a wicked side. And as a very smooth and shrewd Donald Trump might have done, Grandma Sepa made it her business to indulge her customers' whims, not their needs. I still remember how she charmed my oldest sister Macaria without much effort, to "trading-up" the gold ring she had inherited from my grandmother for a collection of fake jewels, hand-crocheted doilies and a blanket, the goods Grandma Sepa peddled during summer. The ring was adorned with a black diamond the size of a toddler pea.

"This ring has brought me nothing but bad luck," my sister reckoned. So she was more than happy to exchange it for goods she supposed were of more worth. In our culture black diamonds were believed to be harbingers of bad luck, some of which had come my sister's way during her first marriage. Grandma Sepa saw the black stone in a different color; white and pure like the snow on Christmas Eve. She knew all along that it was indeed a very unusual stone, because as a peddler, her many travels had taught her well. However, my sister was delighted with the exchange.

Forty years later, I would learn more about my sister's black diamond ring. I read an article about how many scientists believe that black diamonds are rare gems. Supposedly, they are fragments from a diamond-bearing asteroid that may have fallen to earth billions of years ago. Brazil and Central Africa are the only two places where the gems are found.

Three times a year – in May, August, and December – Grandma

⊱ Bittermelons and Mimosas ⊰

Sepa trod down the dusty village road, sometimes with a big clay pot sitting on her head. Inside the clay pot was the delectable dessert called *kalamay*, where pieces of cake floated over fresh coconut milk cooked with brown sugar. The scent of the mouthwatering *kalamay* was so yummy it drove all of us children to run to our mothers and beg, Mother, please even just a small piece." If they obliged, we were soldiers of peace. If they refused, we were the enemies. To ward us off, our mothers brandished swords of bamboo sticks or slippers and chased us to one corner of our house. Words asking for forgiveness and a promise of good behavior would free us from bondage; otherwise we would be confined to that corner until eternity.

On other occasions, Lola Sepa carried a big basket overcrowded with *ikmo* leaves. Older women like my mother and some men in the village chewed *ikmo* or pepper leaves with *bunga* or betel nut and *apog* or lime as a substitute for cigarettes. Finally, when the harvest seasons came, Grandma Sepa returned with a *kariton* to collect the corn or *palay* payments for the goods she had sold for consignment throughout the year.

Twice a year, we also enjoyed the regular visits of migrant rice planters/harvesters from other villages. Their arrival stirred up the sights and sounds of the village mood, which normally was sluggish and staid. Accompanied by stringed instruments on most nights during their stay, bachelors enlivened the streets with music as they serenaded the women migrants.

One of those cold December mornings – and I remember it to be one of the coldest we had in Sumacab – Tomas and Ciano, sitting before a bonfire and stroking the feathers of their pet roosters, were having a serious conversation. Tomas was a married man in his early 50 s and he had six children. Ciano was a bachelor in his 30s. Both were part-time farmers and avid *sabungeros* (cockfight betters).

"Last night, we serenaded Mang Kanor's niece, the one from Munoz. She's here to help in the harvest. Oh, she's very beautiful and she sang pretty nice! She's got beautiful legs, too!" Ciano was beaming as he talked to Tomas.

"How do you know that?" Tomas' face showed doubt. Ciano had always been a joker.

"I was the guitarist because Goding was down with a fever. I sat close to her when she sang. She smelled nice too!" Ciano's grin became wider than the Pampanga River because he enjoyed toying with Tomas's imagination.

"Did you touch her?" Tomas wanted to know more.

"Of course. I pressed her palm with my thumb when she offered a handshake." Cianos's teasing eyes showed the wickedness a naïve Tomas failed to see.

"Were her hands soft? Did she like it?" Tomas leaned forward, getting very excited as he waited for Ciano's next statements.

Ciano told a big fat lie when he nodded his head in agreement.

"Well, I can tell you made it to first base." Envy was oozing rapidly from Tomas's eyes. Little did he know that Ciano was taking him for a ride.

The touch of a girl's hands, even if it was just a handshake, was something men found worth bragging about. What a different world it was then!

Grandma Sepa and the merry migrants taught me about work ethics – and being the best in everything I do. It was a doctrine I would preach to my children when they were growing up, with passion and often teary-eyed. Many years later I would learn that they had coined a title for me – DQ or drama queen. Behind my back they had called me that name, over and over again.

I STILL REMEMBER THE red flatbed truck being tailed by hordes of children bathing in dust as it cruised down our street many summers ago. A Johnny Mathis song ("a certain smile, a certain face, can lead an unsuspecting heart on a merry chase") the melody of which has been wedged in my brain like a microchip ever since it blasted out from a loudspeaker. The vibrant music lured spectators to its destination – which was usually Uncle Pedro's front yard. The driver (whom we called Kiko, the Con Man) was a good-looking guy in his mid-30s. Wearing a black gabardine pair of pants and a neatly ironed white long-sleeved shirt he

ও৳৩ Bittermelons and Mimosas ৩৵৯

stepped out to set up his stage atop the hood of his truck. Much to our surprise, a big python was swaddled around his neck.

"Good day, my friends. I am Kiko and this is my assistant Fortune," he introduced himself and the python around his neck. His voice echoed as far as Marta's house, which was a 10-minute walk from where the extravaganza was. (Marta, a distant relative, had albino twins that provided the entertainment/ridicule in my barrio for many years. My barriomates never knew about gene mutation being the cause of albinism. Instead, they believed the twins were cursed because Marta worshipped the sun during her period of conception).

The python, whose head Kiko held, yawned and then stuck out its tongue. It was black as midnight and looked like the line of a fishing pole ready to hook the audience in a single cast. The split in the middle reinforced the creepiness of an already spine-tingling looking creature. A snake as huge as Fortune was a rare sight for most of my barrio folks who had never been to a carnival. The crowd roared with excitement. Petrified children hid under their mothers' skirts. The spectators, who had almost doubled in number in a matter of minutes, occupied a large portion of the street. They all came to listen to Kiko's testimonial for his "cure-for-all" liquid medicine. My barrio mates saw purchasing Kiko's wonder medicine as a "win-win" solution for them as it was sold in decorative square bottles that could be recycled as candleholders or flower vases.

"This drug has cured the body aches, arthritis, colds, and coughs of people from all over the world, including the nobles of Europe. White and soft skin for women and increased libido for men, guaranteed! And today, I offer you all a special price – and it's just for today." Kiko kept the audience enchanted with his incessant talk so smoothly presented it put the skin of the python hanging around his neck to shame.

My Uncle Basilio was one of Kiko's avid believers. He swore the wonder medicine, which he would take with Cortal tablets, relieved him of the terrible headaches that made him wail worse than a child with a bad tooth. At the onset, no one suspected Kiko of being a con man. So his snake-oil show was able to entertain my *kababayan* for a few years – until one day, Uncle Basilio took a turn for the worse.

Nieves Catahan Villamin

Uncle Pedro, my father's cynical brother, took a bottle of Kiko's wonder medicine to a real doctor to have it tested. After some lab tests, the doctor told us that the liquid would do more harm than good. When my *kababayans* found out his "medicine" was only a mixture of salt, sugar, and water, they threw stones at Kiko the next time he showed up with his python. He never appeared in our barrio again. And so it was, my *kababayans* had been paying money for something of no value.

The lesson I learned from Kiko, the con man, is also a simple one: If it is too good to be true, it probably is.

IT WAS A SUMMER'S day. The crowd was starting to thin out after watching the "cure-for-all" sideshow of Kiko and his python. Then, we heard a commotion coming from the riverbank.

"They're blasting the river!" Eddie Ang jumped up and down in front of their house, shouting as if his pants were on fire. He was talking about dynamite fishing at the river, which was common during summers up to the mid-1960s. We knew why – Eddie thought they would be having *ayungin* for lunch and supper like the previous summers. It saddens me to realize that my *kababayans* thought of survival first before environmental preservation. "*Bahala na bukas.* Tomorrow will take care of itself," we heard this expression all the time.

The commotion at the riverbank, however, was more exciting than dynamite fishing. I was underneath our house, resuming the chopping of firewood that had been interrupted earlier by Kiko's sideshow. I heard Inso Ponyang's call at the foot of our stairs.

"Aunt Ela, Aunt Ela, is Uncle Itong there?"

Curiosity made me stop what I was doing and move closer to where Cousin Ponyang stood.

"Why?" My mother came out of her store to see who was calling.

"Trouble in the riverbank. Tonio forced Berning into an embrace while she was washing clothes at the river. Tonio doesn't want to let her go unless she agrees to marry him. We need somebody to knock some sense into Tonio's head. Is Uncle Itong there?"

"No." My mother turned to me. "Nieves, go get your father. He went to Siano's shop to have his plow sharpened."

"Yes, Inang, right away." I ran as fast as I could to fetch my father.

Because Sumacab was not yet equipped with electrical power during the late 1950s, the influence of western culture through modern communication such as television or radio had not tainted the naïveté of the *probinsiyana* (provincial lass). Before watching television became a pastime among the Sumacab folks, the idea of an unmarried man and woman living together was frowned upon. Virginity, back then, was held a precious virtue, very much a requisite for marriage. So, women touched by men without their permission were labeled "soiled."

I remember a story that was rife in the neighborhood at that time. When his daughter was getting married, Doro asked for a grand ceremony. He then told the father of the groom, "Pare, if your son finds out that my daughter is no longer a virgin, you can return her to us. All your expenses will be reimbursed."

A woman's chastity was a premium in those days. A "soiled" woman was a disgrace to her family. This was what Tonio had in mind. Shaming Berning in front of our barriomates would force her to agree to marry him. He was a million miles off! Berning was no traditional woman.

Upon arriving at the scene, my father called out, "Tonio, let her go. It is not honorable for any man to force a woman into marriage. You know she can charge you with rape. You can languish in prison for that."

Tonio was the son of Uncle Melchor, my father's HUK comrade. He held my father in respect. After some thought, he let Berning go.

The spectators crowding the riverbank and buzzing like disturbed bees let out a collective sigh. Some were relieved. Others were disappointed. There would be no feast in the neighborhood because there would be no wedding. To save face, Berning and her aunt threatened to take Tonio to court. My father mediated again. He and other barrio leaders accompanied Tonio to Berning's aunt to apologize. I knew that if it weren't for my father, Tonio would have languished in prison for years.

I found an ally in Berning. She didn't care what others thought about her. She didn't allow anything to get in the way of her determination for a better future, even if it meant going against tradition and, more importantly, the wishes of her elders.

A TRAGEDY WITH A magnitude like the one involving Kardo and Rowena's family would probably happen only once in Sumacab's lifetime. So heartbreaking that every time I watch a movie of a love affair that ended in tragedy, my memory of my neighbor Kardo and his smiling face rushes back to my mind with sadness.

The Kardo I remember was a friendly neighbor, hardworking person, and very devoted father and husband. He and his family were sharecroppers. To make ends meet, Kardo moonlighted as a tricycle driver after every harvest. Kardo and his wife Rowena and their family of five children lived close by so we saw them regularly. When no grains were stored in their *matong* for years in succession, fragile Rowena was unable to cope. She took the easy way out by openly seeking the company of men who had means. Concerned friends and neighbors who saw Rowena's open flirtations tried to warn Kardo, but Kardo's dare of "Prove it," accompanied with looks that could kill, gave the neighbors reason to call him *pindeho*, a cuckold, behind his back. He could not see the truth through his blind love.

One day, Rowena finally left her family for her jeepney-driver boyfriend. Kardo told his children that their mother would soon see the light and return to her family. Three months passed and Rowena didn't return. Unable to bear public humiliation and the taunting of neighbors, "Apples don't fall far from the tree," a reference to his three daughters, Kardo had a nervous breakdown. Rowena's cheating ultimately ripped Kardo's moral fiber into the smallest of pieces, driving him into madness.

One evening, close to midnight, he did the unthinkable. We believed that her guardian angel led his daughter Agnes away from the place before the massacre happened. Heeding the call of nature, she got up and proceeded to the toilet/shed at the side of their house.

✄ Bittermelons and Mimosas ✄

On her way downstairs, Agnes walked past her intoxicated father who had passed out, his body blocking the foot of the stairway. She remembered being very careful not to wake him up.

"Maybe I had awakened him," Agnes kept telling the neighbors after the tragedy. "As I was about to go back upstairs, I heard my father yelling at the top of his lungs, 'I'll kill all you girls so you won't grow up like your mother.' Then my two sisters yelled, 'No, don't, no! Aaaggghhh, aaagghhh! God! No! Father, no! Have mercy on us!'"

Ditas, the nearest neighbor, who was unaware of the seriousness of Kardo's madness at first, heard the screams and came out to snoop. As she got closer to the house, she realized the tragedy that was unfolding. She saw Agnes through the *gumamela* bushes that fenced the yard crying hysterically with her hands over her mouth, and trying to get away from the place. Ditas reached out to the girl, scooped her into her arms, and moved her quickly out of the front yard. She called on one of the neighbors who she knew had a relative living across the river.

"Take her to your aunt, quickly! Without a *banca*, Kardo has no means of crossing the river. He would drown."

The neighbors came out, but retreated quickly when they saw Kardo came out of his house. Kardo cruised up and down the street cursing Agnes's name as he wagged a bloodied bolo on his hand. By this time, they realized the worst had already happened. The neighbors barricaded their doors to stop Kardo from entering their houses in case he came looking for Agnes. Unable to find her, Kardo went back to his house, even more enraged, and slit his own throat. The massacre sent shock waves throughout the community and put Sumacab in the headlines for days. Two innocent children who were unable to defend themselves became the victims of Kardo's rage and Rowena's self-absorption. Three coffins filled the house the next day, but Rowena stayed away. Burdened by guilt over their insensitivity, neighbors collected donations to give the three family members a decent burial. It was the least that they could do. This tragedy taught me about compassion and understanding for other people's shortcomings. It also taught me that passing judgment is not godly.

Nieves Catahan Villamin

THESE ARE ALL SPECIAL people, these people of Sumacab. They have helped in shaping my life. My memories of them are like photographs in my mind's eye. Every time I think of where I grew up, their names and faces immediately come to mind. They helped make Sumacab a unique place, a place I will always remember and tell my children about. They helped fabricate my values in life and left me with many cherished memories.

I miss the old days, the pure and simple life, the intelligence and charm that came with the simple joys of life in Sumacab, the way people took care of one another because they cared. These people taught me how life should be lived. Money isn't everything. There are some things that money can't buy.

Chapter Three

Country First

Labong ng kawayan,   A bamboo shoot
bagong tumutubo   when young.
Langit na mataas,   Straight up above
ang siyang itinuturo.   to the sky it points.
Kung ito'y lumaki,   After it's fully-grown
masunod ang anyo   and starts aging.
Sa lupang mababa,   To the ground below
doon din yuyuko.   with time it bows.

A poem my father taught me.

My father was like a bamboo tree, pliant and resilient, but proud. He would bow to reason but stand up for his principles. Such admirable traits had earned the respect of his children – and these traits he passed on to us. The first vivid memory I have of my parents when I was almost seven was not pleasant. We were inside the lobby of the Cabanatuan city jail. An almost tearful Tatang squatted on the floor huddling his five younger children, ages three to twelve. The four older ones were standing around him. Inang sat on the wooden bench close by,

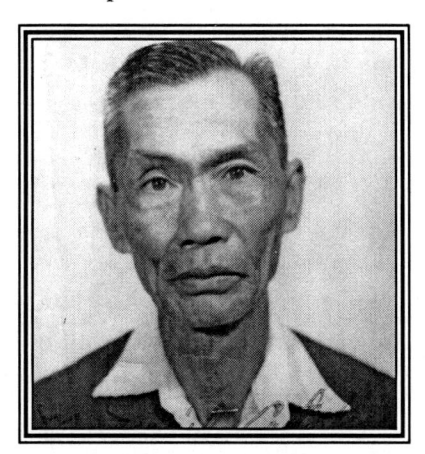

My father, Margarito S. Catahan, a patriot and a great man.

breastfeeding baby Ammie. My youngest sister Beth was three years away from being born.

The door of the office to our right opened and a prison guard came out. "Sign these papers. Then you can get out of here." He handed my father his release papers. "They are all yours?" the guard asked, pointing at us.

I remember him being tall with shaggy brows and a thick mustache that matched his wide shoulders.

"Yes," my father replied curtly. We felt he couldn't wait a second more to get out of there.

Tatang recognized the guard as one of the men who had tortured him some nights before. I remember him gritting his teeth upon sight of the guard. He didn't make any sound, but in my head I heard the same swish I heard when he sharpened his bolo using a big stone. One day, his bolo killed a baby python washed aground during one of the many floods in our barrio. The python swathed around one of our house posts after feasting on Inang's chicks, and Tatang's razor-sharp bolo cut the snake into two halves in a single whack.

The prison guard let us out after Tatang handed back the release papers.

"Don't forget to thank your negotiators, Councilman Quimson and your civilian guard cousin." His voice trailed off as he went back inside his office.

The guard's imposing build, clothed in a neatly pressed police uniform that showed authority, scared me and gave me many nightmares later.

"What did they do to you?" my mother asked as we walked toward the parking lot.

Tatang had bruises on his face, neck, and arms. His eyes were slightly bloodshot, perhaps either from sleep deprivation or too much anger. He completely ignored Inang's question. Tatang was walking in double time scurrying to get away from the building that had been his hellhole for weeks.

Several days later, tears of anger flowed copiously as we listened to him recount the punishments he had endured behind bars.

ᴄ꒰ Bittermelons and Mimosas ꒱ᴐ

"The prison guards tortured me. They subjected different parts of my body to electric shocks. Several times they watered me down until I passed out. One time, one of the guards clapped both of my ears like a pair of cymbals. Blood came out of my eardrums. Still, I didn't 'sing' any of my HUK comrades' names."

We were listening to a man brimming with pride. He held no prejudice against the system that punished him for standing up in opposition to what he believed were injustices suffered by the oppressed and peasant farmers as a result of two major political ideologies being at odds with each other. It was then that I understood why his HUK comrades, who were half the men in our barrio, hailed him as a local hero. The hearing loss he sustained from the prison torture was worn like a badge of honor – it reminded him of his valor. And my barriomates responded to his physical disability with deference and kindness.

I REMEMBER TATANG AS being the best in everything he did. He was endowed with many talents and physical attributes that made farming, hunting and fishing, carpentry and masonry work, arts and crafts, and writing in prose and poetry like second nature to him. His barely 5'7" height cast a long shadow in our barrio. Being the Good Samaritan that he was, he led the group of carpenters in the construction of our elementary school for weeks during the mid-1950s without any remuneration. The only one who understood the complexities of the art of masonry early on, he erected the tombs or houses of my deceased barriomates. I watched him many nights crouched in the *sala* weaving the nets he used to snare the wild quails. My mother sold them at a premium price to the rich folks in the city after the harvest seasons. The same nets trapped native fishes we feasted on when the floods came.

Nieves Catahan Villamin

Tatang's writing skills surpassed those of a college graduate. The most eloquent words he wrote were in verses. The Arakyo manuscript that he left to us was his enduring legacy. His skin was fair, which was unusual for most farmers. His kind face lit like a modern-day *parol*, Christmas lantern, when surrounded with his grandchildren. His offspring and their children saw him as a handsome man endowed with natural talents. His cultural efforts, producing Arakyo for many years, and other spiritual deeds spoke well of his religious beliefs.

As the token priest in our neighborhood, he performed *pagbubuhos* (similar to Saint John's baptism) for the newborns and administered the last rites to the dying. Yet we never saw him attend any church services. He removed curses on people believed to be hexed by witchcraft, guided only by a stone the size of a dinner roll that he believed possessed healing powers. (On his way back to the mountains one night after a visit with his family during his HUK days, he chanced upon the stone on the river shore and felt its electrifying energy.) Had he not had nine female children, I believe he would also have done the laundry.

The shortage in qualified teachers during the American period in 1930–1932 gave Tatang the opportunity to impress others with his superior intelligence. He became a substitute teacher with only a fifth-grade education on his resume, and yet he was able to educate the youngsters in Sumacab just as any certified teacher would have.

Tatang's American superiors discovered his uncompromising principle and discipline that they learned to respect. And those were the days when uprightness – not money or power – mattered most. Paradoxically, these traits that made him an idealist brought our family hardships for many years.

But Tatang was also human. Like most men in a chauvinistic society, he never owned up to his infidelities and stood firm on his ground that his children had no right to question their father. I witnessed his womanizing ways. I saw the hurt it inflicted on all of us, especially my mother. I couldn't help it when my admiration and deep feelings for him began to change. Love combating anger, and admiration battling disapproval – all these turned to compassion when I became a "golden girl."

DURING MY HIGH SCHOOL years, I was once given homework to write a report on the HUKBALAHAP. So, I asked Tatang to tell me about them because he had been a part of the organization for many years.

"It has never made sense to me," I said. "Why were you jailed for fighting against the Japanese imperial army? And why were you hunted like a wild animal after the war? I don't understand it."

"It was like this," he explained. "While other freedom fighters were American puppets, the HUKs stood against both American and Japanese imperialist occupation; and we also fought against the native capitalists and landlords who had been exploiting the peasant farmers for years. Because we were spreading Marxist ideals and communist revolution, the Americans thought we were trying to overthrow the Philippine government."

In college, I would learn that the American government loathed communism, which at that time was gaining ground in some parts of Europe and Asia. Therefore, the Americans considered HUKs terrorists who had to be eliminated at all costs. It made it tougher for the movement that political ideologies during the early 60s were seen mostly through the eyes of American writers. Young minds like ours were led to believe that communism or any economic doctrine that wasn't capitalism was evil. However, with the advent of heightened activism during the Marcos's martial law regime came new information and the rise of anti-American sentiments. Therefore, appreciation for my father and his comrades' ideals became inevitable. Had I belonged to his generation, I am sure I would have been one of them. I would have trod miles and miles of the same dirt roads and climbed the same hills. Sweat would have poured from the same glands in my body. I would have shared any bounty with the people I loved. And I, along with my companions, would have died willingly to protect what was rightfully ours.

To appreciate Tatang's involvement with the HUKs, I found it essential to educate myself about our family's past and the ghosts that haunted it. I learned from him that the Catahan family tree once grew sturdily in Bulacan, a suburb of Manila. But firm conviction, a Catahan trait that I am proud of, almost destroyed our family tree.

The HUKBALAHAP movement had deep roots in the *encomienda* system, a thinly veiled form of native Indian slavery, which the Spanish colonizers had practiced in the New World with devastating results before coming to the Philippines. At first contact, the Spaniards thought the natives were incapable of living a Christian life (the centerpiece of their colonization) because they were savages and pagans. To ensure that Christianity would be spread, the Spanish colonizers were granted pieces of land. The land grantees, called *encomienderos*, were to look after the welfare of the natives, as well as educate and teach them about God. In return the natives were to farm and pay taxes to the *encomienderos* so they would have something to live on. The *encomienda* system was begun with good intentions and seemed to be a fair exchange. When the Spaniards settled on staying in the Philippines permanently, they decided to grant the Spanish soldiers, who had worked for their motherland for years, lands as remunerations. The Philippine natives were exploited and abused just as the indigenous people of the New World had been. Often, *encomienderos* arbitrarily increased taxes to whatever amount they desired to support their lavish lifestyles. When the natives became overburdened and refused to pay more taxes, they were punished severely, sometimes beaten to death. (Many isolated revolts had been taking place although a few failed at the start because some women would tell the priests about it during confession.)

The *encomienda* system was abolished in 1720, and succeeded by the hacienda or large landed states. This time the hacienda owners directly employed laborers, which eventually became their "servants." The system had good intentions when started; however, this was quickly exploited when the hacienderos realized their unlimited power. The haciendas basically kept their "servants" in debt until their death, when the debt was passed on to their children. The same barbarous cruelty that the natives endured from the Spaniards during the *encomienda* system was applied to the servants of the *hacienderos*.

Before a harvest season in the mid-19th century, my ancestor was

Bittermelons and Mimosas

begging from his *haciendero* master another loan so he could bring his very sick wife to a hospital. My ancestor was refused the life-saving loan. He was already heavily indebted from previous loans that had accumulated huge interest. Like most *haciendeross*, his master was a usurer. In addition to being refused, my ancestor was berated for his poverty and slapped several times. Pedro, his son, barely 18 years old, witnessed his father still begging in spite of the cruel treatment he was receiving. Blinded with rage, and without giving any consideration to the consequences of his action, such as a possible death penalty, he jumped to his father's rescue and killed the *haciendero* with his machete. They both fled in different directions. After walking northward for almost two days and one night, Pedro found himself in Sumacab. Neither Pedro, nor any of his children, ever returned to Bulacan. Nor did they try to find out what had happened to his family he left in Bulacan. Thus the family tree was transplanted to Sumacab, and eventually became a respectable one which the mother tree had she known about it would have been very proud of.

On December 10, 1898, the Treaty of Paris formally ended Spain's sovereignty of the Philippines. The Filipinos soon learned that only a changing-of-the-guard had taken place. They were still slaves in their own land. The Filipino-American war raged from 1899 to 1902. After the dust of the Filipino-American war had settled in 1902, the Americans set up a new government. The key players placed at the helm were from the same families of *encomienderos* who governed during the Spanish era. The exploited peasants and workers were more outraged than ever. They began to organize themselves into labor unions with the hope of improving economic conditions.

But the wheel of change that was turning slowly was interrupted by another foreign invasion. Filipino lives again went into a tailspin. With the advent of the Second World War in 1941, the peasant leaders of Pampanga, Tarlac, and Nueva Ecija saw the need of protecting their homes from Japanese invaders. On March 29, 1942, they formed HUKBALAHAP. The main objective of the organization was to fight for a free and independent Philippines. (Most history books give credence to the mistaken belief that the HUKs wanted to overthrow the Philippine government.) The HUKs gave the Japanese plenty of headaches due to the hit-and-run battles they fought throughout Central Luzon. The Japanese forces eventually feared them more than the guerilla units.

Tatang's affiliation with the underground movement (using the code name Vallarta) began in 1943 when he was appointed as a HUK logistician operating in our barrio and nearby villages. His burgeoning family made him a reluctant member in the beginning. However, when the Japanese invaders became serious about putting an end to all anti-Japanese activities by placing the villages under *zona* raids (men from the villages were forcibly rousted and rounded up by Japanese soldiers and herded to the village schoolhouses), he decided to become a full-time HUK. In principle, he declared he would rather die fighting for his country as a HUK than be killed during a *zona* for no cause.

Tatang would disappear from the barrio for a week or two to avoid the *zona* and then come back home through the protective watch of our barriomates, mostly HUK sympathizers, to attend to his farming duties. At the height of the *zona* in December 1944, when news about the landing of American forces was being smuggled onto the Japanese airwaves, men, women, and children from other villages were being beheaded with the help of MAKAPILIs.

Before the American Liberation Army arrived in January 1945, the HUKs had recaptured areas of Central Luzon from the Japanese. In each liberated town, the HUKs immediately installed a municipal government system with their leaders as administrators, only to be replaced by the Philippine Civil Affairs Unit (PCAU) and the American Army with their favored Filipino-USAFFEE guerilla members.

HUKs were labeled as communist terrorists and the Americans loathed them. The HUKs annoyed the American soldiers even more after they almost foiled the liberation in progress of POWs from the Cabanatuan prison in January 1945. HUKs stopped the fleeing 512 POWs freed by Army Rangers, Alamo Scouts led by Lieutenant Mucci, and rival Filipino guerrillas led by Captain Pajota. The HUKs maintained that only Americans could pass, and Pajota's men had to stay, for a reason that was never revealed. Knowing Japanese forces were pursuing them, the American lieutenant threatened to call in an artillery barrage and level the village. The HUKs reluctantly let both groups pass and the 512 POWs marched to freedom. Situations like this led to more vigorous campaigns against the HUKs.

On February 22, 1945, disarming of the HUKs began, followed by arrests. In 1948, President Manuel A. Roxas declared the HUKs an illegal and subversive organization. President Elpidio Quirino opened negotiations with the HUKs but nothing was accomplished. The HUKBALAHAP became the HMB (Hukbong Magpapalaya ng Bayan or People's Liberation Army) in 1950. Beginning in 1951, the movement began to weaken. During the popular Ramon Magsaysay administration, many HUK leaders surrendered and the HUK rebellion came to an end in 1954.

However, the failure of President Elpidio Quirino to implement a secret agreement his brother Judge Antonio Quirino made with the HUK leaders in June 21, 1948, sent Luis Taruc and the HUKs back to the hills. Once more, the HUK movement regained strength, and skirmishes between the rebels and government troops intensified.

When one of the cadres in my father's group that was stationed in Malilio, Santa Rosa, was killed by the civilian guards, most went into hiding, except my father. His bravery earned him a promotion. He was taken by the HUKs to the Sierra Madre Mountains to preach as well as evade the civilian guards who were hunting him down. Little did he know that he was also a marked man within his organization because our non-HUK no-supporter no-good barriomates were feeding the leaders bad information that would make him run for his dear life back to the lowlands where the civilian guards were waiting. By then the HUK leaders knew that Tatang's oldest brother Basilio (a man loved and respected in our barrio for his political savvy and above all a HUK supporter) was the acting Teniente del Baryo or barrio captain of Sumacab. Because of his blood relationship with Jesus Ponce, the head of civilian guards in Cabanatuan City, people with HUK relatives came to him for help for military concessions.

Jesus Ponce was a civilian guard known for his strong stance against the HUKs because they had tortured him early on. He was one who would do everything in his power (which the government had granted him in abundance) to quell the resistance.

The supposed dots were there, and the HUK leadership just had to connect them. Tatang's superiors accused him of being a spy embedded in the organization. He was caught in the crossfire of politics and ideologies between the HUK organization and the Philippine government. He had been dealt a double-edged sword. Whichever way Tatang chose spelled doom. The thought of the camp he had considered his second home becoming his prison cell, and the leaders that he served with utmost loyalty for many years now becoming his enemies, disillusioned him. His testimonies of his loyalty to the organization – that he wasn't and would never be a spy that would defame an ideology he chose over his family – fell on deaf ears. He grew desperate, especially after his superiors set a date for his trial in the HUK court. But the trial for deceit, which carried a possible death sentence, was avoided.

Late one night, a flurry of bullets being fired by the HUKs, not the military police, hounded him as he sped down the mountainside into the lowlands and across the river. The gunfire echoed throughout the region and frightened those living nearby. Our family, which was camped inside the *lungaw* for safety, had no idea that the bullets were meant for Tatang. His trusted comrades, Razon, and Alto, had helped him escape. Upon reaching the barrio Tatang hid inside an abandoned house close to our neighborhood. When daylight came, he called to a passerby and asked the man to summon his brother. Basilio took him to the Cabanatuan City officials to surrender.

Tatang escaped from the HUK's prosecution, but not from that of the Philippine government. The law now considered HUKs as terrorists and enemies of the country. In spite of his brother's and cousin Ponce's connections, he was imprisoned for almost a year and was occasionally tortured like a common criminal. The government officials wanted him to name other renegades still hiding in the mountains. That, he never did. His brother and cousin, together with

Bittermelons and Mimosas

Councilman Andres Quimson, Sr., a Sumacab native, all worked to seek his early release.

The year 1953 saw our family riding a seesaw of emotions. Although we were elated to know Tatang was alive, we were despondent over his incarceration. We were fully aware of the hell to be found inside his prison cell. Tougher than a nail, he endured the water-cure-torture and the other punishments dealt him by the Philippine Constabulary. The punishers might have broken his body and bones but never his spirit. At no moment did he waver and disclose the names and whereabouts of his comrades because he knew that would compromise innocent lives. Besides, he was a man of integrity. The HUK leaders who had accused Tatang of being a spy changed their tune when no arrests were made as a result of his surrender. Finally, Tatang became a free man.

In 1954 Taruc emerged from the jungle to surrender and the HUKBALAHAP Rebellion, for all practical purposes, came to an end. HUKs surrendered and were dealt punishments, which were imprisonments for a period of time. The crossfire of bullets on the once blood-spattered river shore was neither heard nor seen anymore.

RAZON, ALTO, MINATULA, AND Vallarta were a few of the Band of Brothers of the HUKBALAHAP era. They were ordinary farmers who under extraordinary circumstances left their families and took to hiding to fight for what they believed was the right cause. Before they were HUKs, Kanor (Razon), Melchor (Alto), Feliciano Julian (Minatula), and Vallarta (my father) were law-abiding farmers and close friends, as had been their parents. They had adjacent rice fields. (In the old days, adjacent could mean miles and miles of distance between places.) My father was the overseer of a hacienda that lay in close proximity to the Vejandre community in Cabanatuan City where my civilian guard uncle, Tatang's second cousin, lived. My uncle, who would eventually make their lives miserable, knew Razon, Alto, and Minatula because of my father.

At the height of the campaign against the HUKs (1948–1953), the Philippine Army and Constabulary and the civilian guards were given enormous powers and equipment to get their job done. The army and the constabulary ultimately merged in 1950, the time when Central Luzon, a primarily agricultural area, was virtually under HUK control. The civilian guards that were hired by landowners to protect their crops from HUKs who now were in control chased farmers, mostly HUK families and supporters, away from their fields. Upon the relocation of these people into communities, the civilian guards stole or burned their crops in the hope of breaking the HUKs' spirits so they would surrender. Most farmers and HUK families were left with nothing other than the possibility of starving before the next harvest came.

Blood, however, again proved to be thicker than water. My civilian guard uncle and his cronies left his Sumacab relatives' crops alone, so we didn't starve as most HUK families did. Meanwhile, Razon, Alto, and Minatula's families weren't as lucky. For safety and protection from the civilian guards, Tatang decided to place Razon's family under his wing. He offered Razon (he was more than happy to do it) the opportunity to move their house next to ours. Razon was Pascual's uncle. Pascual was my sister Clarita's boyfriend and had once saved Tatang's life when both were serving with the HUKs. HUKs took care of each other as a way of survival. Tatang courted danger upon settling what he believed was a debt of a lifetime. If he had any regrets doing so, he never told us.

LIFE WITH AN ABSENTEE father was tough. As expected, my father's allegiance to the movement brought misery not only to our home but to his brothers' as well. Although his younger brothers, Gorio and Pedro, were under the watchful eyes of the law, they still helped with our farming duties. Luckily or unluckily they had small families. Uncle Gorio had an only son. Uncle Pedro had two boys and a girl. With their help, it was almost as if Tatang had been present during the farming seasons. Still, I give the most credit to my mother, whose strength and calm disposition was the family's guide to safety and decency during troubled times.

However, all of us were forced to grow up. My older siblings tended the farms and animals. I still remember the times my older sisters, together with my two brothers, cleared the farm of thick bushes by using long and sharp machetes almost bigger than them.

✥ Bittermelons and Mimosas ✥

They toiled from sunrise to sundown in preparation for plowing. They were young and female, but they worked in the fields as hard as most farmers. We younger ones did the household chores and assisted my mother in peddling vegetables and other food items in the market and neighborhood to make ends meet. I was my mother's "crier" as we peddled mangoes, eggplants, string beans, tomatoes, and other vegetables. "Vegetables, vegetables for sale, come buy them now, cheap only." In between their farming chores, my two brothers became newspaper boys in the city.

Hard times taught Kuya Lino to be clever. Kuya Lino, as the elder of the two boys, became the symbolic head of the family in my father's absence. Although he was frail and skinny, his survival instincts went way beyond his 14 years. On days when he didn't make any commission from his newspaper route, he played *cara y cruz* (heads-or-tails coin-tossing game), with children in the streets for small bets so he could buy Ammie's milk. (My mother's milk started to dry out early because she was in her mid-40s when she had Ammie.) Luck seemed to be on his side until the day the children figured out that the coins he was tossing were double-faced; either side would let him win. "Cheater, we don't want to play with you no more." They avoided him as if he were a leper.

With no children to dupe, Kuya Lino did what he thought was the next best thing. On days that he didn't have the money to buy Ammie's milk, he stole it. He was able to do this twice but was caught on the third try. Although tears of shame flowed from Kuya Lino's eyes, the storeowner wouldn't budge.

"It's either your mother or the police," was what he told the frightened boy.

My brother appeared on our doorstep with the angry storeowner yanking on his shirt collar as though he were a dog on a leash. As Kuya Lino held a can of milk in each hand, my mother immediately figured out what he had done. She tried to break the ice and said, "Hello," but the storeowner rudely interrupted her and started cursing. He stopped short upon the sight of a smiling baby bouncing happily on my mother's hip with both eyes focused on the cans of milk my brother held. Cooler words and kinder hearts prevailed. In the end, Kuya Lino gained a new elderly friend. Ammie had her milk for the next few days. And, Kuya Lino never stole again.

Our mother tried her best to comfort us, especially at times when the bullet-ridden bodies of HUKs were brought home inside a cart pulled by a *carabao*. She fended off our worries by always telling us that Tatang was indoctrinating new members, not engaging in combat. My father was such an intelligent man, he must have known what he was doing. At least, that is what I tried to tell myself over and over again. We all worked hardest as a family together during those trying periods. Difficult days indeed, yet the best learning days as well. Like a blessing in disguise, those adversities inspired us to strive harder and eventually guided us to the successes we have achieved today.

Surviving HUKBALAHAP members: L-R: Estanislao Francisco, Ben Sangueza, Edmundo Pelayo, Roming Pascual and Matias Buan.

Chapter Four

The Young Ones

Youth is the best time to be rich,
and the best time to be poor.

Euripides, Greek Tragic Poet (480–406 BC)

After my father got out of jail, he and the older siblings resumed full-time farming and planted rice, corn, and other vegetables. The farmland, back to my father's management, became more giving than before, and bountiful harvests soon appeared, overfilling our granaries. These extra yields were sold to finance the bigger house needed for our ever-growing family. Among my father's many natural talents was carpentry. By observing his elders, he taught himself how to make bricks, use scales and measuring tape, and estimate costs. Using a pointed stick in the dirt, he sketched a rough blueprint of our family's bigger house. The simple design mirrored our simple lifestyle. Gifted with his hands, my father depended on nothing more complicated than a few hand tools and the help of our neighbors, whom he had helped before, to complete the project. One afternoon in March 1954, after school, I came home and found ten cement posts braced with steel bars planted in our lot where once a *nipa* hut stood. A shed at one side of our lot became our temporary shelter where we waited with much anticipation the first rainfall in May.

The house he built with the help of neighbors and relatives was elevated three to four meters from the ground, allowing air to circulate beneath it. This space underneath the *silong* served as a workspace, a storage space, a granary, and sometimes a pen for livestock. It later became my mother's variety store. Wood posts that stood on cement foundations secured by steel brackets held the house together. Parts of the walls were made of bamboo and some wood. No sheetrock was used. This type of material was unavailable in Sumacab. The roof was covered with sheets of galvanized steel, each nailed securely on the exposed wood beam ceilings. Like most houses in the barrio, our house had four rooms: the kitchen, the living room, the sacred room, and the *matong* or grain storage. Our house had bamboo floorings spaced an inch between the slats. However, to protect our privacy, my father used tightly lined hardwoods in the living room to seal off the floor space. This was to stop any "Peeping Tom" from getting a quick look under my older sisters' skirts while they did their nightly chores.

"They wouldn't dare," my father assured my mother. "They know I wouldn't give a second thought about hunting those 'peepers' down with my bolo."

Securing the harvests was as equally important to my father as safety for his children. August, one of the monsoon months, was when we harvested our corn crop. To circumvent challenges from the unpredictable weather, my father hung his corn harvest tied in its husks to dry (in preparation for milling) on the exposed beams from our house's ceiling. My older sisters complained about this, saying the hanging corn made our house look like an unkempt barn, which could tell a lot about their housekeeping habits. We were embarrassed to entertain company, especially possible suitors, with food hanging from the ceiling.

The kitchen was actually the kitchen and dining area, cramped into one room with every inch of space used day in and day out. Three times a day, burning firewood heated the clay stoves that cooked our simple meals of steamed rice, fish, or vegetables that were more flavorful than today's meals. It was during these meals that my mother lectured us endlessly about morals and Christian values. Respect your elders. Love thy neighbor. Among Filipino families, tradition dictated that mealtime was spent together at the table as a

Bittermelons and Mimosas

family – the children would learn while everyone shared the grace from Above.

Our biggest room, which was the living room, served as a multi-purpose room. Our elders received guests here during fiestas, Christmas, and other holidays. At night, we switched the room over to become a large bedroom for the children. None of us ever enjoyed the luxury of a private room in that house. We shared everything, from pillows and cotton blankets to food, problems of the day, and – the most-looked-forward-to commodity – gossip. Adjoining the big *sala* was what we referred to as the sacred room. The only space in the entire house boasting the luxury of a door that could be closed for privacy, it kept pillows, blankets, and personal accessories. It was a very sacred place. The silid served as the honeymoon suite for the family newlyweds. Sisters Clarita and Macaria and brother Lino all retreated behind that door with their new spouses. Danny and I also enjoyed the privacy of that room during our honeymoon nights. If walls could talk!

The *matong* room over in the right wing of the house was our little Fort Knox or grains safe house. A large bin my father built of rattan and bamboo stored the *palay* grains, our food until the next harvest. Like hanging the corn from the ceiling, storing food inside our house was preferred by my father for safety reasons. During a few bountiful harvests, I remember that the *matong* room overflowed, and sacks of stored *palay* lay on the floor. To prevent the *matong* room from yielding to the weight of the grain, my father reinforced that part of the house by adding more posts to the space underneath. Then that area was filled with firewood to conceal the overflowing *matong* room. If neighbors discovered that we had extra grain, they might have decided to use it as their source of food too. My father wasn't a selfish man, but with eleven children, he had to be prudent.

There were dangers associated with being too cautious. The stash of firewood became a hiding place for snakes that crawled up to the flatland from the nearby woods to seize mice and sometimes chickens for food during the dry season. Twice I remember his killing snakes with a sharp bolo. I was too young to understand the price we paid to safeguard our food.

We moved into our bigger house before New Year's Day in 1955. Our house of wood with a galvanized iron roof stood like a peacock, proud and distinguished, overshadowing the surrounding houses in our neighborhood because of my father's skill. Finally settled in, our lives became normal again, but not for long.

In mid-March, my oldest sister Macaria and her three-year-old baby boy Andoy escaped from Pedring to live in Sumacab. Her husband had again battered my sister; she was bruised from head to toe. As Macaria was trying to build a new life, Clarita was planning hers. Unruffled by our older sister's fate, she eloped with Islao, a farmer who was five years older than she.

However, the unexpected changes in our family structure were offset with excitement raised by the crowning glories the younger siblings brought home from school. Soon, framed certificates of scholastic achievements, instead of paintings or photographs, hung on the walls of our living room/bedroom. I was never athletic like most neighborhood girls my age. It didn't matter though because in those days, athletic skills were not only unimportant but even looked down upon. Athletic girls were teased and called "tomboy" or boyish. Most parents hoped for academic excellence for their children. My parents acknowledged our certificates of scholastic achievements with unspoken love and pride. We knew that each award ceremony they attended made them proud and tall, higher than a kite trying to reach over the moon. Punishments such as "sermons" or lashings became fewer – even when we fought with each other and all hell broke loose, and we called each other awful names.

AS A CHILD, I was teased a lot because I was clumsy. Also, most children

Bittermelons and Mimosas

my age thought I was some kind of freak. I had six toes on my left foot because my mother said she ate a lot of ginger when I was in her tummy. "You are what you eat." That's what everybody told me often. "Ebeng ginger toes, last again to finish!" They teased me nonstop because I couldn't escape from being "it" in a game of bring the guard down before our school recess was over. The few times I fought back, I ended up kissing the ground with a heavier girl on my back pulling my hair while the rest of the group cheered her on.

I still remember the brawl during the fourth grade when one of them threw me into the tilapia pool the sixth graders were constructing as a science project. Humiliated and dripping wet, I screamed to the group after I got out of the pool, "Someday you will look up to me and beg for my friendship!"

To which one of them replied, "Look you up where? On top of a *kamatsile* tree?" I pretty much know that was an insult. Kamatsile trees are very tall and thorny.

I got my revenge in the fifth grade. Everybody wanted to be my friend after I took the first honor ribbon in that class. Enemies today, friends tomorrow. We drew a line on the dirt and spat on the ground and then we were friends again. Because there wasn't a park or recreation hall available in Sumacab for growing children like us, we were forced to kiss and make up soon. Otherwise, we would not be welcomed in someone else's backyard, which on most occasions was our playground. Boys seldom played with us girls because if they did, they would be teased mercilessly as either weak or *bakla* or homosexual.

I still remember the many times our mothers called and called for us to come home for dinner, only to be ignored because we were in the heat of our games. Then our fathers showed up, waving a big bamboo stick with which to spank us if we did not obey. At the sight of the bamboo stick, we ran in different directions like startled cats, only to face our mothers, who wanted our blood for penance, waiting at home. Our heads bowed down like Sunday communicants, we washed our hands in a hurry and rushed to the *dulang* to devour our waiting supper. Before transistor radios filled our ears, our night entertainments after helping wash dishes and clean the kitchen were more games, and sometimes fighting over the first chance to read the local magazines. The older children bullied the younger ones, who were forced to stay up late for their turn to read the precious magazines.

On nights when the moon glowed over our world, we filled it with laughter and zest as we took our tag and block game into the streets. The excitement from the fantastic ideas put into our heads by our favorite magazines or from the games we played in the streets tired us beyond exhaustion. Even the loud noises of dishes toppling down on the bamboo floor or the yowls of stray cats hunting for food in the middle of the night could not disrupt us from our deep slumber. Loud voices from our older siblings, which could be heard within a mile distance, woke us up the next morning. We had to either go to school or help on the farms.

To avoid playing with bullies after school, I stayed home and read anything I could put my hands on. Books for reading pleasure were a rarity then, so I would read any printed papers – even the *tinapa* (smoked fish) paper wrappers that my mother recycled for use at her *sari-sari* store. Many years later, my mother told how she had bribed the smoked fish vendor to make sure her next order was wrapped with the next issue of *komiks* (cartoon magazine) that we read. It delighted her tremendously to see how happy we were, and I was able to find out what happened next to Rosing and Kenkoy, my favorite *komiks* characters. I borrowed Cousin Casio's songbooks and memorized the lyrics of Tony Bennett's "Rags to Riches," belting it out on my way home from school. (I could sing the high notes until after puberty.) Then, there were the ones that gave me the most pleasure, old notebooks that held Kuya Lino's romantic thoughts written in verses and prose. (Kuya Lino gave me an earful when he found out because he didn't think it was right for me to read his private thoughts without his permission.) All this reading gave me more wisdom than any institution of higher learning could have ever done.

When I felt restless because there was nothing else to read, I walked to the river to cool down. I don't know why, but even at a young age, I felt a special bond with the river. Like an ice-cold root beer during a toasty summer day, the river had a calming effect on me, especially during the almost perfect December weather when it looked glorious. I felt inner peace looking at the receding water that formed into tiny currents as it was ruffled by a gentle breeze. As the currents drifted further away, I often wondered where they'd end up. Many years later I would still ask myself the same question.

DURING OUR ELEMENTARY DAYS, Nora, Ofelia, Naty, and I were the neighborhood *haragans* (the tagalog version of the Little Rascals). We walked the same road almost every day and sometimes we skipped school. We planted the same stalks of rice and teamed up to steal watermelons. We sometimes quarreled because we didn't agree on certain points. Naty and Ofelia believed in destiny and folklore like Juan Tamad, or Lazy Juan, who waited for the guava fruit to ripen and fall into his mouth as he lay under the tree. I would argue it was foolish of him to do that. Destiny could intervene – a hungry bird could peck at the guava fruit before it ripened, leaving Juan with nothing.

As farmers' daughters, we were no strangers to all agricultural adversities while growing up. We all experienced how pests and bad weather destroyed our crops and robbed us of our livelihood, thus forcing hand-to-mouth living until a bountiful harvest came along. Farming for a landlord was what was in line for me. And I had trouble accepting this destiny. Behind my back, I knew Ofelia and Naty had been impertinent and changed my nickname to "Ebeng Mapangarap" or "Ebeng the Dreamer." They laughed at my dream – my obsession, they would say – of becoming someone better and not just a farmer's wife. In time, they would understand me.

Our parents' inability to provide us a life of plenty, no matter how they wanted to, taught us how to hunt for food at an early age. And during our hunts, Mother Nature and her offspring toyed with our imaginations and resolve. As ten-year-olds, our silhouettes hardly

✦ Nieves Catahan Villamin ✦

The grown-up *haragans* 60 years later. L-R: Ofelia, me, and Naty.

rose above the rice paddies, so our parents, like a broken record, warned us about the dangers and consequences of wandering from home. But finds from the streams and the rice paddies that our elders brought home after fieldwork put the idea in our empty heads and stomachs that we could do that too! Food was scant. And if we sought it ourselves, we thought for sure our plates would be fuller than usual during supper. The thought was more than enough reason to disobey our parents.

  Hundreds of snails drifting on the streams like black pearls floating on a bowl of sago drink excited us. Catching a bucketful was painless. St. Nicholas, the Guardian of Children with his angels of mercy, was always a step ahead of us, ridding the streams of leeches and mosquito hives that preyed on children's blood for their own food. Tiny crabs, although harder to find, were not really smart. They left footprints around the holes they had dug on the side of the elevated dike. Farmers built the dikes around the rice paddies to hold rainwater for the rice stalks' subsistence inasmuch as irrigation hadn't come to our region yet. And if luck were on our side, we would see snakes emerging before we put our hands inside those holes. (Forget you leeches and snakes! When steamed, the tiny crabs had more flavor than the big ones caught on the Alaskan reefs today. Snails

Bittermelons and Mimosas

sautéed with cooking oil, lots of garlic, sweet onions, and ginger were tender and a lot more flavorful than the escargots served at a French restaurant.) We weren't aware that snakes usually shared the crab's holes for their domain. Again, St. Nicholas and his angels made sure the holes we invaded were the safe ones. How else would someone explain that?

With Father Sun's help, nature's bounty leaped from the ground to the trees in spring. When it happened, we made sure to be there to enjoy it. Of the three of us, Ofelia was the youngest, yet the biggest and strongest. It was a common joke in our neighborhood that her parents fed her *guano* (cave dwellers and sea birds' droppings used as fertilizer) when she was a baby and so she was much bigger than other girls her age.

My bell rang much later when I found out that guano was a kind of nourishment for the rice stalks and other crops, certainly not for human consumption. My guano friend was also the best *salagubang* (edible beetle) trapper among the four of us. I remember one May when our backyard tamarind trees swarmed with *salagubang* in the thousands. It looked like a scene from the Ten Commandments during one of those plagues. Ofelia made a hook from a 20-foot bamboo pole and anchored it to every branch of the tamarind trees along the backyard row. Each time she pulled the hook with a force only she could muster, hordes of *salagubang* perched on the tree leaves fell freely on the ground like raindrops. Pickled *salagubang* was the side dish of choice for supper that night.

Our neighbors' told us many times that we were our parents' daughters. Ofelia was the quick thinker and had a disposition that matched. Naty, even at an early age, was tactful and knew how to handle money. Nora was sweet and petite like her mother. I was the most scholarly and knew what I wanted to be when I grew up. Ofelia was very protective of her friends. Children who poked fun at Naty, Nora, and me had to answer to her.

When I became older, I realized that perhaps protecting us was her way of acting out the anger against her father that she had held in for so long. Her father, who had languished in prison after accidentally killing an uncle by striking him with a bamboo pole, ruled his roost with an iron fist. Black marks from five to ten lashes were often tattooed on Ofelia's behind. Her father's wooden cane, used only to punish his children, painted the artwork. Before I brought home honors, I was spanked quite a few times too, but they were nothing compared to Ofelia's lashes.

Naty was the most pleasant and well mannered among us. Her parents taught her early on that hard work and getting along spelled success, especially if you were in business. As one of the most trusted *viajeros* in the barrio, her father never had resorted to illegal means to collect payments, as other merchants frequently did. Naty's mother, in addition to taking care of the house, helped in the business enterprise. They were unlike the typical husbands and wives who were idle after planting season. Hence, their pantry was always stocked with food.

Nora was the precious one. She was the smallest and the cutest, with the fairest skin. When the three of us spent long hours in the river helping our parents or playing, Nora's sunburned skin turned beet red instead of dark charcoal like the rest of ours. She looked like a China doll with brownish wavy hair and small brown eyes complemented by her small, pointed nose. Nora's parents were very ambitious and adventurous, so unlike most farmers in our neighborhood. They wanted to have their own land so they could raise more crops for their growing family. When they heard about *kaingin* (slash and burn farming) from relatives who had done it, they didn't think twice. *Kaingin* were virgin lands given to farmers by the national government to win them over to their side. Farming the *kaingin* would give them the opportunity to better their lot. Nora's parents were fed up with the tenancy system where at every harvest they gave 30 to 50 percent of the crops to the landowner. What remained of their harvest was not even enough to pay off debts because of the outrageous interest charged by their landlord. Nora's family knew that in time one of the children could be taken in as a servant to pay off the family debts.

I was the dreamer. The one who was willing to do anything to avoid being a farmer's daughter for the rest of my life. The one who they labeled "Ebeng The Dreamer." The one who would travel half

Bittermelons and Mimosas

the world only to settle in a foreign land for the life I despised in my youth. Only this time, the situation would be reversed.

As the 1954–1955 school year was ending we were busy planning activities for the coming summer vacation as in the past. We had no inkling that summer would be best remembered by us with tears not cheers because Nora would be leaving us for good.

HOLY WEEK, 1955. IT was the last time when my friends – as a gang – took an active part in the rituals. Our early indoctrination into the Catholic faith taught us that Holy Week was the period when we would commemorate the passion and death of our Lord Jesus Christ through weeklong religious rites.

Aunt Gertrudes, our barrio holy woman, would preach to the youth the teachings in the Bible. "Fast or give up meat on Good Friday so your souls will be cleansed and sanctified."

To which my father would argue, "Don't take the Bible literally. That's not what it meant. It has more to do with being intimate."

Truth or not, to this day, that's what I practice.

Good Friday or not, having meat on a designated religious day was never a problem for us because we seldom had it in our daily menu. If fasting for one night was difficult for my sweet tooth, I knew it was a bigger challenge for Ofelia, who liked food better than she liked her parents. Her gluttonous appetite increased as the arrays of meals and snacks streamed endlessly into the makeshift kitchen of the church for five nights. It wasn't an exaggeration when others noted that often Ofelia's appetite was bigger than all the *Pasyon* (Passion of Christ) chanters and worshippers combined. After Holy Week, she could hardly fit into her skirt.

While Ofelia was busy in the kitchen, I was chanting with the worshippers. Naty and Nora frequented the many snack booths that stood around the church purposely to check out who was stationed at which booth. In reality, the booths were a tacit way for bachelors to check out the prettiest girls in the neighborhood. This disguised display of romantic overtones added zing and spirit to an otherwise serious and grueling five-day *pasyon* marathon. Before Good Friday came, the two girls were able to complete a roster of who was dating whom, replete with the juiciest information.

On Good Friday morning, hooded penitents paraded down the road. They beat their backs with whips tipped with sharp objects as a form of self-flagellation to ask for the forgiveness of their sins and to express gratefulness for favors granted. Hardly had the procession passed by us when Nora made an announcement. Her face was paler than a white sheet of paper.

"We are moving to Santo Rosario a week after the May Arakyo. My father wants to farm a *kaingin*."

Nora's pronouncement caught us by surprise. We were too shocked to follow the parade of devotees on its way down to the church to watch the re-enactment of Jesus' nailing to the Cross. I saw Ofelia look down at the ground to hide the tears trying to sneak out from her eyes. Naty was wide-eyed and visibly upset. And I almost threw up from being anxious. Later that evening we pulled ourselves together enough so that we were able to watch the *pasyon*-chanting contest. But we did not wait to see who won prizes. I went to bed thinking about Nora and how I would miss her.

"How far is that place?" I asked her the following day as we bathed in the river with picnickers commemorating Glory Saturday. "And are you sure you can still watch the Arakyo with us before you go?" Arakyo was our favorite fiesta show because it was always staged when the temperature was perfect for eating a big glass of *halo-halo*, our favorite cooling aid.

"It's about fourteen kilometers from here," she said. "And yes, I promise to watch the Arakyo with you just as we have in the past. You guys can come and visit me also." She tried to mask the sorrow in her voice with a smile.

Right after Holy Week, Nora's family packed everything they owned, put it all inside a *kariton* hauled by their only *carabao*, and moved to Santo Rosario. Ofelia, Naty, and I cried aloud as their *kariton* passed by. Only three of the rascals took to the streets and showered under the downpour when the first rainfall in May came flowing down. However, we anticipated the four of us would be up on the stage to dance for a blessing as we did the previous year when Arakyo day comes.

⁂

AMONG MY FANTASIES WAS to be an Arakyo performer. However I was short, dark, and with six toes on my left foot, definitely not princess material. Yes, the face could be covered with make-up. With tons of it, my face could look smooth and lighter. My arms wouldn't be exposed because the costumes had long sleeves. The delicate fabric was woven tightly enough so that one couldn't see through it. High heels would give me additional height, and could disguise my dark legs. However, I could mess my dialogue, or miss a step and fall down on the stage. I would be the laughing stock of the performance. And no sympathy from my family adding insult to the injury! How cruel would that be?

"Give it up," Naty and Ofelia teased me incessantly. "And besides, your father won't let you,"

They were right. None of us nine daughters played a part in the Arakyo presentation. He didn't like the idea of amorous males ogling his daughters as they acted on stage. I was smart enough to forget about being an Arakyo princess. Being on my father's bad side wasn't the place I wanted to be. So I celebrated Arakyo every May with my friends from a distance.

I can remember my father writing the Arakyo script. This chronicles the pilgrimage Saint Helena of Constantinople made to the Holy Land in search of the real cross on which Jesus was crucified. According to legend, after Saint Helena's army battled many unbelievers, a bright star appeared and led them to the place of the crucifixion of Jesus. This is where they found the three crosses – Christ's and the two thieves' – buried underneath a mountain that the Jews had made to erect a church they called Venus. After subjugating the

Nieves Catahan Villamin

First Arakyo cast in 1958. Uncle Basilio holding a baton third from right.

My father took the baton after Uncle Basilio died. Father sitting fourth L-R. Uncle Gorio standing at the back fourth, last row.

church guards that were led by Herarkyo (as time passed, the name became Arakyo), Saint Helena and her army destroyed Venus and dug until they found three crosses with inscriptions and nails. Jesus' cross was identified when a gravely ill woman immediately got well after touching it. Saint Helena had a church built on the site. The church became the Cross's permanent home. The cross later became the symbol of Christianity.

Clearly influenced by the Spanish colonization, Arakyo was one of many cultural expressions Filipinos nurtured through the years. The performers were dressed like the kings and queens on a deck of cards, each outfitted with a sword that made them look like real warriors and a crown or hat lavishly trimmed with sparkling beads. The finest of yarns reproduced the elegant costumes of a once-flourishing kingdom. White and green colors dominated the Christian wardrobes, perhaps as symbols for spirituality and advanced civilization. Red is the color for the non-Christians, perhaps symbolizing their courage for fighting the war to the very end. These interpretations could be the reason why pale-skinned and wholesome-looking individuals always played the Christian roles. The non-Christian actors were muscular, taller, and darker.

Nora's absence during Arakyo made us miss her more. We planned on going to visit her until our elder siblings warned us about the vampire who was rumored to cut off children's heads and collect their blood to pour down the cement posts of a bridge then under construction. Folk belief said that doing so would make the bridge sturdier and strong enough to last several lifetimes. Without an elder to chaperone us during our trek through kilometers of open space, we would be the perfect prey. We didn't fancy seeing ourselves with our skulls chopped open and put inside a sack hanging on top of a *balete* tree. We heeded the elders' warnings. We didn't see Nora for a very long time.

Chapter Five

Missing Coins in the Year of the Bounty

> Dreams never hurt anybody,
> if you keep working right
> behind the dreams
> to make as much of them
> become real as you can.
>
> *Frank W. Woolworth*
> *Founder, F. Woolworth Company*

As the Catahan family enjoyed the blessings of being a whole family again, my sister Macaria's fortune was improving as well. By this time, she had remarried and had Andoy's baby sister. Her second husband, Tomas, was a mestizo from Aliaga whose mother was my grandmother's close friend. In spite of Tomas's poor eyesight and hearing problem, my grandmother handpicked him because she thought his family was well-to-do. Tomas's mother was a *pensionado* or retiree who received a monthly allowance.

My oldest sister Macaria resisted at first. "My God, he is deaf and blind! Forget it." However, my grandmother thought there might be some advantage to a pre-arranged marriage, particularly after the life Macaria had led with Pedring. Besides, she was a single woman with a child and so she could not afford to be choosy.

After their church wedding (her HUK marriage with Pedring

wasn't recognized by the church), Tomas built Macaria and Andoy a small house in Bibiclat, a village near his parents' place. Farming would be their livelihood. Away from the people she trusted and overwhelmed by her farming duties, Macaria cried out for Tatang when it was time to reap their first *palay* crop. Tatang heeded and sent Conchita, my third older sister, and three of my older cousins to Bibiclat as soon as the December harvest started. For the next few years, our family took turns in visiting because Macaria missed us terribly. While the older girls appreciated the nightly serenades by the bachelors from other villages, who later became their friends, I found my thrill from climbing up the *sampalok*, *kamatsile*, and *atis* or sugar apple trees spread around my sister's big backyard, especially when their fruits were in season. One visit was very memorable because it was during Bibiclat's fiesta celebrations.

I remember that June in 1956 when I visited Ateng Macaria and her family during a religious festival in their barrio called Pagsa-San Juan, which was celebrated in honor of Saint John the Baptist, Bibiclat's patron saint. My sister's guests were participants in a ritual called *Taong putik* festival, and they had requested *sinampalukang palaka* (frog dish cooked with tamarind blossoms) for lunch. With modesty aside, my sister's *sinampalukang* tasted heavenly even without frog meat, the dish's main ingredient. We have had it a few times in the past. Then again, anything tastes good when one is starved.

Early that day my sister's husband Tomas had left to pasture his animals in some nearby fields. He wouldn't be back in time to pick tamarind blooms for the main dish she was preparing for her guests. I volunteered for the chore to ease her worries. With a big piece of cloth tied loosely about my neck as my basket in which to put the blooms, I climbed the tamarind. Up there I picked only the healthiest of blooms, Macaria's secret spice for her frog dish that many thought was the best that they had ever had in Bibiclat. Not enough tamarind blooms would have been disastrous for the dish.

I was busy doing my job up the tree when I felt a sting on the back of my neck. I thumped the insect with my right hand but missed it. This made me lose my balance, but being young and agile, I quickly regained my footing with the help of my left hand. I heard a shriek sound from below that made me look down. I was aghast to see Juan, one of her neighbors, standing beneath the tree and looking up with his mouth and eyes wide open. Furious words poured out of my mouth as I shouted at him. I knew what that no-good, despicable man was up to because my sister had already warned me about him. So I yelled down at him.

"Peeping Juan, you want to see if I am wearing underwear? Here, look!" I raised my skirt so he could get a good view of what was underneath my skirt.

All Juan could see were my brother-in-law's fatigue-colored shorts. It was a good thing that my sister had advised me to wear them before I did any tree climbing. Perhaps she had had a feeling of what might happen. When Macaria heard me shouting, she came running from the house.

"Horrible man! Get off my property and never come back, or I will tell the other neighbors what you tried to do. My sister is just a young girl." Juan was long gone when I climbed down from the *sampalok* tree.

I received another scare around noon when two people who I thought were native hunters (because they were garbed in banana leaves and vines with their faces smeared with mud) showed up at the foot of the stairs asking for alms.

"Alms for candles," they begged.

"Hunters downstairs asking for alms," I called out to my sister. They resembled the indigenous people who came down from the mountains to steal food during the drought season. My sister came out and gave each a ten-centavo coin.

"No, they're not the natives. They are called *taong putik*, or mud people. They are devotees of Saint John the Baptist. They transform themselves into "mud people" as part of Pagsa-San Juan. They go around the neighborhood on the day of the fiesta to collect money for candles for our patron saint." The *taong putik* thanked my sister and moved on to the next house. My sister continued her story about them.

"The name Bibiclat came from the Ilocano word *biclat* meaning a snake. A long time ago, poisonous snakes cohabited with the townspeople. After the first Ilocano settlers brought the image of Saint

Bittermelons and Mimosas

Taong Putik during the festival begging for alms.

John here, people noticed that the poisonous snakes that had been the menace of the village were gone."

"How much money do you think they will collect? How many candles can they buy with their money? Are you sure they light all those candles for Saint John and not make them into floor wax?" I asked Macaria.

"Ssshhhh." She motioned to me. I followed her gaze that shifted to other *taong putik* walking toward the house. They were her guests. My sister recognized them even though their faces were smeared with mud.

It was a brief visit for me because school had already started but my mini-vacation that year was very memorable, as I had met the *taong putik*. Although their appearances were worn and ragged because of their shabby costumes and mud-smeared faces, I thought they were righteous people because they were ethical and faithful to their beliefs, unlike Juan, whom I thought did not possess a decent bone in his body because he was just a step short of being a pedophile.

Nieves Catahan Villamin

RICE FIELDS IN BIBICLAT, as in most barrios including Sumacab that year, flaunted rice stalks that were taller and healthier than they had been in many years. Inspired with the prospect of a great harvest, most radio stations began playing holiday music in early September, although Christmas was still a few months away. When harvest came, the whole neighborhood buzzed with excitement as huge piles of rice stalks lined up and waited for the rice thresher to come after Christmas. I remember my father and Mang Kanor comparing the size of their piles and the number of grains each rice stalk had generated. With only their toes and fingers to help count, they projected a 50 percent increase over the previous year's yield.

For many years, my mother put up a native dessert stand outside her small variety store during the Christmas seasons to supplement our farming income. That year, our neighbors' cravings for *bibingka* or rice cakes were more robust than the vigorous harvest in progress. The rice cakes like fruitcakes in the United States were a vital part of a Filipino Christmas celebration. I still remember how all of us children did specific tasks, which we happily performed and for which we were rewarded with leftover *bibingka* at the end of the day.

My sister Huling ran the hand-cranked stone rice grinder that processed the rice paste, the main ingredient. To make the mashing of the rice grain into a liquid form easier, it had to be soaked overnight. Operating the rice grinder required the use of both hands with swift steady motions. Using her right hand, Huling filled the funnel on top of the rice grinder with soaked grain, and then cranked it with her left. In between motions, she put droplets of water inside the funnel with her right hand to achieve consistency in the ground rice. She repeated the process until the rice paste became soft enough to bake evenly on the open stove, a task my mother always did to perfection. My job was to gather firewood.

On weekend afternoons, I meandered along the bank of the yellow winding brook and searched for dried bamboo stumps or partially burned tree branches struck down by lightning during recent storms. My mother specifically told me to collect this kind of firewood because it burned longer and more uniformly, allowing the rice mixture to cook slowly and evenly.

My younger sister Gertrude was the expert coconut grater. I still remember how she straddled a *kudkuran* or coconut grater and scraped the coconut flesh upon the grater with gusto. One of my father's handiworks, the *kudkuran* stood on four wooden legs topped by a 14" x 6" sheet of metal. An iron blade with sharp corrugated teeth protruded on one end. Because the user had to sit astride the wooden stool, the *kudkuran* is also called *kabayo* or horse. Gertrude grated the coconut meat into fine shreds very artistically, carefully following the contours of the coconut to get to the innermost part of its shell. Like the liver-based sauce that made the roasted pig taste flawless, the grated coconut meat was the perfect foil for the *bibingka*'s sweet and smooth buttery taste.

My mother always cooked her *bibingka* with such great skill that their aroma never failed to tantalize the neighbors and children. It was not surprising that on most evenings, we children had only the leftover tea to share with each other. Yet, it brought us pleasure and pride for Inang's *bibingka* when all were sold out. For a homemaker with many children, her *bibingka* venture was an important source of income during the Christmas to New Year holiday season.

EVEN THE DEW ON the spiny stems of the *makahiya* anticipated the great harvest. The weather turned extra cold that year, and the fog along the riverbank where the vines grew plentifully was thicker than usual. Had I seen snow in pictures, I would have known about "White Christmas" and I might even have thought that it also could happen in Sumacab. I remember how our family, the size of an army squadron, prepared for the feast as if we were having the president of the Philippines as our special guest.

"Get out of the way. Play somewhere else." I recall how my father shooed away the other children who were watching him slaughter Osang, the pig I helped fatten up by feeding it with rice chaff and leftover farm vegetables. Osang wailed and kicked its legs in protest, but my father didn't budge. He was determined to make a feast out of the beast.

"Huling, careful not to set our house on fire," my mother called to Huling, who was boiling water in a vat. The cooking vat was nestled on an improvised stove of three big stones positioned in a triangular fashion on the ground. My father would use the boiling water to dress the slaughtered animals that were stacked on top of Unti's small cart which was parked close by. Consequently, a variety of sumptuous pork and chicken dishes inside aluminum containers surrounded with milk custard and sweet sticky jam-like purple yams graced our dining table.

I remember vividly the pain from Conchita's pinches as if it was yesterday, when I wouldn't own up to eating portions of the desserts before it was time to serve. I had seen "whodunit" but my lips were sealed. I could bear the pinches but not Diko Unti hitting me on my nape with one of his hands. Without a doubt, he would have let me have one if I ratted on him.

Because of the holiday season, we had to do the cleaning better. Nothing was overlooked, from cobwebs and small beehives hidden in the ceiling to bird droppings on the stairways. My father had built a birdhouse near our well pump so his doves would be closer to their drinking water, but the birds preferred roosting in the roof's eaves. My father consented and built small boxes around that corner in which they could nest. Soon, bird droppings from two dozen doves strewed the stairway leading to our porch and became Huling's daily nightmare. Like an insult the litter seemed to double on days when her suitors came to visit. Nevertheless, she couldn't complain no matter how much she wanted to. The doves were not pets (and I'd even like to think they were my friends because they gave Huling headaches). We sold them for money.

Tidying up the inside of the house was equally grueling. For a cleaner and smoother look, the walls, floors, and windowpanes were all scrubbed with Pakiling leaves. Pakiling worked like sandpaper. But clean and smooth was not enough for the hard floors. To achieve a shiny and rich-looking color and sparkle, Huling applied homemade wax (leftover candles from All Saints' Day dissolved and mixed with kerosene oil) to the floor. She buffed the waxed floor with *bunot*, the native floor polisher that worked better than any commercial one. She held her right foot firmly on the flattened top of the *bunot* or half the side of a dried coconut husk making dozens of consistent motions to assure a deep and even polish. The result was a floor so shiny and smooth that a falling grain of rice would bounce like a rubber ball.

Our windows opened to a big garbage bin that was the whole yard. We threw food scraps through the window so animals could feed on them. In the morning, my sister Mila swept up the litter and gathered it into a big pile to be burned away from the house. During cold December mornings, the bonfire warmed Mila, soothing her asthma. She performed this task daily without fail, even on mornings when she could hardly breathe because of the dust.

As a final touch of an almost weeklong cleaning, Conchita hung new curtains she had made especially for the holiday. All that was missing was the tree, which happened to be my favorite Christmas decoration from the time I first saw one in the fourth grade. Since then I made sure we had a tree every Christmas for as long as I lived at home.

Uncle Melchor's big backyard boasted a variety of banana plants. Bananas were the best plant for that land because they could withstand small floods. All parts of the banana plant were useful. The fruit could be fried or barbecued. The leaves were generally used to wrap and line the *bilao* for *bibingka*. Pieces of the trunk could substitute as plates during picnics. Once ripe, the bananas produced a pungent, sweet scent that drifted half a mile away and drove children playing at the nearby riverbanks frantic for tastes of the ripening bananas. But they seldom ventured into his banana farm because Uncle Melchor had dogs roaming loose in his backyard during the day. These were not cute dogs from the local pet store and at that time most dogs in the Philippines did not have immunization shots.

Nieves Catahan Villamin

Our parents had told us that dog bites could infect us with rabies, which would kill us, so few children dared to venture into his property. However, unless your nose was plugged with mucus or your parents had done a superb job of brainwashing you about the consequences of stealing, no child easily could turn away from the sweet smell of ripened bananas. I fit neither category and the aroma was making my mouth water. Besides, I was sure Uncle Melchor wouldn't mind if I helped myself to some of his bananas because he had been my father's HUK comrade. And I had done in the past.

With a bolo in my hand, I made a detour to pluck a couple of yellow ones from the bunch. All at once, I heard a chorus of barks. I turned to where the barks were coming from and saw a hungry pack of dogs zeroing in on me. They seemed ready to tear me to pieces, their shining fangs showing through their wide-open mouths. I ran away faster than the speed of light, the monsters close behind me. Feeling trapped, I was about to strike out at them with my bolo in self-defense, only to hear Uncle Melchor's authoritative voice calling to them to stop. He had heard the commotion and recognized me instantly from where he was standing. The dogs headed toward their master with wagging tails.

"Go ahead. Help yourself," Uncle Melchor shouted to me.

I stood there in shock, unable to move, before finally turning and rushing away. When I think back on those dogs, my body still quivers with fear, but I learned my lesson – "stick to Christmas trees in December and listen to your elders."

NATY AND I WERE gathering firewood from a nearby grove a few days before Christmas Eve that same year. Naty told me about Santa Claus and his sleigh and reindeer. She was in high spirits, unlike previous times when she complained endlessly about her parents' frequent

Bittermelons and Mimosas

business trips. Barely 11 years old, she took care of the house when her parents were away. I was sure that Santa Claus was just a figment of Naty's overactive imagination. I had never heard about him before nor had my parents. Besides, I was sure my parents would dismiss Santa as being another "Kiko" fraud. Sumacab had little means of communication with the outside world until it was equipped with electric power in the early 1960s. Expensive batteries made most families choose necessities over transistor radios.

"Are you hanging a sock tonight on your kitchen eaves?" she asked on our way home, as if I knew exactly what she meant.

Trying not to step on *carabao* dung while crossing the sandy but still muddy brook with our *bilao* full of firewood on top of our heads was not an easy feat. Her strange questioning made me miss a step.

"What for?" I hissed under my breath as I rubbed the dirt off my right foot onto the ground. I was very annoyed.

"Sus! So Santa Claus can put coins inside the socks like he did to mine last year. I can't believe you! An honor student who doesn't know Santa Claus!"

I heard the sarcasm in her voice as if she were telling me, "I am smarter than you are." Maybe she was. I had never heard about him until that day.

"So who is Santa Claus? Is he a ghost or a magician?" I sneered at her to hide my embarrassment because she made me feel stupid.

"No. My parents told me he was a chubby, white-bearded old man who rewards well-behaved children. They told me I had been a good girl, taking care of our family when they are away. So Santa gave me plenty of gifts last year – most of the money was ten-centavo coins.

"So you are hanging a sock tonight?" I volleyed the question back to her.

"Of course." Naty's confidence and optimism were contagious. I started to calm down. Coins this Christmas? Wow ... I would like that much better than sweets or the native delicacies we had received as presents from relatives during the previous Christmas.

Although it sounded like another "Kiko" scam to me, I began to imagine coins inside my sock the minute I unloaded the firewood in the kitchen. My mind was on overdrive counting the things I could buy with the coins. Perhaps some velvet ribbons and shiny hairpins to pretty up my plain ponytail. There was a boy in school that I liked very much. I was short and dark, a chubby girl with a moon-shaped face, nothing close to being pretty. But it gave me the creeps when I thought of being called Mrs. Tinga for that was his surname. (Tinga meant food particles lodged between the teeth.) Still, the colorful ribbons and hairpins would make me look attractive enough for him to start noticing me.

Acting on Naty's instructions that Christmas Eve, I hung one of Kuya Lino's socks (without his knowledge) on one end of the kitchen eaves before I curled up on the mat on the wooden floor to sleep. I was very careful not to attract attention because I knew that, just to annoy me, my younger sisters would tease me mercilessly by calling me, "Idad Luka-luka Baho," or Crazy Idad with bad smell, the name they called the crazy woman who lived alone in a big house with a yard planted with trees and vegetables year-round across from our school. Lying there, I whispered my sincerest prayer and asked Santa to grant my wish: coins inside the sock, my reward for being a good girl. I had gathered firewood on weekends and had fetched water for cooking and drinking almost every day. That should be more than enough for my name to be included on Santa's list.

I tossed and turned on the hard floor, listening for any sound in the hope I might catch a glimpse of Santa putting coins inside the sock; I saw again the optimism in Naty's face. I was very excited because I was sure Santa would grant my Christmas wish as he had done to my friend Naty and other children. I waited and waited until my eyelids got very heavy. No sign of Santa came. Then I fell asleep. Voices that seemed to come from nowhere woke me up. I let my imagination ran wild. I did not want to hear carolers, who during those years made rounds close to midnight and into the wee hours of the morning. I wanted to see the silhouette of a chubby old white-bearded man tiptoeing and putting coins inside the sock. I shot a glance at the one dangling from the kitchen eaves through my half-opened eyes. Its position hadn't changed. From the looks of it, Santa

Bittermelons and Mimosas

hadn't come yet. As the carolers' voices drifted farther away, so did my thoughts.

The morning light seeping through the windowpanes woke me. I vaulted from my sleeping mat and hurried toward the kitchen. The sock was there, its hanging position still unchanged. My heart beating fast, I reached up and yanked it down. It dropped to the floor. To my dismay, there was no cling-clang of coins when it landed on the hard floor. It was empty. I broke into tears. Naty got her coins. I was too young to know it was her parents who put the coins inside her socks, not Santa. I don't think she knew it either.

The incident made a Santa Claus non-believer out of me. I told myself I would not tell my children stories or create fantasies because I didn't want them to experience the pain I felt as a child when Santa had ignored me.

Although the year ended on a bittersweet note as far as I was concerned, our family waited the anticipated bounty with much excitement.

Chapter Six

Farmers in the Dell

Planting rice is never fun
Bent from morn 'till the set of sun
Cannot sit and cannot stand
Cannot rest for a little while

Planting rice song

It was the New Year's Eve of 1957. The moon was sharp yellow, intense but dream-like, adding to the happiness overflowing my heart. I was certain that the odds for obtaining a high school education were better than the odds of the sun rising up in the morning after a storm had cleared overnight.

I was resting on sacks of *palay* piled on top of each other, my bed that evening. I could feel the mist touching my face like my mother's hands stroking our hair to calm us down during the monsoon seasons when lightning and thunder kept us awake all night. The sounds of fireworks crackling from miles away and the fact that I wasn't at home firing bamboo cannons with my friends to greet the New Year didn't bother me. I was with my older siblings guarding the sacks of *palay* that would be transported to our granaries at daylight. The threshing had taken longer, right up to New Year's Eve, because many heaps of rice stalks were bigger and rounder than usual.

"Here, your rewards," my mother said as she handed each of us an apple, an orange, and a box of raisins after we had stacked up the last sack of *palay* earlier in the day. She felt so generous that she didn't

Bittermelons and Mimosas

mind paying the peddlers with *palay* grains for the fruits instead of money even though it wasn't a fair exchange. I would relish the taste of my first apple, orange, and raisins for many years. Never did it occur to me that that bountiful harvest was a prelude to the long and winding "Bittermelon and Mimosa" journey that would eventually bring me back to my agricultural roots: the life that I despised very much when I was a young child.

***

THE INTERMEDIATE GRADES 5 and 6 of only one section for each class were added to Sumacab's elementary school curriculum after the Japanese occupation. Before then, the fifth and sixth graders, most of them barefooted, walked approximately a ten-mile roundtrip to Santa Rosa to the south or Cabanatuan to the north to attend school. I remember being either in the third or fourth grade when my father and some of our barriomates constructed the fifth and sixth grade classrooms. I was among the selected pupils who helped our teachers cook meals during the period of construction.

Miss Ortiz was my first grade teacher. I remember that her skin was as white as a radish. She was plump and round with rosy cheeks. I swear now that she looked like a brunette Mrs. Claus. Miss Ortiz was kind and always smelled nice.

However, her perfume wasn't enough to cover the awful smell that hovered inside the classroom one morning when we were having our ABC drills and word recognition recitations. One of the pupils was so nervous she wasn't able to wait until recess to use the bathroom lcated oitside the school buildding. She was too embarrassed, just as anybody would have been, to admit to causing the odor. So, Miss Ortiz had no choice. She made us all stand up. Using her stick, she lifted the girls' skirts and peeked on the boys' behinds until she found "whodunit." The shamefaced pupil transferred to another school and we never saw her again.

My second-grade teacher is a blur to me. I do remember learning my early multiplication tables in her class. My older cousin Nick, to ward-off my constant borrowing of his, copied the tables on a piece of paper in a *"hueteng*-like" (illegal numbers game) list because the back of my cheaper notebook, unlike most, didn't have them.

In the third grade, the unexpected death of our teacher, Mr. Ramos, from a car accident shook up all his pupils. On Friday he bade us goodbye and said, "Study your homework, and see you on Monday." Monday afternoon we had a new teacher because Mr. Ramos wasn't coming back, ever. It was the very first time I felt the pain of losing someone from death. I still remember his chiseled and tanned face and his two front teeth capped with gold.

Our fourth grade teacher, Mr. Fajardo, was a good dancer, a cha-cha expert. Like most of my male teachers who greased their *hair* with *brilliantine*, or *pomade*, Mr. Fajardo's hair was well managed, always shone like newly polished silver, even in the middle of a storm.

My archangel was waiting for me in the fifth grade. Mr. Patricio Navarro, as I recall, was a patriotic, genteel and fine-looking, spectacled teacher who embodied the model Filipino of bygone years. After an attendance check one day he told me in front of the class, "Your father is a very intelligent man. I don't see any reason why you haven't been on the honor roll."

He is? I asked myself after he made that pronouncement.

Perhaps Mr. Navarro truly believed that with some encouragement he

Mr. Patricio Navarro, my 5th grade elementary school teacher.

~ Bittermelons and Mimosas ~

Class of 1957 50th elementary school reunion. Seated L-R: #7 Gloriphine wearing sunglasses; Mr. Pablo Fajardo, our fourth-grade teacher; me; and Esperanza.

could show me that I could be the best. And with the right motivation he thought he could squeeze the juice out of this *kalamansi* or acid orange fruit to make a delicious thirst quencher. I remember that he nurtured me by assigning tasks that might have seemed impossible for a fifth grader to carry out.

Like that one afternoon when he spoke to me in front of the class and said, "You will lead the pledge of allegiance starting tomorrow during our morning flag ceremony." That was unbelievable to me! The task had always been performed by one of his co-teachers ever since I could remember. (I led the pledge in high school also.)

I was so proud as I led the oath the following morning: "I love the Philippines, the land of my birth, the home of my people."

Then a couple of days later he asked me, "Could you please write the lectures on the board for me? I have an emergency meeting now. I'll let you take my notes home so you can copy them later." My fingers were light yet firm when the chalk curved its lines on the face of the blackboard. My writing glowed with pride. I got additional praise from him when he came back a couple of hours later.

It was understood. I was his pupil assistant starting that day. He

Nieves Catahan Villamin

trusted me implicitly like the counting of monies from the school canteen receipts, and delivering confidential letters to the rest of the teachers. In spite of the interruptions, I was able to catch-up on my lessons because I was motivated. Mr. Navarro's act of trust and his constant praise of my abilities built my confidence and lit the fire in my belly to get great grades. He was right. I had slept through the fourth grade. I needed to wake up from my long nap and start burning the midnight oil.

When school ended that year, I had the highest marks among the fifth graders. Along with my medal was the aspiration to become a teacher, one just like him.

I continued my hard work all through the sixth grade and held on to my dream of becoming a teacher. It paid off, and my reward was winning the Medal of Honor for being the best student. During the graduation ceremonies Mr. Navarro and Mrs. Perez commented to my father, "*nagmana sa ama, matalino* – she took after her father, intelligent also." His smile told me that I made him happy and proud.

IT WAS A TYPICAL sunny day in late March 1957, a few days before our graduation from the sixth grade. The older folks were still reeling from the death of Ramon Magsaysay, our beloved president whose plane went down in Mt. Manunggal in Cebu in the early morning of March 17, 1957. I remember that it was in the afternoon and we were taking our final exams when the principal came into our room and announced that he, together with the other 25 passengers, hadn't survived the plane crash. I knew Ramon Magsaysay through his signature song "Mambo Magsaysay," which people were singing during his campaign for the presidency a few years back. I can still picture my father and his comrades' sad faces because they lost an ally and a hero.

Bittermelons and Mimosas

Meanwhile, the *palay* and vegetable harvests were almost over. People were still in high spirits in spite of their heavy hearts. And like any day during the dry season, the sun on that day promised high temperatures by half-past eight in the morning. On this day, however, we didn't notice the increasing heat. It was our graduation day. We were all keyed up. Graduation was a big event then and we all brought our parents to witness the ceremony.

"There she is. Almost late, but she made it!" called Fely, my classmate and friend who gave me guavas in exchange for helping her with homework. We turned to follow Fely's finger pointing at the gate.

Milaflor, the class of '57's third honorable mention, was making a grand entrance in her vintage dress. Embarrassed for drawing such attention, she quickly blended into our group, by putting her head down and pretending that she was watching her steps. She tried to avoid eye contact as we stared at her dress because it was like nothing we had seen before. She remained quiet until she found her place, and then broke the silence by explaining, "This was my mother's wedding dress. She gave it a face-lift so I could wear it today." She was apologetic and close to tears as she spoke.

"Don't be embarrassed, Milaflor. It looks very nice on you," Teresita tried to make her feel comfortable. We other girls rallied around her when we saw what Teresita did.

Tears began streaming down Milaflor's face, showing the heartbreak she was experiencing at that moment. We knew that Milaflor's mother would be pinning her ribbon of honor on her chest for being No. 3 in the graduating class. She was the only fatherless sixth grader. Members of the Philippine Constabulary had gunned down her father, a HUK, a few years before, thus tearing apart the family. With no land to farm, they had no future in Sumacab. An uncle in Bulacan promised financial support so the family could get back on its feet. Thus the whole family would be leaving for Bulacan after the graduation ceremonies.

The sixth-graders, 30 girls and 26 boys chatting in chorus like *pasyon* chanters during Holy Week, were assembled in small groups on the school grounds. The girls wore white dresses like we had for our first communion. The boys wore long-sleeved white shirts and black pants for the first time, making them uncomfortable in the heat. We all had our shoes on, some made of vinyl or leather. Some were new, some already used.

The "star" of the day was my godsister and classmate Gloriphine – not me – who was leading the graduating class. Gloriphine, in her pristine white lace dress, looked like a movie starlet I'd seen featured in *Liwayway* magazine. She was pretty and affable. Many of the sixth-grade boys surrounded her.

Obviously enjoying the attention, she called out, "Renato, check my satin sash to see if it is wrapped straight around my waist, please." Renato complied.

As he walked around her touching part of her dress, everybody cooed. "Wow, he touched her. They are now boyfriend and girlfriend."

Gloriphine laughed her heart out. Renato played along, giving everybody the impression the two of them were sweethearts. Esperanza, Gloriphine's adopted cousin and the class of '57's second honorable mention, stood with her lips held tight, staying away from Gloriphine's limelight. Esperanza knew that to be assured of peace at home, there could be only one star. Their dresses were identical, showing their matching tastes, but their personalities were as different as night and day. They lived together in a big house my father and some of our *kababayans* had built for them when we were in the fourth grade. It was obvious. Their futures looked brighter than mine.

Naty, the busiest of bees, after assessing every girl's dress like a fashion connoisseur, said to me, "Gloriphine and Esperanza's dresses, very pretty, must be very expensive, huh?"

I nodded. Of course, I knew they were. My father had told me that Gloriphine's family owned plenty of land in the barrio. That's why I had chosen her parents to be my Confirmation godparents, hoping I would take home generous presents for many Christmases to come.

I glanced over to a small group standing underneath the huge acacia tree. Ofelia, Norma, Matilde, and Maria were talking as noisily and simultaneously as a flock of quacking ducks. Ofelia towered above the other three. All had ditched their usual ponytails for a perm at

Bittermelons and Mimosas

Mila's Beauty Salon the weekend before. Their faces were generously covered with waling-waling face powder. The perfumed scent of the face powder had somehow given confidence to the young women who at that moment hardly looked anything like the girls I went swimming and clamming with down at the river during the dry season. Penny, Violeta, and Mercedes looked like cherubs in their white dresses. They were petite and the most passive of all the members of the class of '57. The three stood quietly near the flagpole, waiting for the flag ceremony to start. The bells rang, and it was time to assemble.

Miss Bautista, our school principal, called the crowd to attention. "Everybody fall in line. Let's have our flag ceremony so we can start the program. It's getting hot."

Victorina and Graciano, the Cajucom cousins whom we nicknamed "short rods" – because they were both quick on their feet and fist – dashed past the rest and claimed their rightful places in front. Miss Enriquez, our music teacher, led the national anthem. I led the pledge of allegiance, a task assigned to me since the fifth grade. I felt so proud.

"Nieves, did your parents roast a pig in your honor?" Mrs. Perez, our homeroom teacher, managed to ask me as we passed by her on our way to the ceremony area.

I pretended not to hear her. There would be no roasted pig, not even a roasted chicken to be cooked in my honor for being the No. 1 student. That I was sure of. A big harvest for a big family would not last long if my parents didn't conserve. Mrs. Perez respected my silence and was sensitive enough not to ask me the question again.

We took our assigned seats and waited for the program to start. From where I sat, I threw a glimpse at my parents, who together with the others were standing patiently behind us ignoring the heat. I saw their faces were lit up brighter than the mid-morning sun. They had anticipated this day. Tomorrow, their children would be working with them in the field.

Graduation from elementary school marks the beginning of a better life for some and the end of the road for many: a college education for the well-offs like my godsister Gloriphine and farming and manual labor for the farmers' children. Our society, which was shaped by hundreds of years of colonial rule, had placed farmers and manual laborers as second-class citizens who were looked down on because they were always dirty and charcoal-burned. Thanks to my parents, I would be one of them, a full-time farm worker after graduation. It would have been different had my parents been landowners, not tenants. For the non-farmers, their children's prospects were even bleaker because they would end up as sharecroppers. The little wages they made barely put three meals a day on their dining tables.

The program started and we breezed through it. Then came the part I had waited for all morning – the recognition ceremony. My mother walked up to the stage with me. She pinned the ribbon of honor on my chest. The audience clapped their hands as my mother and I walked down from the stage. Back in my chair, I savored my two minutes of fame.

Then the inevitable came: the end of the ceremony. The graduation march was played again. We dispersed and gathered in our schoolroom for the last time for an after-graduation party. It was then I realized my school days were over and what that day truly meant to me. Reality hit me even harder when I heard Gloriphine, Esperanza, Maria, and Renato talking about which high school they would enroll in. As I watched them from across the room, the thought of maybe ten children clamoring for my attention at the same time, and my husband nowhere to be found because he was out drinking with the neighbors, flashed before me. I was supposed to be celebrating, but the uncertainty of my future made me absolutely miserable.

As I dragged my feet on my way home, I knew that my dream of becoming a teacher, not a farmer's wife, was an impossible one. That night, a flood of tears that was more bitter than Milaflor's soaked my pillow, then chilled my inner core because I had been assured by my family during supper that sixth grade would be the highest education I could ever attain. How I wished that Milaflor had seen them so she would know she wasn't the only graduate who was sad. One thing was certain. The day after my elementary school graduation

Bittermelons and Mimosas

in March 1957, I would become a full-time member of the Catahan labor force. It would also be the day I became an adult.

Looking back, I know I should not have felt so bad. None of my elder sisters went beyond the sixth grade. However, we knew that even if Kuya Lino's bad health didn't render him useless on the farm, my parents would still support his dream of pursuing a higher education because he was a male. Someday Kuya Lino would carry the Catahan name in the limelight for everybody to honor. After all, he was very smart.

In June of 1957, Kuya Lino enrolled in the city after having been out of school a few years. All I could do was wish for the same opportunity every day as I saw him ride his bicycle to school. As days went on, the hopelessness that was digging into my soul made me anxious and desperate. I became weepy like the skin of a just-picked green papaya at the slightest cut. My tears flowed each time I begged my parents to allow me to enroll in high school. My pleas were answered with rejections. "Shut up. You will just marry young like your older sisters." They argued that my future husband would be the one to reap the fruits of our family's sacrifices after I had become a teacher.

My brothers and sisters, though sympathetic, thought I was wasting my energy and not being realistic about the family's financial situation. Public education was not free like it was in the United States. Although schooling was subsidized by government funds, my parents could not afford to enroll me because of other stiff fees. The most elite public schools were for children from families of businessmen, government officials, and other professionals, not from farmers like my parents. Some private institutions offered scholarships, but what about the daily allowance and books? The more rejections I got, the more obsessed I became to continue school. I was determined to elude a life as a farmer's wife. Aside from not wanting to be treated as a second-class citizen, there was too much about agriculture that seemed unpredictable. This was no life for me. I knew I could have security and comfort if I worked hard enough. At 13, I was willing to do almost anything to have an education. I wasn't expecting a free ride. I just wanted a chance.

Nieves Catahan Villamin

"Tatang Nene, father of my child," my mother called out to my father one day before supper when she could no longer put up with my crying and refusing to eat. "She might go insane. Make her stop." My father heeded and rushed to the corner where I was crouched sobbing like a little child.

"What is so bad about being a farmer?" he asked. I saw the anger flashing through his eyes. I was smart enough to recognize the danger sign and its consequences.

"*Patpat o tsinelas?* Stick or slippers?" For sure, I'd get one of them.

With my head bowed down, I joined the rest of the family waiting at the dining table. I told myself, "Okay, if this is my fate, then I am ready to be a farmer's daughter.

When we got together during the May Arakyo, Ofelia told me that Maria, Renato, Gloriphine, and Esperanza had enrolled in high school. When classes started during the middle part of June that year, I pretty much accepted the fact that Mother Earth would be the one to educate me about life, not the schoolteachers. It was painful to see my friends riding a jeepney on their way to school. They passed by me on my way to the field. They waved their hands but I looked away. I continued learning daily lessons about life as I worked in the fields.

FARMING AND POVERTY. THEY chase after each other like a hunter and his prey. The year that I was off from school I became a part of Sumacab's many cycles – rain and floods, planting and harvesting. I saw how everything became lush after the first heavy rainfall in May. I witnessed how nature's clock brought the July rain that all farmers prayed for. The rivers, streams, and rice paddies overflowed, becoming a breeding pond for tiny crabs, varieties of shellfish, and many types of native fish. These gifts from Mother Nature were one of the lifelines that sustained us through the next harvest season.

꧁ Bittermelons and Mimosas ꧂

My first full planting season (from July to mid-August) was very strenuous. It was my first time working in a bent-over position all day long. Because I was the slowest planter, my older sisters would come and help me finish my column. My back often hurt to the point of collapse. My fingers went numb from the thousand strokes I made into the soft ground to plant the rice seedlings firmly. The heat made me dog-tired. What kept me going was the thought of morning snacks of native delicacies around 10:30 and lunch, often made up of cold rice, fried dry fish and smoked fish, *kalamansi* juice, and shrimp paste. To ease my aching back, I often took naps after lunch. At times, the rain came rushing from nowhere to energize me somehow, until my wet clothes took the last bit of heat from my bones, and then I chilled. When the sun showed again, the day was almost done and it was time to head home.

As days passed by, I discovered one element of the planting ritual that was very entertaining. We called it *bagay*, or harmony in the art of rice planting. Like a perfectly orchestrated symphony, everybody delivered planting strokes at precisely the same time, often accompanied with songs and guitars. Maintaining the tempo, the strokes became harmonious and melodious, making planting rice fun, easier, and faster.

Courtship while planting rice was a tradition that entertained planters to keep their mind away from the tediousness of rice planting. It happened this way: A bachelor would take the column next to the girl he was wooing and start planting. Making strokes faster than the bullets spewing out of a machine gun's mouth, he gained a much, much longer lead, fencing the girl inside in her column. He would then come back and help the girl. Hidden from everybody else's view, boy and girl would find this the perfect time to discuss affairs of the heart. This was an accepted tradition, especially at times when parents wouldn't let suitors they deemed unacceptable talk to their daughters.

Courtship in the rice field sometimes became the only means for men to woo women. This practice resulted in romances blossoming during rice planting season. Goding and Clarita were one of the couples I vividly remember with fondness. Goding would play the guitar during the rice planting *bagay*. Clarita would sing native songs. Goding was a versatile guitarist who had taught himself how to play the musical instrument. Although cross-eyed since birth, he was popular among the barrio maidens. He was the only guitarist in the barrio. He played his guitar during many barrio activities: at weddings, baptisms, fiestas, church rites, and vigils for the dead – wherever people congregated and sang songs. In time, after one planting season, Goding and Clarita married.

There were Dado and Fresca, too. Felisa (Berning and Fresca's aunt and adoptive mother) was so strict that Dado only found time to woo Fresca during rice planting season. Dado was not allowed to court Fresca at her house. But Aunt Felisa could not plant rice anymore because of health problems. That left the two of them free from her watchful eyes. During those planting days, their courtship turned into romance. Dado and Fresca eloped one day and returned home several weeks later. What could Aunt Felisa do but accept the marriage? Dado and Fresca became man and wife, all because of rice planting.

Another practice of the planting season was *batarisan* or volunteerism. In *batarisan*, volunteers were always fed great food. I still remember that day when we helped plant the rice field of Aunt Juana, my mother's younger sister. The aroma of our lunch – chicken stew that I loved but got to eat so rarely that I could count the number of times I had using just the fingers on my right hand – was driving me wild. I broke through the line of starving field workers and went to Aunt Juana. I tapped her arm and called her, "Hoy!" – thinking she was somebody else – and asked her to fill my plate first. "Hoy" is an impolite way of addressing people, much more if they were elders like Aunt Juana. Aunt Juana turned around and glared at me.

"Did you want some food, ma'am?" She looked at me like she was ready to attack. I had seen her do this after several shots of her favorite gin. Her irritation served me right. I should have waited for my turn.

"Sorry, Aunt Juana, I thought you were Cousin Elmer." She was wearing Elmer's raincoat and a big salakot, making her look like a man.

IN FILIPINO CULTURE, BEING impolite and disrespectful to anyone older

Bittermelons and Mimosas

justified a severe punishment. I addressed my older siblings formally – *Ate, Ditse, Sanse, Dete, Kaka, Kuya, Dikong, Sangko*. I did not dare raise my voice or answer back to them. My parents expected our unconditional obedience. We may have learned many things from years of schooling, but my parents would always tell us they knew better.

"I have drunk more water than all of you," my father liked to say in his unique Filipino logic when we doubted him and tried to prove him wrong by doing exactly the opposite of what we were told. His decisions regarding important issues always prevailed since whatever happened to one member of the family affected all. Making a decision regarding education, marriage, investments or a job without consulting our parents would simply not be tolerated.

Growing up in this Filipino traditional setting had programmed me to seek the approval of other people and be dependent upon others. This, I know, is the main reason for my lifetime struggle with indecisiveness. My older brothers and sisters were expected to assume parental roles with the younger siblings, even making sacrifices on their behalf. I learned about household duties from my older sisters, who learned them from our mother. Even after the older children married and left home to start their own families, they were still expected to contribute financially to the education of the rest of us. In turn, we looked up to them with awe and respect, to the point of even overlooking their character flaws.

The intense planting months were only a small part of our hard work because a farmer's work in reality is a never-ending process. The tedious process of maintaining the rice and then harvesting other farm crops simultaneously left the farmers practically no time to rest or relax all year round.

ONE AUGUST SATURDAY DURING the corn harvesting season, Ofelia, Naty, and I had a surprise visit from Nora. Nothing could stop us from hugging her even if we smelled like a salad dressing mix of rotting cornhusks and body sweat. (That was how one smelled when one had to work on the farm all day.)

It had been almost three years since she left and we were so ecstatic to see her again. Nora looked very grownup compared to us, and very pretty, too. We soon found out why.

"You are what?" I heard what she had said. I was just teasing her.

"The fiesta princess. It's our first-ever grand barrio fiesta to celebrate an extraordinary harvest. Please come. All my relatives are coming."

"I can't wait to see you wear your crown," I told her as she was leaving. She smiled. We watched her fade from our lives for the second time.

Our first visit during the fiesta was one of the two visits we ever made. On Santo Rosario's fiesta day, we left Sumacab at sundown, after finishing our farm chores. Cousin Bining, Spinster Sena, Fermin, Dado, Nesto, Lucing, my sister Mila, Ofelia, Naty, and I composed our group. The shortcut to Santo Rosario was accessible only by foot. We walked the two-hour route that sprawled across kilometers of rice fields to save on bus fare. We finally arrived at Santo Rosario, barely making it to Nora's house for dinner. The few dishes left on the dining table for us "late birds" left our stomachs only half-filled. It didn't bother me one bit because I was more excited about seeing Nora than I was about having more food. After thanking our hosts, we proceeded to the plaza.

Nora was on the stage looking every inch like a princess, not a China doll. Seeing her being cheered on by adoring males, mostly sharecroppers, made me think she would marry young and have half-a-dozen babies before I would have one. (I learned many years later that she died an old maid.) That was the last time I ever saw or talked to Nora. Our communication stopped after the fiesta night as our lives took different paths. We watched the rest of the show, which ended shortly after midnight.

On our way back to Sumacab, the harvest moon hung low like a jackfruit from Spinster Sena's backyard when the fruit was in season. The moonbeams chased us across the meadow. Bining and Dado, who had done business with some farmers in the area, had assured us earlier that they knew the way. We marched down the road talking and laughing at Spinster Sena as she sealed her future husband's fate.

"If I caught my husband cheating on me, I would definitely cut

Bittermelons and Mimosas

his "you-know-what" with a very sharp blade like the ones Old Saring uses for circumcision." (For many years, Old Saring, not a nurse, circumcised males in our neighborhood.) "Killing myself is what they would have wanted, those sinners." Spinster Sena was talking about the stage play we had just watched where the wife killed herself after the husband left for the other woman.

"That's probably why you cannot find a husband. You are extreme," I teased Spinster Sena.

Truth had been told and everybody laughed at it. After the laughter had died down, we began to realize we had been walking for more than an hour. Still, there was no sign of the river we had crossed before. We were trained to tell time, so even without a watch, we knew that by now we should have come to the river, or at least be close to it.

Cousin Bining and Dado became leery. Their doubts fueled foreboding among the others. Tired and antsy, we sat down at the roadside to rest for a while. We gathered our thoughts and concentrated on the road. Looking around, we saw the same trees and bushes we had passed almost an hour ago. We were not making progress, just walking in circles. Somehow, some magical force held us in that area. It was as if we were in a twilight zone.

Cousin Bining bravely broke the news to us in whispers. "*Tikbalang* (a half-man, half-horse supernatural creature that makes a traveler lose its way) is here toying with us."

Like people of other cultures, we believed in supernatural forces co-existing with humans on earth. My parents told us about them. And I had read about them in books and magazines. And from what I read, I knew they could harm us, or even kill us. The predicament unfolding before me scared me worse than the time when I saw Aunt Juana sticking out her tongue down to her waistline because a witch was punishing her. She had refused to lend a neighbor, who many believed was a witch, money earlier that day. I started to sweat. I reached out for sister-in-law Lucing's hand. She felt my body shaking and gave me a hug.

"Don't be afraid," she said. "They're the good and playful ones.

Nieves Catahan Villamin

If they were bad, they would have tripped us while we were walking or hit us with stones. None of us has been hurt; that's a good sign."

I felt a little better. The younger members of the group let out soft cries, "Oh, God" while the older ones whispered their prayers: "Hail Mary, full of grace..."

"Take off your shirts and wear them inside out. This will confuse them enough to leave us alone," Kuya Bining ordered very quietly. He didn't want the *Tikbalang* to hear his mumbo jumbo.

We obeyed. "Please let us pass." Again and again, Cousin Bining and Dado spoke to the *Tikbalang* in their most respectful tones as they asked them for the right direction.

The bushes and trees along the path did not stir as we walked by. Yet, soon enough, we found our way to the river. Were we just tired and sleepy? Or were there really elemental beings with magical powers that shared the universe with us? If it hadn't happened to me, I would never have believed it. Before I could hit my mat bed, I heard sister-in-law Lucing talking to my parents, who were already up and getting ready for their farm chores.

My mother retold a similar experience during lunch, perhaps to reinforce the existence that "others" really do exist with us. I had heard the story before but hadn't paid any attention to it. I had goose bumps bigger than the chicken pox that attacked me at age ten as I listened to her story.

Sanse Conchita was eight years old when she went missing one weekend morning while playing with other children at a neighbor's backyard close to a wooded area. For hours, many neighbors combed the area where she was seen last. But there was no Conchita in sight. Like a rabbit that vanished during a magic routine and later was pulled from inside a hat, she reappeared before dusk, dirty and looking tired. She told my parents about little people with long white beards and wearing pointed caps. She said that she had been playing with them for hours. Our elders would later tell the younger children that the *duwende*, the little people who abducted my sister, liked her unusually white skin and cherubic face.

Another experience with the *duwende* occurred after the birth of

ᑫᕐᐧ Bittermelons and Mimosas ᑫᕐᐧ

my sister Beth. My mother developed a mysterious illness. Doctors and hospitalizations failed to improve her worsening condition that lasted for weeks. She was wasting away and almost bedridden. Through my mother's prodding, my father finally summoned an out-of-town *arbularyo*. The *arbularyo* performed the *pagtatawas*, a form of energy cleansing, for my mother. He dropped a lemon-sized alum crystal, called tawas, into a small aluminum basin of water.

I remember how white bubbles surfaced on the water, showing the outline of a person's face. In a language that only he understood, the *arbularyo* mumbled what I thought would be prayers. He then asked us, "Wasn't there an anthill in your backyard?"

"Yes," my mother answered, proceeding to tell the story of how she had it leveled because it was underneath the big guava tree where children gathered around. "I thought it might be a breeding ground for snakes, especially after a flood."

"You are being punished by the little people that used to live there. To appease their ire, make food offerings, candles, and prayers on the leveled anthill for seven days." The *arbularyo*'s prescription was simple and my mother heeded.

My mother recovered fully after a couple of weeks. However, the guava tree that once sheltered the little people's mound-house didn't live long after my mother's recovery. One stormy night, a lightning bolt shot down and burned the tree. Charred fruits and ashes on the ground, where once our favorite tree stood and watched children enjoy its fruits, greeted our sight the next morning. Yet, the surrounding bamboo trees close to it were unaffected by the lightning.

WHEN OCTOBER WANDERED IN, our encounter with the *Tikbalang* was old news. The glint of hope of being in high school with my godsister Gloriphine was eclipsed with thoughts of the approaching fiesta and the upcoming harvest that wasn't promising. The drought in September stifled the growth, and the influx of insects deflowered most of the blooms. As a result, the rice stalks were spawning shorter stems. The farmers knew it too well. Shorter *palay* stems yield less harvest, as there will be fewer grains after the chaffs are removed. For small farmers, this means less income after the harvest. Before the November fiesta got on its way, most farmers had started the harvest cycle.

Fiesta, a Spanish religious practice handed down from generations ago, started as a way of thanking our patron saint for well-being and an approaching bountiful harvest, but not this year. The colonial mentality saw it as an opportunity for the less fortunate to shine and become the "toast of the barrio" as they spent lavishly on the fiesta. This often resulted in their breaking their bamboo banks and then being famished until the next harvest came around. Religious rites, musical and theatrical entertainment, sports or local game contests and, surprisingly, gambling, made up the calendar of events in our yearly fiesta celebration.

At the church backyard rose the stage. It was built with happy hearts and strong arms by my barriomates using six *mulawin* posts with one-foot wood boards as flooring. It stood with open arms promising to deliver the finest of shows – shows that hoped to elicit endless guffaws for two evenings. Betting games' gazebos, *halo-halo* and rice cakes' open booths draped with bamboo exteriors and cogon grass tops fenced the whole churchyard. The booths teemed with bachelors at nighttime and women and children during the day.

The streets were dressed up with endless multi-colored streamers of various designs. They hung on bamboo poles planted every 20 feet along the sidewalks. Two city firemen came on a firetruck and doused the dusty street with water both mornings. As expected, not a speck of dust rose from the ground when the brass band marched up and down the street, their boots pounding the dusty road to the tune of a native song. A mini-skirted *bastonera* or (a majorette) with legs that measured longer than one of their award-winning bottle gourd vegetables and a flawless skin almost as white as the vegetable's flesh led the band. A gang of children followed closely behind.

Bittermelons and Mimosas

The church was packed with worshippers during the morning feast mass. Seated in the front rows were the *manangs* who prided themselves for being the "anointed ones" by Father Hernandez, our mestizo parish priest. Most members of the religious women's group called Sumacab Sodalists revered Father Hernandez. In their white uniforms I thought they looked like angels of the fields because most of them were farmers. The occasional churchgoers and children occupied the middle rows. Parents, infants, and future godparents shared the back seats with the choir. After Father Hernandez told the worshippers to "go, the mass is ended," parents clutching their infants rushed in front of the altar, with future godparents in tow. The baptism ceremony moved quickly along like some sort of holy assembly line being pushed by the infants' loud cries for food and water.

At five o'clock in the afternoon, floats of fresh flowers and multicolored lights carrying the statuettes of Santa Catalina, our patron saint, and two others, were paraded around. Barrio folks of all ages with lighted candles in their hands joined in the procession, reciting prayers aloud. "Dios te salve, Maria. Hail Mary full of grace." The same brass band played spiritual music in the background, softly, though occasionally being disrupted by the bang of fireworks. After the procession, a spectacular display of fireworks for 30 minutes ended the religious rites of the fiesta.

After the smoke settled, the *zarzuela* (a musical dramatic play performed live on stage), the highlight of the fiesta pageantry, got on its way. Looking around, one could see the tail-to-tail caravan of *carabao*-pulled carts surrounding the church plaza. All were occupied by people watching the stage play. You could hear sniffles as the crowd reacted to the emotionally charged roller-coaster feel-good stage play. As expected, a beautiful rich and powerful couple adopted Orphan Maria, and they all lived happily ever after.

For the two days of fiesta that year, Sumacab barrio folks lived in a fantasy world and forgot all about their problems. Reality would set in only the morning after, when husbands awoke with hangovers and wives with headaches because the *matong* underneath the house, once brimming with precious grain, now stood empty. And the coming *palay* harvest didn't look promising at all. It was also the first time I noticed the empty cooking pots lining our kitchen sink at the end of the fiesta. I thought to myself, why lavish on a fiesta, not my education? But I knew the answer to my own question. Tradition, tradition, tradition.

WE RESUMED HARVESTING THE day after the November fiesta. Stooped once more over the field and holding tight sharp sickles by their handles, we tediously cut every rice stalk until the last one standing bowed down. We spread them thinly on the rice paddies for drying. After the heat of the sun baked them golden, we bundled the rice stalks and formed them into a heaps. Soon the rice thresher would come to complete the harvest cycle.

There were delicate treasures the children went after during the harvest routine. As the harvesters rushed for home because the evenings came so soon during the harvest months, they randomly dropped a few of the stalks they had cut. Knowing how precious these cuttings were, we cleaned up after them the following day, sometimes filling up our bamboo baskets with *palay* twigs. In a pinched harvest like this one, these cuttings, after threshing, would bring extra grains for our food.

As I sorted the *palay* twigs inside my basket, birds darting from one stem to another, following the beat of the rustling wind as they plucked *palay* grains for food caught my attention. The birds were very careful in gathering the grains, pressing each piece tightly between their beaks. They kept coming back, even though we shooed them away many times. That scene made me think that I wanted something out of life, I should go for it and go for it hard like the birds. But how?

The question hounded me all during the threshing period that had come earlier than usual because the heaps mounds were smaller.

Bittermelons and Mimosas

The grains racing down into the mouth of the jute sacks we held weren't like an endless waterfall as in the year of the bounty.

Small farmers like us toiled for landlords, whom we called *kasama*. In the *kasama* system, the landlord and tenant farmers share the fruits of the labor – not a fair deal but that is how it was. The tenant farmers prepared the field, planted and looked after the grains, and then gathered and got them ready for threshing. They shouldered all the expenses that went with the work. Since they didn't have much, they often borrowed money from the landlord. This had to be repaid with steep interest rates. More often than not, debt payments were deducted from the farmer's share of the harvest. Different places in our country had their own specific arrangements in the *kasama* system. In our case, our landlord took 30 percent of the harvest.

"Hu ... Hu ... Hu ... Oh, dear God ... Hu ... Hu ... Hu...," my sister Conchita sobbed like a child as she watched our *kasama* take his share and the rest of our harvest to cover our debts. None in the *kamada* (pile) or heaps was left and November hadn't ended. Farm harvest was almost four months away.

"Please leave us some grains for food." Our landlord turned a deaf ear to my mother's plea.

Our landlord visited the field only during threshing. And when he came, he wore a gun latched to his belt and guarded the grains like a hawk. On the way home, I walked behind Kalakian, our hardworking *carabao*, as he pulled a cart filled with hay instead of sacks of *palay* grains.

Like a mantra, I told myself, repeatedly on the way home. "I won't be a farmer for the rest of my life; I won't be a farmer for the rest of my life."

Putting the harvest dilemma behind us, our whole family found other ways to survive. Tatang worked as a carpenter in the city, where house repairs and other masonry work around the Christmas holidays were plentiful. Sanse Conchita helped our relatives in Aliaga harvest in exchange for grains. My two brothers took Tatang's instructions to a "T" in cultivating the farm for the next crop, working the soil thoroughly for better plant growth and fewer weeds.

Although not the superstitious type, Tatang always believed in ethereal beings as far as I can remember. He told us the story (before he went hunting for golden chicken with Inang) that in the old days, the *silong* – or open ground floor of the house – was used as a workspace, a storage area for our *matong* filled with *palay* grains, a coop for livestock, or living quarters for the extended family when their children married. He also told us that long before he was born, the *silong* was used as a burial place for departed loved ones so families could be close to them. This was perhaps why the *silong* was the subject of many amazing stories about hidden treasures and ghosts. As dire straits caused fewer dishes to appear on our dining table, my parents' optimism started to fade.

I vividly remember the shimmering light of the golden moon glowing over the bamboo trees and part of our backyard. It was past midnight, in mid-December. We heard Tatang and Inang talking in hushed tones speaking nearly inaudibly sounding almost like stray cats trying to find leftover food in our *banggerahan* (open-air cupboard).

"There they are again. I heard them. Come quick." We saw Tatang following Inang down the stairs.

It was past midnight. They were not carrying any lights to avoid startling the creatures basking in the light of the *bilao*-sized full moon.

"There, there, golden chickens! Let's follow them. They can lead us to pots of gold!"

We heard Inang cry out softly and saw her pointing to something at the foot of the thick bamboo plants fencing the area between our backyard and the riverbank. Feeling their presence, the golden chickens dissipated like soap bubbles blown into the air.

"Yes, they are real," Tatang later told us. And so we believed the golden chickens existed. "That means there were ethereal beings guarding hidden treasures buried close to the sacred anthill your Inang had leveled. Remember how she got sick?"

It was also common talk around the neighborhood a few years later that the deepest part of the river where eight-year-old Sonia drowned was only a few meters away from our back yard. Perhaps little Sonia was stunned upon seeing Inang's golden chickens and

Bittermelons and Mimosas

fell into the water. Maybe the whole area was inhabited by ethereal beings – rich, ethereal beings.

I don't believe the golden chickens were common knowledge in our neighborhood. So when Uncle Bito, a distant relative who lived four houses down the block, experienced similar visions in a dream, Tatang understood. Uncle Bito had seen a short, white-bearded man in his dreams, who told him there was gold and silver buried in his *silong*, and he should dig them up. Acting on his dream, Uncle Bito asked our neighbors to help him tear up the *silong*. Yes, they were cynical about this, but what if Uncle Bito's vision was true. Then they would all partake in the treasure.

Thus one crisp December morning, the men dug as if they were on an archeological expedition. Tatang was one of the diggers. Women and children watched. Inspired, the excavators hardly noticed the first two hours of digging time. By late afternoon, they could hardly lift their shovels. The rectangular hole reached almost eight feet in depth and a pile of dirt rose next to it, but there was no sign of any buried treasure, not even a piece of dead wood. Hoping against hope, they dug some more. When darkness fell, the tired and hungry diggers decided to retire. They finally realized there was no treasure to be found, only broken expectations from the unrewarding ground. The truth was far more than sad. When the digging stopped, Uncle Bito cried like an angry child.

Uncle Bito became the laughingstock of the neighborhood. That broke him completely, and he was never the same again. A few months later, he moved his family across the river, far away from us, to escape the humiliation brought on by the dream that failed him.

My mother never caught one of her golden chickens. Uncle Bito never found a gold nugget in his *silong*. When one was so hard up in life, he or she got to see things like golden chickens and gold nuggets. They were false hopes but believing in these things somehow made them feel that one of those days their lives would be better.

The year 1957 left most farmers with their granaries half-filled and thoughts of starvation before the next harvest. The scant harvest chased my dream further away, making it seemingly impossible to reach anymore. There was nothing left for me to do but pray for a miracle and hope that my prayers would be heard in the soonest time possible.

Chapter Seven

A Year of "Halo-Halo" Blessings

*Learning is a treasure that will
follow its owner everywhere.*

An English Proverb

My parents' sighting of golden chickens was a sign of better days ahead. Dark clouds seem to have a silver lining; and when the clouds burst, the bright lining shines through. Thanks to my father, who hated the expression, "that's good enough," the growth of our farm vegetables from the well-cultivated soil showed no signs of slowing down since the seedlings had sprouted from the ground. The seedlings from the kernels that Tatang insisted on being planted exactly so, "too shallow and the new plants would die from heat, too deep and they wouldn't grow fast enough," promised an abundant yield. Sprouts from the planted corn, turnips, beans, and watermelon seeds were healthy, with leaves of shiny green and robust stalks pointing straight up to the sky like an exclamation point.

Three months after the drought, my mother's bamboo bank once again was filled with silver coins. And it looked like even after we had paid off the money we borrowed from our loan-shark landlord, we would make it through the next corn harvest. Had we not had the farm, the loan with compounded interest would have grown much larger as time went by. Others were not as lucky as we were because they didn't have any land to farm. With one harvest to depend on, sometimes they starved. In our case, with eight children still living at home, whose lives depended on the yield, my parents had to be sure the farm got all the necessary care so harvest would bring us the bounty that we so badly needed.

ORGANIC FARMING I BELIEVE was a common practice in the Philippines before it became popular in the United States. It was the only method of farming we used when I was growing up because chemicals were expensive and organic materials were plentiful. Weeding by hand using only a hoe was routine among farmers. My sister Gertrude (she quit school after the third grade), our human weed whacker, hated those killer weeds especially when they appeared in turnip beds healthier and greater in number than the seedlings, as it happened that year, 1958. She knew she would be baking under the sun by herself for many days pulling out those dammed weeds because Tatang said they would take over and kill the turnip plants. She didn't want that on her conscience. Although Gertrude had some flaws, good heart wasn't one of them.

The rest of the children were either too young to do farm chores or had school and would help only on weekends. Weeding alone sometimes made Gertrude paranoid, and she would begin to think one of the elder siblings had sown the wild seeds in the turnip beds on purpose, to punish her because she didn't want to attend school anymore. Being in school is more fun than weeding. So, at home we kowtowed to Gertrude like she was a princess. It worked like magic! And we knew she deserved it.

When the whole family worked at the farm as we did on weekends in December 1958, my mother brought us hot lunch from home, which was a good two-kilometer walk. A basket filled with food on her head and a pail of water on one arm made quite a heavy load for a small woman to carry. Clay pots containing our meals and

Bittermelons and Mimosas

the ceramic plates we ate from made Inang's load heavier. And lately, Inang had been having severe backaches. Almost every night, my father would massage her back with a pack of hot ashes crammed inside a clear drinking glass, called ventosa cupping. He rolled the base of the glass on my mother's back just as if it were a hot pad similar to those used in today's therapeutic treatment.

In mid-January, the whole clan was at the farm weeding the turnip beds again because Gertrude couldn't keep up with the weeds. And Gertrude wasn't happy about the situation.

"Ebeng! Tone-deaf! Mother is calling you," Gertrude cried out to get my attention. Her turnip bed was closer to where my mother stood under the shade of an old mango tree.

"I'm coming, Mother." I didn't let her call out to me again because I didn't want to hear another barrage of insults, which I was sure I'd receive had I dilly-dallied. I was known to play deaf when I wanted to escape errand calls from my older sisters and sometimes even our parents.

"Here." She handed me the bolo as I got near her. "Cut some banana leaves so I can lay out our lunch. I know you are all starving."

We had been weeding nonstop since eight o'clock that morning. With the sun directly on top of my head making my shadow almost disappear, I could tell it was nearly noon. I could have just walked toward the banana plant farm that was only a few hundred feet away. Instead, I ran like the time when I was being chased by Uncle Melchor's dogs. I was very hungry.

The banana tree was a lot taller than I was. Without any thought about danger, I jumped up to reach the branch and hewed the first leaf with the razor-sharp bolo with force. I underestimated the softness of the shoot, which was not hard like the bough of a tree. I did not anticipate my grip on the bolo would loosen because its blade cut through the leaf rapidly. The jolt that resulted when my feet landed on the hard ground shook my body and loosened my hold on the bolo.

The bolo chose my right shin for its landing strip instead of the *carabao* dung spread around the banana farm. I saw blood shooting from my shin faster than water gushing from a natural spring. I screamed for my mother, and then passed out.

Nieves Catahan Villamin

Kariton Airlines transported me up the road. At a much faster rate than his regular speed, Capt. Kalakian tried his best to make my ride as comfortable as possible, carefully avoiding bumps on the ground. Up the road was a jeepney to take me to the hospital in the city. I regained consciousness and I felt mushy like the almost crushed *duhat*, our local black berry. (The *duhat* is my favorite berry. The berries make good munchies after they are shaken with a sprinkling of salt inside a container.) I glanced at my mother sitting beside me. She was tending the tourniquet my father had applied on my right thigh. Making certain that the bleeding on my shin was kept under control in spite of our bumpy ride, she pressed the already bloodied rag on my shin hard.

"Were you trying to kill yourself?" my mother asked the minute she saw me open my eyes.

Why didn't I think about that? I don't have any future anyway, I told myself. I was in pain and scared to death, and still my mother was castigating me, not in the least comforting me, for what happened. But I remembered how most mothers played their game. By showing tough love, they thought we would grow up strong and brave, capable of standing up for ourselves. They didn't want anybody pushing us around.

My father's tourniquet worked. I didn't lose too much blood, and I didn't need a transfusion. The cut on my shin was a hairline close to a major artery. I could have bled to death, the doctor at the hospital told my father after he cleaned and bandaged the wide cut on my shin.

The wound left a frown-shaped scar after it healed. Another scar made a permanent home of my right leg. When you are in puberty, such things would affect you terribly. I was then at the lowest point of my life. I know I fell into a deep depression even though I had never heard of the term at that time. I had no education. I was small and dark and looked like a starved kitten according to Tera, my snobbish cousin. And now, I had ugly scars on my right leg! No handsome suitor would ever take a liking to me!

Bittermelons and Mimosas

IN MID-MARCH OF 1958, Kuya Lino's friends came over for a picnic at the river during the Glory Saturday of Holy Week. My family welcomed them with open arms; later, we sent them home with plenty of fruits and vegetables. While helping cook lunch, I didn't hesitate to tell anybody who would care to listen how much I wanted to be in school like them. Kuya Lino was tolerant. He knew how badly I wanted to attend school because he shared my passion for education. He had planted seeds before the big rain, and when it poured, the seedlings sprouted. A few days later, my brother came home for supper with the news I had hoped to hear since the picnic.

"My two friends who came to the picnic, Bert and Alfredo, have promised to help me solve Nieves' predicament. Inang, Tatang, with your permission, I would like us to try it."

Kuya Lino continued while everybody listened. "Bert's aunt owns a private high school that offers free tuition to deserving children from poor families. Nieves qualifies. She graduated at the top of her class. Alfredo's sister is a university professor. She can provide for Nieves' board and lodging. She'd even provide Nieves with a stipend for daily allowance, books, school uniform, and shoes. But Nieves will have to work for her as a house helper." So Kuya Lino had it all figured out. "Mind you," Kuya Lino told me, "you'd be taking on quite a responsibility. Alfredo's sister has six children, with ages from six months to eleven years old."

I knew I had little of the experience required for becoming a house helper. But I was a good student and I wanted so much to continue my schooling. Why, I could even tutor the professor's children who were of school age. The professor's eldest child was close to my age; we could get along well. And Kuya Lino was right in saying that it would be quite a responsibility. It didn't matter, however. It could have been taking care of a hundred children and I still would have jumped at the opportunity. This was my ticket out of the fields, my path to higher education that could lead to a better life. Everything about this proposed arrangement seemed perfect. Sitting at the table, I could only look over to my father, pleading with my eyes. My eyes popped out like steamed mussels from a mixture of shock and delight when Tatang announced that he was amenable to the idea. He must have seen the desperation on my face. Deep down inside, my father must have sensed that it was time to let go and take a chance on me.

Soon after Tatang gave his blessings, I prepared to leave home for the first time to begin my new adventure. School was scheduled to begin in June, but Alfredo's sister needed me to start work right away. I packed the few pieces of clothing I owned. I had not really thought about how I would juggle the demands of being a student with everything expected of me as house help. I was too young and naive to truly appreciate the challenges that loomed.

Serving a family of eight turned out to be incredibly tough and demanding for someone as young as I was. I was only 13. Back in Sumacab, I didn't do many household chores because I was working in the fields. And there I was, listening to my new employers as they outlined my everyday duties. I was to wash and iron their clothes, cook lunch and dinner, do all the dishes, and clean the house. The cooking itself turned out to be a bit more than steaming the rice. Oftentimes, I cleaned the fish or poultry or cut vegetables to be cooked while taking a break from my laundry chores. The work was nonstop and I had little, if any, free time. It didn't take long to realize I had bitten off more than I could chew.

Washing machines were not yet common household appliances. Washing large bundles of clothes was rough on the hands. Soon I had small lesions on my fingers. These hurt and never seemed in a hurry to heal. My back ached from pumping water from the well and carrying the buckets inside the house. The long hours spent at the ironing board left my shoulders tight. The children couldn't help me do chores, but I did not complain. I knew I was too young for this enormous task. With each passing day, my brother's grand idea seemed less and less attractive. Yet, I was determined to succeed. He had opened an important door for me, and I had to walk through it. There was no turning back.

~ Bittermelons and Mimosas ~

Alfredo's sister was very nice and sympathetic during my period of adjustment. She knew I lacked experience. She was willing to be patient with me to a point. Her husband, though, was far more demanding. If he could yell at his children for the slightest infraction, he then would have no qualms about reprimanding me. Often his voice would rise higher than the star apple tree standing at their front yard when he gave me instructions about cutting vegetables the right way or preparing the fish properly. He was always stressed about even the smallest thing such as recycling the cooking oil and serving cold rice during meals. I felt I was a lowborn, coming from a servile class and that I didn't deserve any respect. Somehow, I made it through those first three months, settling into the daily routine, keeping up with the workload, and trying to block out the shouting.

At night, I lay awake, wondering how I would add school into all my household chores. Such thoughts certainly dampened my excitement. I thought my body went into shock from the non-stop physical labor when one night I felt like I was peeing in bed. But when I looked at the stain at the back of my skirt, I saw the color red, not yellow. Almost a month shy of being 13, I hadn't anticipated becoming a woman so soon. I had heard stories about "the stuff" from my other older sisters, so I wasn't scared.

IT WAS EARLY JUNE, just before classes were to begin, when I received quite a surprise. In the midst of my morning chores, I looked up one day to see my mother's face peeping through the window. At first, I thought I was dreaming, and that the work must have been getting to me. But then she called to me. What was this? No member of my family had come to visit me since I started working. I didn't know how to react as I opened the front door for Inang. Alfredo's sister was equally surprised.

"I've come to take Nieves home," my mother announced, her eyes trying to avoid my employer's bewildered stare.

"Why?" I asked dumbfounded.

"Your father has sent for you," Inang replied. "His exact words were, 'None of my kids will work as a housemaid for as long as I live.'" Inang didn't mention anything about my education so I protested.

"But, Inang, I'm not the only one in our barrio who is doing servitude in exchange of education. Look, neighbor Cora's son Rico (a neighbor who became a successful lawyer and educator, married a doctor and had five beautiful children all with equal success) had lived with the Veneracions since 1954. Why can't I do the same?"

"That's different. He is a male. Now, get your things before I lose my patience," my mother commanded.

The colonial culture considered domestic helpers second-class citizens then, especially if you were female. On the way home, I learned from Inang that my father had been mortified since I left. People were constantly asking about me, and he had been reluctant to tell the truth – to have to explain that his daughter was working as a house helper.

My own feelings were mixed. I was happy to be out of that house and away from the daily workload. However, I was also worried about what waited for me at home. Would I ever get my education, or was I about to be sent back to work in the fields? I hadn't put away my clothes yet when my father, sweaty and muddy, came home from the fields. It was way past noon. He, my brother, and some friends had just finished plowing the rice field in preparation for planting after the heavy downpour of a few days ago. I didn't have to ask. He explained in a few words.

"Helping neighbors in exchange for loose change for your allowance is more honorable than having you work as a house helper."

I didn't say a word. I simply nodded my head. I knew that was his way of telling me to "go follow your dream; we will be here to help you."

I REMEMBER IT BEING the last Monday of June 1958. I had slept only a few winks the night before. I kept waking up because I was so excited. The morning light couldn't come soon enough. I would be on my first bike ride with Kuya Lino to Liwag College, the place that would give me a glimpse of what my life could be if I worked hard and followed the rules. Classes had already started many days ago, but that didn't dampen my spirits. When the moment finally came, I felt my heart jumping in my chest as we rode the bicycle Kuya Lino

Bittermelons and Mimosas

had bought from Uncle Tura for the eighty pesos he earned from sharecropping during the harvest season.

That Monday morning, he was going to drop me off at the gate of Liwag College, where his friend Bert was waiting for us. The day I had dreamed of for so long was finally here – I was returning to school. My parents, thanks again to my brother's intervention, had decided to honor their promise concerning my education. I remember that the gate had already been closed as classes had already started when we arrived. We were late because we had underestimated our biking time. But true to his word, Bert waited for us at the gate. Looking at him talking with my brother, I noticed his good looks. I saw he could be a double for Romeo Vasquez, one of the hottest movie stars in the 1960s and my favorite actor. (Romeo was a charismatic guy of the right height, dark with wavy hair, and more than handsome.) Bert must have many girlfriends, I thought to myself. I smiled at him when my brother signaled, "*Sige, Bert, bahala ka na sa kapatid ko.* Okay, Bert, take care of my sister, I have to go now." My brother shook Bert's hands and took off. He was late for his classes himself.

Bert ushered me into the office of the owner and director of the school, his Aunt Susana Liwag. Being inside that office meant I already made it to first base. It would be all up to me now to make it to home plate. After I heard the best possible news that morning at Mrs. Liwag's office, I realized my dream wasn't impossible anymore.

"Nieves, this will be our arrangement," Mrs. Liwag explained. "As long as you maintain good grades, you will not have to pay tuition for your schooling. Is that acceptable to you?" The excitement on my face had to be obvious.

"Oh, yes, Ma'am," I replied, trying to stay calm. "Thank you very much."

"We expect you to study hard." She wasn't smiling when she said that.

"I will do my best because I want to become a teacher," but stopped short of finishing my sentence. Not a farmer's wife like my older sisters and most of the girls in my neighborhood. From what I had heard from my brother, Bert's aunt was a farmer's daughter from Talavera. I didn't want it to be thought that I was ashamed of being a farmer. I just didn't appreciate the "perks" that went with the occupation.

"I am pleased to hear you say that," Mrs. Liwag said. "I think we can help you become a very good teacher."

Our brief exchange of words lasted for five minutes or less. Other people were waiting inside her office for their turn to talk to her. However short the conversation was, I still got the impression that she would make good on her promise if I kept my end of the bargain.

I was feeling proud as Bert escorted me to my first class, which was already in progress. He introduced me to Miss Yambot, the teacher-in-charge, a woman in her early forties with a very kind face that made first timers like me feel welcome. Then Bert bid me goodbye and left.

As I sat on my chair during that day I was in awe watching Miss Yambot, our adviser, and the other teachers that stood before us. It was the same feeling I'd had one night in March 1957 at the provincial fair when my favorite actors, Nestor de Villa and Nida Blanca, danced rock and roll while I watched from the front row with Maria, Gloriphine, and Esperanza. Yes, this was exactly what I wanted to do with my life, study and teach. I knew I could be very good at it, too, like Miss Yambot and my favorite elementary school teacher Mr. Patricio Navarro.

On most times during our way home I was forced to let out the "uugghh" sound after every bump our bike ran over as we traveled along the rough road. This made Kuya Lino very concerned about my safety. One hand clutched a bundle of notebooks and books on my lap while the other held tightly to the edge of the bike seat. "Look Ma, no hands." Bam! I could wind up down on the bone breaking if I wasn't careful.

I would have been a goner by week's end if my brother hadn't come to my rescue. One morning he gave me part of his wages from his side job before he dropped me off. I hotfooted it to the market during my lunch break and bought a stainless steel basket. He pedaled

Bittermelons and Mimosas

home that night with a basket full of school things bolted on the bike's handlebars and a much safer-feeling passenger riding behind.

I can remember clearly the perspiration dripping from my brother's face and back, making marks on his neatly starched and ironed white polo shirt, when the weather registered to above 80 degrees Fahrenheit and it was only eight in the morning. I am sure that pedaling an old bicycle for an hour while carrying over 90 pounds of baggage on a bumpy dirt road was a great challenge to him. Still, I didn't hear him complain.

Besides the daily rides, Kuya Lino befriended an elderly couple who owned an eatery close to school so I could work there in exchange for free meals. I still remember how before washing them I'd sweep with my hands the bottom of every aluminum pot for scraps so I would have lunch that day.

Kuya Lino helped me with my theme writing homework occasionally. During those homework sessions we both discovered that I had the natural ability to transfer my thoughts into words in spite of my youth and inexperience. I started to dream of being a journalist instead of being a teacher.

"You are way over your head. Liwag College might help you build the foundation for that course but college is another thing. Besides, jobs for journalists are hard to come by unless you are extremely good. You might end up going to bed with an empty stomach sometimes like when we were kids." Kuya Lino nipped my new dream in its bud. And I didn't have any qualms about what he had said.

LIWAG COLLEGE'S ENROLLMENT AT that time was fairly small. There was only one section for each year of high school. So, we became a second family as days went by. Our class of about 40 was a combination of young and older students, our ages ranging from 12 to

༄ Nieves Catahan Villamin ༄

26. There were Eduardo A. and Cornelia K., two of the smallest, brightest, and the youngest members of our class. I was neither tall nor small, but more mature than most because I had one year of practical education under my belt. And there was Ernesto D., who at 26 years old was the oldest of all Liwag College's students. I was the English buff because I liked reading both the Tagalog and English magazines. He was our Algebra and Math wizard. I remember how we fought with each other for a seat close to him during our quarterly Algebra and Math quizzes. We were like a relay team with Erning as the leader as the rest waited to get of hold of that tiny piece of paper with answers to the questions of multiple choices. Until one day when we got caught and our adviser assigned us our permanent seats.

Our adviser didn't realize the depth of our smarts and boldness. Soon the blackboard replaced Erning's tiny pieces of paper because we had thought of another and better way of outsmarting our teachers. During our English exams, I had written the answers in secret codes that I developed on the blackboard for everyone to take advantage of. It worked fine and everybody was happy, that was until a crab of a classmate told our English teacher about the scribbles on the blackboards. My English teacher thought nothing of the doodles when she first saw them, until she was told about it. (Over the next three years we would face immaculately clean blackboards in front of us during our exams.) The incident did not have an effect on my grades. My scholarship remained intact at the end of the year. The "whistleblower" took the Most Loyal award during our end of school ceremonial rites.

༄

AT LAST, LIFE WAS good to me. I was finally living my dream – going to school on weekdays and helping with the family chores on weekends. Except that a Saturday without an exchange of harsh words

Bittermelons and Mimosas

between Huling (who was living her dream also) and me – normal teenagers that we were – was as rare as having a side dish of meat for supper on special occasions. On weekends, Huling's many suitors came calling every hour like clockwork. So she was under extra pressure to make our house shining clean. That Saturday, however, I had other plans besides fetching water for her cleaning chores. It was the start of our holiday school break and I had planned to meet with my friends Rosita, Gloriphine, Esperanza, and Maria to sample some sugar cane from my Godfather Ode Tumibay's farm before the *viajeros* who bought the lot would have them harvested in a week or so. We hatched the plan that Friday before the school break when I saw them at the jeepney station waiting for their rides. Godfather Ode's sugarcanes were extra plump that year, and we intended to munch the sugarcane until our teeth fell out and everybody in our group knew Godfather Ode wouldn't mind. I was his favorite goddaughter.

So staying around for more servitude to Huling after fetching water like I did in the past wasn't going to happen that Saturday morning. My mistake was telling Huling that I would be meeting my friends by the riverbank close to Tanda Menes' backyard before I even started fetching water for her. I knew my plan made her edgy. She stood at the top of the stairs wearing a big frown, watching me like a hawk as I hurriedly struggled to bring the water bucket up to the house.

With her left hand on her hip and her right hand clutching a cleaning rag, she yelled, "If you let even a drop of water drip from that bucket, I'll empty it on top of your head. Oh, and after you finish, take some firewood up the kitchen."

I felt she was delaying me on purpose. "But the firewood has to be cut into small pieces, I don't have time to do that." I protested.

"I don't care, just do it." She insisted. She was determined to keep me at bay so I could be her weekend slave. I got very angry and started cursing her under my breath. At least that's what I thought until I heard my mother, who was feeding the chickens nearby, calling me.

"Come here, you bad mouth, did I hear you curse your older sister? Cursing an older sister was like cursing at me." My mother was coming at me like she was ready to swat a big fly. She immediately reached for a stick from the pile of firewood underneath the *matong* room and headed my way. She was yelling and waving the stick wildly in the air. I knew I was in for some lashes – just how many depended on what I would do the next few seconds! I couldn't move, nor say a word. I set down the water pail. But before her stick would touch me, I ran away toward the river to avoid her.

"Bad child. You'll regret doing that when I catch up with you." As I kept running away from her, I thought she would get tired of following me and just let go. She did exactly the opposite; she pursued me with intensity like Mang Agaton chasing a passerby who couldn't resist helping himself to one of the jumbo watermelons on the vines crawling wantonly on his farm. Trapped, I backtracked toward the house and waited for my punishment.

Lying on my belly, tears rushing down my cheeks, I received a series of quick lashes as my mother reminded me that I had to respect my elders.

"You will not curse her no matter how much she has provoked you. Always keep in mind that she is older than you." And so I promised myself that would be the last time my mother would give me a stick session, even if it would mean not returning to the house forever. That incident intensified my craving for the saccharine evil cane that I had to remind myself I could go to jail for stealing a stick when I passed by the fruit stalls during school days. However, I was deathly afraid of the punishment I would be dealt if I got caught of stealing. And a stick of sugar cane is not worth risking my education.

I stayed clear out of trouble and focused on my studies more than ever after that incident. (When school ended in March 1959, my mother went up the stage with me [the third time since the fifth grade] during our commencement exercises and pinned another ribbon of honor on my chest. I had finished freshman year at the top of my class.)

Sometimes good news could be a harbinger of troubles to come. In December 1958 a textile company from Tenejeros, Malabon, a suburb of Manila, posted a wanted for work sign at Kuya Lino's

Bittermelons and Mimosas

school. He applied and was one of the select students who were called for an interview after the holidays.

That year, a Doris Day Song, "Que Sera, Sera" (Whatever will be, will be), was one of the most played songs over the radio. As the song had implied, the future would be all mine to see. I wasn't worried. Kuya Lino would be in a better position to help the family if he landed the job he interviewed for.

Thank you God! My school days of potholed-bicycle-ridden trips would soon be over. Yiippeee! I was elated, yet very apprehensive.

Chapter Eight

Beautiful Dreamers

Meme na, Bunso, Tatay mo'y malayo,	Sleep, my child, your father is away
Bumili ng bukayo sa hulo.	He bought candied coconut from where the river begins.
Tulog na, Bunso, Tatay mo'y malayo	Sleep, my child, your father is away
Bumili ng pakumbo, para kay Bunso	He bought candied coconut for you, child,
Sa hulo.	from where the river begins.

A lullaby my mother used to sing to my sister Beth.

Kuya Lino's crusade to lift our family from poverty didn't stop with me. Before he left for work in Manila, he had negotiated a deal for my older sister Huling with the owner of a Cosmetology School in Cabanatuan City who was also his friend. Huling would cook and wash dishes for his friend's family of six in exchange for board and lodging and classes in Cosmetology Science. So in June 1959, my sister and I became city students: she with her Cosmetology Courses, and me in Second Year high school.

That summer of 1959, after Kuya Lino left Sumacab for Manila, I became my mother's partner in every venture to whatever place it took us, which was mostly hunting for natural goods to be turned into silver coins. Inang made sure I would not miss school just because I couldn't pay the jeepney fare. I saw my mother up close and personal during these many outdoor times together.

I don't remember my mother singing any other songs except this lullaby and the All Soul's Day song she taught me while we gathered *zacate* from the farms. I don't think she even knew some words of the

Bittermelons and Mimosas

national anthem that every Filipino sang with heartfelt fervor after the World War II. But she had a very gentle and loving voice that put my sister Beth to sleep even on an empty stomach. The lullaby exemplified her simple delights. Love for her husband, children, and the earth, in that order.

EVERYTHING ABOUT MY INANG was pure and simple. Inang always wore loose flowery cotton skirts and a delicately woven kimona or overgarment that she took pride in sewing herself. I have always pondered how much prettier she would have looked in a pink dress. The pink color would have matched her ever-rosy cheeks made healthy – not burned – by the heat from the field. Her petite figure, made more attractive by a tiny waistline, never lost its shape in spite of her giving birth eleven times. I surmise that her secret beauty formula was the uneven mix of pleasure and pain in raising eleven children. It helped her maintain her petite figure all through the years. She kept her hair in a bun at the back of her head, anchored by a decorative comb. Like most women of her generation, she never wore lipstick. As a girl, devotion to the farm she loved kept Inang away from school. She never learned to read or write, but she was extremely clever and street smart. She taught herself to recognize and count paper money by its colors. Touching each individual shape, she memorized the value of every coin.

From bits and pieces I heard from my elders, what attracted Tatang to my mother (he was already betrothed before they met), in addition to her simple and appealing beauty, were her resourcefulness and immense love of working in the soil with her bare hands. Better

My Inang.

than a man, she could tolerate intense physical labor. She was exceptionally hard working and was knowledgeable about farming. Tatang saw her as a cut above the rest of the women in our neighborhood, a strong partner he could depend upon to work in the fields and run the household at the same time. This feeling proved to be right when Inang was both father and mother to her children during his HUK days. Most of all, my mother was very much in love with him. She was willing to do anything to make him happy, almost to the point of sharing him with another woman had her children not objected.

As so often happens in the rural Philippines, my parents met during rice-planting season. Newly separated from her legal husband, my mother went to her relatives in Sumacab and worked as a rice planter to earn money to support her daughter. She met Tatang during an evening serenade. Within the year, they decided to move in together as common-law husband and wife. It was a decision that would affect their children's lives later on. During the HUK period, couples lived together, started families and had their union solemnized by the church after the war.

In those days being an illegitimate child was like the kiss of death in our culture. Because of my mother's marital status, it was understandable that in the beginning they lived together as man and wife without the sanctity of the church. Much later after the war, my older siblings insisted upon a church wedding. But a nuptial never happened. For whatever reason he had, my father held out.

I believe my mother's love for my father was the cause of her greatest anguish. However, I also believe that the love she had for her eleven children was equally great. In contrast with a modern-day mother, Inang rarely tucked us into bed. She never read us bedtime stories or helped us do our homework because she was untaught. But even if she had been educated, there was little time after fieldwork and housework. Her day job included helping my father farm and taking care of our animals or hunting for nature's bounty for food. At night I remember seeing her hunched over on the floor weaving *banigs* or sleeping mats, which she sold to our neighbors or to families

Bittermelons and Mimosas

in the city during market days. She was always hustling for things to do and sell to help take care of her platoon's growing needs.

There were many other motherly duties she relinquished to make sure we didn't go to school with empty stomachs, as did some of the neighborhood children. She wasn't around to send us off to school in the morning because she had already gone to the fields long before we were up. But she made sure there was food on the table for breakfast and lunch. My older sisters, who were school children themselves, cooked breakfast and fed the younger ones before trekking along the dirt road to school.

My mother, bless her soul, was a loving person in her own way. She never wiped away my tears of pain and shame or gave me a hug to make me feel secure at times when bad thoughts and insecurity ravaged my brain after my elementary graduation. But I knew that deep inside her she understood my fixation to not lead the life my parents had been destined to live. She saw many times how the curse of poverty had mercilessly broken a farmer's spirit to pieces after a bad harvest. When it became clear to her that I wanted a different and better life and I was willing to work hard for it, she became my ally.

Had I become even half the woman my mother was, I am more than convinced I would have risen to more noteworthy situations because I had an education she lacked. Yet my mother was comfortable in her own skin despite her educational handicap. She owned and operated a small variety store on the ground floor of our house. I remember on market days, she would ask my older sisters to write her grocery lists which she handed out to the different vendors in the city. Then she would come back later to collect her purchases. We always checked the lists against the goods she brought home. And nothing would be missing. Except for her immediate family, nobody knew about her disadvantage.

In a way mother was lucky, as she didn't see a world of wars, death, and hunger in print. She was also spared from the intricacies of the everyday life, as she did not have to worry about attending to any legal matters. My father took care of all that – from paying real estate taxes to reading our report cards. My father, despite his shortcomings, made most of their married life uncomplicated. His wit complemented my mother's industry.

It was one of those early Saturday mornings after a long Friday night of reading and listening to the transistor radio, my newest and most wonderful form of entertainment. Mine was pocket size and apple red in color. I had always been a "night owl"; therefore I got to enjoy listening to it by myself until my favorite station signed off at midnight. So come Saturday mornings, I felt like a *nilasing na hipon* (pan-fried flour coated shrimp with head marinated with whiskey or gin) dish from lack of sleep.

It was still dark outside when I heard my mother calling from underneath the house. She had just finished helping my father milk Dumalaga, our nursing *carabao*. Her voice was decibels louder than Old Conrado's, the milkman to whom we sold our *carabao*'s milk. At the same time every morning, Conrado came to the village and collected *carabao* milk in the neighborhood.

"Nieves, get up. The early bird catches the worm." My mother's words sounded more righteous than Father Hernandez' homilies during Sunday mass.

"We have to be there before the others." My mother was talking about the other farmers who had trailed us on previous mornings because they knew Inang could smell fodder grass better than a stray cat could sniff the leftover fish from supper my sister Conchita had hidden inside the cupboard. My body craved more sleep. However, I was fully aware that my mother wouldn't hesitate to wave her slippers before me if I dawdled because she had done it before. This unpleasant thought catapulted me out of my mat from a zero-to-sixty-miles-per-hour speed.

"Go drink your ginger tea. You will have stomach ache if you cross the river on an empty stomach," she reminded me as usual. A cup of our hot morning "tea" sat on the *dulang* waiting to warm my stomach before we ventured out to the farms.

Although the barrio was still asleep, most farmers were already up. Like us, they had to start farm work early to beat the rising heat. At midday, with no breeze stirring the air, the ground could get hotter

Bittermelons and Mimosas

than the Arabian Desert. Walking barefoot at noon, which my mother and I had done often, made me loathe poverty even more.

"Inang, it's cold, very cold." The freezing water from the river that merged the barrio to the farms chilled my warm feet and made every hair in my body stand.

"Keep your clothes dry so you don't catch a cold. Raise your skirt up to your waist." She assured me that nobody was watching because it was still dark.

Puberty denied any likely "Peeping Tom" with an undoubtedly earthly pleasure because I chose to be wet rather than be seen naked from the waist down and teased about it. Dripping wet and cold, I walked behind Inang echoing the morning greetings she exchanged with the farmers we passed on our way.

We were weeding faster than a weed whacker when I felt thorns rip into the palm of my hand. I hadn't noticed the *makahiya* plants embedded with the grass because it was not yet daylight. "Aray! Ouch!" I shouted in pain as I pulled out one by one the mimosa thorns sticking like needles in my palm. The sting stirred my blood and warmed up my body. I licked the little blood that came out with the thorns and resumed weeding like crazy. Before the temperature rose to the 90s, my mother and I each had a sack packed full of fresh *zacate* grass that we later sold for two pesos. I was very happy. Besides earning my next week's school allowance, I was bonding with my mother.

During these times, I realized that although my mother was petite and appeared fragile, she wore her pants like any man. I had heard stories repeatedly from my older siblings of how she took care of our family during my father's absence. But seeing with my own eyes how she worked non-stop until our sacks bulged at the seams with the precious *zacate* grass to make sure we would have something for the horse owners, made me believe that Tatang had the right instincts about Inang. She became my heroine because she had a heart bigger than those of all her children combined.

One thing I always did to endure the double-digit heat that made me sweat like a waterfall was sing. I liked to sing even though songs didn't like me. I remember one evening during my first week at Liwag

Nieves Catahan Villamin

High School I was so happy I started to sing in front of the stove while cooking rice.

My mother stopped me. "Don't sing in front of the stove. You will end up marrying an older man. You are not going to school just to be a caregiver for a much older husband, are you?"

No way. Why would I want to have that kind of life? I asked myself.

So I stopped singing altogether. Coincidence or not, one of my most ardent suitors when I was in my early twenties was 13 years older than I. I have always thought that had I continued singing in front of the stove while cooking, I could have had a May-December marriage. Fine if he was rich, but a farmer like me? Not in my lifetime. (I picked up singing again one day when my granddaughter was in my arms and I was trying to put her to sleep.)

"Hum like whistling" was something my mother did when the heat became more than we felt we could bear and home was nowhere near because our sacks were only half-filled with *zacate* grass. She said she hum-whistled to call the wind to cool us off. I was astonished when the wind came and fanned us.

"How did you do it?" I asked her.

"I'll teach you," she said.

But I never learned the trick because when I pursed my lips as she did hers, my saliva would get in the way. Can she really call on the wind when she needs a breeze? I asked myself. Why not? She was my mother. She could do anything.

One time in mid-October, I helped her pick turnip pods. Then we gathered and dried the seeds. During the turnip-planting season the following month, we would sow them in moist soil. In time they would grow into the big, round roots that became the turnips sold in grocery stores. The turnip leaves have the poison ivy effect. They irritate the skin upon contact. I was itching badly so I needed some diversion to take my mind off my discomfort. I asked my mother if she knew any Halloween songs since All Saints' Day was just around the corner. She said she knew a few verses and started singing softly. She stopped after the fourth line and told me to ask Kuya Lino because he knew more about Halloween songs. We sang these only during the *pangangaluwa*, a practice similar to "trick or treat" in western countries. When All Saints' Day came, I had the best Halloween songs in the area, which I later taught to my neighborhood friends. The following year we were all singing about souls in purgatory.

Maybahay po'y huag magagali,	Homeowner please don't get upset
Sa pagdulog at paglapit,	With our plea and our presence,
Kaluluwa'y humihibik,	We are the restless spirits,
Ginggin ang ipagsusuli.	We ask that you hear our laments.
Nang kami po'y nabubuhay,	During our existence,
Dito sa Lupang ibabaw,	On this wonderful earth,
'Di namin napaghandaan,	We did nothing in our might,
Itong sasapiting buhay.	To prepare for the afterlife.
Araw-gabi pawang layaw,	Day and night mostly comfort,
Hangad ng lupang katawan,	Was what our body sought the most,
At 'di po nagunam-gunam,	And we never even gave a thought,
Pagsapit ng kamatayan.	When death would knock on our doors.
Itong araw nang sumapit,	And then the dreaded came one day,
Kamatayang Mapanganib,	The gloom of death stopped our way,
Kalulway ay nabulid,	Grabbed our souls wallowing in sins,
Sa bangin ng madlang sakit.	Down the abyss of agony and dim.
Sana'y huag n'yong pamarisan,	We hope you won't duplicate,
Ang nagawang kasalanan,	The wrongs we had done on earth,
Upang sa kabilang-buhay,	So that in the afterlife,
Ang langit ay inyong makamtan.	Heaven would be on your side.
Kaluluwa kaming tambing,	We are kindred spirits,
Sa Purgatoryo nanggaling,	That came from purgatory,
Doon po ang gawa namin,	All we did there,
Araw, gabi'y manalangin.	Was pray day and night.
Kung kami po'y lilimusan,	If you would give us alms,
Dali-daliin po lamang,	Please hurry up,
Baka kami mapagsarhan,	Because we might miss,
Ng pinto sa kalangitan.	The closing of heaven's gate.

By watching my mother do her rituals on the Day of the Souls, I learned the practice of offering candles and prayers every November 1 for my relatives who had crossed to the other side. Through the glow of the lit candles guarding our altar, I remember seeing my mother on bended knees praying for our departed relatives as she wept softly. She didn't have to remind us, her ritual participants, to behave during the rosary. A painting of Jesus Christ hung over the altar and His piercing eyes seemed to follow us wherever we went. They were more than sufficient to keep us alert during the hour-long ritual.

For several years, we spent All Saints' Day visiting my grandmother's tomb in Aliaga, my mother's birthplace. Like most graves, my grandmother's lot was cleaned and freshly painted, making the gravesite look respectable. The gravestone was five feet above ground, my grandmother's name intricately carved on the front side. Statues of Jesus, saints, and angels stood around it. We always brought her homegrown flowers in wreaths or colorful bunches, mostly marigolds and *palong-palonga*n or cockscomb, and placed lighted candles arranged like Christmas lights around the grave. Through the luminous candlelight, the prayer session lasted for hours.

When evening fell, we did our version of "trick or treat." We called on every house in the neighborhood to beg for alms that were either coins or native delicacies, not candies. We donned no Halloween costumes. Happy faces, floating above the glow of candles, were all the costumes we needed. And there was the other group of trick-or-treaters. They were young men and women who serenaded the neighbors with Halloween songs while some of their friends stole chickens nesting under the houses, some just for fun, others for malice or payback because of the strictness of the parents of the maiden who lived in that house.

As a child, I learned that this holiday was associated with ghosts and spirits and mythological monsters. I can only assume that part of the reason behind this was the fact that All Saints' Day fell at the tail end of the monsoon season. On most nights before November 1, dark clouds filled the skies, later bursting into heavy rains punctuated by intense lightning bolts and boisterous thunder. The stormy weather usually kept us close to home, since our parents understandably did not want us outside. We read stories of Lola Basyang from *Liwayway* magazine. These stories became so popular that they were adapted into

ᎨᏍᎪ Bittermelons and Mimosas ᎨᏍᎪ

a radio program. So we knew Lola Basyang before we heard her voice on the radio. "*Oh... Efren, huwag ka nang malikot ... Ito po ang inyong Lola Basyang.* Efren, don't move ... this is your Grandma Basyang."

I can still hear that voice in my head, old and tired but crystal-clear, like water cascading down a waterfall during summer. Grandma Basyang was actually a pseudonym of Severino Reyes. He was a well-respected playwright who told his children bedtime stories. Later, he decided to write down his stories so other children could experience them. He wrote children's stories using the name Grandma Basyang, after a family friend who would gather her grandchildren around her for a nightly storytelling session.

Many of Reyes' Grandma Basyang's stories tell of supernatural beings and so-called creatures of midnight – many times giving nightmares to us children and causing us to wet our *banig* because we were too scared to get up and pee in the middle of the night. There were stories of *kapre*, the black hairy giant with big eyes, sharp teeth, long fingernails and a huge body sitting atop the *balete* tree and smoking a cigar; the *Tikbalang*, a half-horse, half-man cigar-smoking creature that made a traveler lose his way; the *manananggal*, a self-segmenter, usually a woman, who divided herself into two, her lower half remaining on the ground while her upper half, with webbed wings like those of a bat, searched for human victims; the *tiyanak*, the hobgoblin who appeared as a beautiful baby who cried lustily to attract passersby and then turned into a hideous creature when picked up; and the *duwende*, *nuno sa punso*, or *lamang-lupa*, diminutive creatures that could be benevolent to humans who won their favor or cruel when offended by them. (I had my own experience with the *Tikbalang* and the *duwende*.) For us children, these stories drew out cogent fears, complete with genuine chills racing throughout our bodies.

On the Cajucom farm a mile past the river to the west, there once stood a huge *balete* tree the size of a centuries-old California redwood. In spite of the distance, the tree was in plain view of most houses along the riverbank. It was like a lighthouse helping to measure distance and at times guide lost animals and *carabao* shepherds. "A big *kapre* used to sit on top of that *balete*, smoking a big fat cigar. The cigar light was the beacon that guided your father and all the other HUKs on their return to the mountains after visiting their families in the lowlands," Uncle Basilio used to tell us when we were kids.

"That wasn't a tall tale. I saw it myself." my father confirmed what we had been told. He had seen the smoke coming out of the top branches of the tree during his many late-night visits to his family.

IT CAME AND SHOCKED our family in many ways unimaginable. Jealousy, dressed in a bright green suit, had appeared the first time at our door one night in January 1960 and stayed. Its seeds were sown for the first time and later grew so strong and wild it was next to impossible for us to rid our home of them, no matter how we tried.

It was Sunday and almost midnight. Outside the rain was pouring in sheets, trying to compete with my mother's tears. I heard Inang moaning in her sleep as I was still up fanning my half-dried skirt with a big *bilao*. It was the only skirt I had for my uniform, and it had to dry. I couldn't go to school bottomless.

"Sanse, Sanse, wake up. Inang is having a nightmare. I called out to my sister who was fast asleep at the other side of the room.

Both half awake, we hurried downstairs and found my mother trembling on the mat and crying. Tatang was nowhere to be found. He had gone to the fiesta in Gapan, and had not returned. During the ensuing time, we heard Inang's muffled weeping almost every night as she slept alone. At first, Inang tried to suffer in silence, holding everything in, but the green monster that possessed her aroused violent emotions. She could barely breathe at times. On occasions, the sobbing also awakened some of the younger children. We gathered around her, some massaging her chest and stomach with a pouch of warm ashes from the stove so she could breathe regularly and the others preparing *salabat* tea for her to drink.

Bittermelons and Mimosas

We all knew what would make her feel better. Yet we felt helpless. We didn't know where Tatang was. Then one night, Inang passed out with her arms and legs stretched out stiffly. Terrified that she would not regain consciousness, we bundled her up and dragged her toward the hospital even though it was in the middle of the night. She awakened before reaching the hospital, so the doctor treated her by simply prescribing plenty of rest and avoiding more emotional flare-ups.

As soon as she could talk about it, Inang told us her gut feeling was that Tatang was off with an old flame from his bachelor days. Tatang did not believe in – much less participate in – church practices such as festivals. But off he had gone to the town fiesta of Gapan. Days before the fiesta, Inang had overheard Uncle Lope telling my father he had chanced upon Tatang's old flame selling farmers' supplies at the Gapan market.

On the day he came back after a week of forbidden romance, his clothes, accompanied by Inang's curses, flew out the front window. "Here are your clothes, you S.O.B. Go live with your mistress." After she had thrown the last piece out the window, Inang passed out, her body stretched out and stiff. Tatang hurried up to the house, put Inang on his lap, and massaged her whole body. Having the right medication hastened her recovery. That was the first time the entire neighborhood learned about Tatang's womanizing ways. However, it wouldn't be the only time the drama about their love-hate relationship would be played out in front of the children but behind closed windows.

By tradition, Filipino men were generally promiscuous. Our culture tolerated a married man having a mistress, despite the heavy Catholic influence throughout the country. So it wasn't as though my father was the only husband who strayed from his wife. My father's vice was nothing compared with the others in our barrio who lusted for younger women, some even spending lavishly on them. However our family, who thought the world of our father, could neither believe nor accept his philandering ways. After all, he was a man with intellectual integrity. My aunts and uncles tried to talk to my father about their marital woes. All fell upon his deaf ears. Other than his

Nieves Catahan Villamin

philandering, everything about him was the same. He was still the same resourceful, articulate, hardworking and loving father anybody could have asked for.

It was August 1960, only the third month of my sophomore year, but I had already seen from my mother's worried look each morning that providing me with my daily school allowance would be difficult sometimes. Kuya Lino and his bicycle were gone, so no more free rides to school for me. If I wanted to stay in school I felt I had to find other means to get financial sustenance. I also didn't want to add any more stress to Inang's already troubled life. Traditionally, we helped family members without compensation, but during that period, it was the most logical way for me to earn my school allowance.

"Brother-in-law Islao, can I help you harvest corn today for money?" I asked my sister's husband one day during the August corn harvest season.

"Yes," he said gladly. "Harvesting has to be finished soon because the corn is decaying in its husk from the unremitting rain. Some of the kernels have already sprouted into inedible seedlings. I need your help badly." I heard the relief in his voice because there was now an extra hand to help him.

Dark clouds had been hovering in the sky for almost a week. Except for the occasional downpour, there was no indication that a storm had been blowing down trees and flooding the mountain basins, causing an overflow onto the shores of Dingalan, a town approximately 65 kilometers from us. (Many farmers did not own radios then.) So it was business as usual for most of the farmers in our neighborhood. The water was still shallow when Siyaho Islao and I crossed the river in our *banca* that morning. Soon after, however, water streamed from the Dingalan Mountains and filled all the rivers

Bittermelons and Mimosas

and waterways within its course to the lowlands. By late afternoon, the water had risen past the riverbank's waistline and blanketed the shore fronting the adjacent land, even beyond Mang Agaton's farm. The cement block where we anchored our *banca* was buried deep beneath the water.

The sight of the never-ending body of water in front of us and the knowledge of the missing *banca* sent chills up and down my spine. I looked at brother-in-law Islao expecting to see the same fear I felt. But he was calm as a clam burrowed into the sand. As he was perhaps thinking of the best possible way to cross the river safely, my head was spinning out of control because I felt in my gut the worst of the danger that lay in front of us.

I looked around and noticed the darkness starting to engulf us; the likelihood of receiving immediate help seemed naught. Realizing the predicament we were in, I began to panic. I screamed until my lungs almost collapsed.

"Help, help, anybody there listening, please help us!" I hollered. And hollered. And hollered. But to no avail.

"You are just wasting your breath," brother-in-law Islao told me before I could deliver another wave of screams. "The wind gusts are blowing in our direction. No one will ever hear us," he said matter-of-factly.

Even if my screams for help were heard, rescuing us without the *banca* could be an impossible mission. In a matter of hours, the water would possibly be deeper than ever before. The only means to cross to safety was riding on the back of Baguntao, brother-in-law Islao's young *carabao*. He had done this many times in the past. However, now he had more than himself to worry about. It was getting late and he knew if he didn't take a chance, we would end up staying overnight in a *nipa* hut – wet and hungry – with a good chance of getting sick, perhaps even joining Jose, our neighbor's son who had died of pneumonia the year before.

"Be ready. We'll cross the river while there's still time." Brother-in-law Islao had finally made a decision. He inspected Baguntao's leash and tightened it, then turned and gave me his final instruction. "No matter what happens, do not let go of his tail!"

"Yes." My voice hardly cleared my throat. My body was shaking from fear, not from chill. "What if my hands get tired and I loosen my grip, I can drown and never be noticed." The unpleasant thoughts made me hold on to the tail so tightly I felt as if the veins in my palms were about to pop.

Brother-in-law Islao's jerking of Baguntao's leash signaled Baguntao to swim even faster. This caused a sudden jolt that slackened my grip.

"Aaawwww," I sounded off after I almost let go of his tail. I closed my eyes and prayed so I wouldn't face the seemingly endless body of water we had to cross before we could be safe. "God, please do not let any big wave run us over." My palms were glued to the *carabao*'s tail.

Brother-in-law Islao kept Baguntao alert during our journey to safety by pulling his leash occasionally and talking to him incessantly. I was certain the animal felt our desperation. Without a pause, the big, strong animal swam us safely to the other side. The compassionate river made sure none of its giant waves crossed our path. My sister, who had been oblivious to our danger, cried with joy after her husband told her the whole story during supper.

Although that was the longest and most dangerous swim I ever had in my life, the danger I was subjected to became a closed subject. I was paid good wages for my efforts. My school allowance was secured up to the end of the year.

MY SISTER HULING'S COSMETOLOGY classes worked in the beginning, but her discovery of the opposite sex happened more quickly than Kuya Lino had anticipated. Although it was also her dream to escape poverty, her plan did not include hard work and a degree from a

Bittermelons and Mimosas

fashion school. She wanted an easy way out. The warning signs were written in big letters all over our walls, but no one in our family noticed them. Huling had hardly finished cosmetology school when she eloped with Babad in 1960, a few days past her 17th birthday in August. Babad was a Sumacab native who lived his adult life in Manila and worked there as a jeepney driver. Perhaps my sister thought that by marrying her life would be better. The whole family was very disappointed, Kuya Lino especially.

"I told you so!" It was the first of a series of recriminations from my father after Huling's elopement.

WITH ANOTHER ONE OF her babies flying the coup and faced with her five younger daughters' growing needs, my mother had to find another means, in addition to her small and sometimes ailing variety store, to meet our daily necessities. She bought a female pig and decided to breed it. As I remember, included in her bevy were Tatang's doves, native chickens, and Mama Pig with eleven piglets.

I still recall the conversations between my mother and her animals during feeding times on mornings we didn't forage for *zacate* grass. It sounded very sweet. Wanting to be fed all at once, the chickens would cluck, "*Tiktilaok, tiktilaok.*" And my mother would answer, "*Krrrruukyaa, kkrrrruukkyaa.* You'll all have your share." Then the pigs would cry, "*Iiiikkk, iiikkkk.*" And Inang would croon, "*Lleeeegan, leeeegan.* Be patient. You'll have your turn."

Through the slits of our bamboo kitchen floor, I could see the pigs eating at their *labangan* or trough one side of our *silong*. Inang poured their food – a mixture of *darak* or rice chaff and hugas (water drained from washing rice before cooking or from washingd ishes) into the trough. All day the animals roamed our yards and nearby farms for additional food, then they rushed home for supper. Come daylight, they called for food as if they had not been fed the night before.

Next it was time for attendance check. Inang looked around and found none of the pigs was missing. She went on to count the chickens. "One, two, three, four, five, six..." My mother's voice drifted back: "Where has the grayish brown hen gone to? Nieves, see if all the nests are empty." I peeked through the kitchen floor to see the nests below. One of the baskets that *Tatang* had nailed on the wooden beam was occupied.

While the rest were enjoying their morning feast, one hen stayed and sat upon its eggs. "Inang, one hen up here making baby chicks," I called back. As I looked from side to side, my eyes focused on the smooth white eggs inside the baskets. I didn't think Inang would notice if I took one egg for my lunch. *Just for today so I can have a different lunch*, I told myself. *Was I so-o-oo wrong in taking just one egg! One egg gone!*

When Inang found out that I had stolen one of her babies, I found myself listening to an unusually loud sermon prior to Sunday mass.

"That egg would have grown into a fat chicken had you not boiled it! I could have sold it and bought sugar, salt, and vinegar for our daily use, etc., etc."

But still – a fresh egg boiled and eaten with rice and salt was a perfect lunch and a rare treat for me. *Sarrrap, sarap*. Delicious, delicious! It was well worth a scolding.

WITHOUT AN ELDER SIBLING to talk to, I crept away and sought the comfort of my dear river-friend, Pampanga, on many tranquil evenings. One side of the cavern that was sculpted like a giant hammock on the riverbank wall became my sanctuary. During my visits, I discovered nature's many personalities. The most spectacular of all showed up in December when the river was crystal clear and the weather was breezy and mild. The sky was brightly illuminated by a full moon and galaxy of stars. So bright were their beams that inhabitants nestled safely underneath the castle rocks were awakened. Enchanted by the brightness, the shrimp and fish came out, jumped up and down above the water with joy. They seemed to be trying their best to make me feel better. Everything around my small cave was serene and magical. The evening breeze carried the fruity smell of the ripening *palay* and the scent of flowers in bloom during the December harvest season. The night was so serene that I could hear Christmas carols and church bells from the city miles away.

The sights inside the cave calmed me, but the sounds made me restless and angry. Why is it so hard for me to pursue a higher education? I was not destined to be a farmer's wife – no way! Nature never tired putting on a show while I was inside my cavern to keep my mind off my school worries. During the wet season, I watched how the *talahib* grass faced the relentless hammering of the gusting wind and the pouring rain, fearless and dignified. I knew it would only be a matter of minutes before the overflow would drown the grass. Yet, the *talahib* would come back, growing taller and more vigorous than the previous year, ready to take the punishment from the strong wind and heavy rains again and again. Like the *talahib*, my quest for education got stronger with trial after trial. Pampanga River at other times could fill me with fear. Yet, it was my safe haven for many years. Because my friendship with Pampanga was deeper than its water, it was my faithful river-friend I would always call on first every time I returned back to Sumacab for a visit.

WHEN THE 1960 CHRISTMAS season arrived, I was feeling good about myself. Johnny, my closest rival on the junior year honor roll, gave me a surprise gift, his prize-winning lantern fresh from a Christmas *Parol* (Filipino Christmas five-pointed lanterns traditionally made out of bamboo and colored paper [papel de Japon and cellophane]) contest at school. I was proud to have it, although my classmates told me he had cheated to make the honor roll. They added that someday if I wasn't careful, he would cheat me out of a medal. The lantern looked worth every bit the prize it had won. It was bright yellow with yards of fluffy Japanese crepe paper wreathed around it.

Before the day ended, gossip about me being Johnny's girl swirled around the building. Before school closed, I knew the first thing I had to do it was exercise damage control before the gossip found its way to my parents' ears. In a small town like ours, this could happen quickly. I had been in stickier situations than this, and I knew what had to be done. I told Johnny I wouldn't hesitate to slug him if he encouraged such a tale. Instead of getting perturbed, he replied, "You are welcome," as if he was teasing me. And to further appease me, he said something like even if it were true; he would just keep it to himself, because he had heard about how strict my parents were. His demeanor got me confused enough to have a change of heart.

Nieves Catahan Villamin

School had been dismissed for the holidays, and that evening I watched as Johnny's lantern danced with a gentle breeze outside our window. It might have been the wind, but I swear I heard Paul Anka serenading me. I was so tired from the excitement in school that I didn't move to get up. Lying on my mat bed, I relished every word of Paul's serenade to me. *Put your head on my shoulder, Hold me in your arms: baby...*

My mother's voice recalled me to reality. "Nieves, it's almost midnight. Turn off the transistor radio. Batteries are very expensive." She was awake waiting for my father to come home. *Oh Paul, how could you make a joke at a time like this?* I lamented before dozing off.

On a more serious note, the wound inflicted by my father's fling left scars akin to a cracked vase that never looks the same after it's been repaired. Friction replaced the normally pleasant atmosphere at our house and it was never the same again. The continuous arguments between my parents and their storm-tossed relationship that came into full view provided the drama that gave me many sleepless nights and ultimately caused my school grades to drop. When the 1959–1960 school year ended in March, I lost my full scholarship. My teachers were in shock because I got very low scores during our finals. I felt so much shame I couldn't tell them about what was happening at home. Again, a college education seemed to be just another figment of my imagination.

I ADMIRED MY MOTHER'S emotional strength as she shed many silent tears from the wounds inflicted by my father's infidelity. Unlike many women in the barrio that chastised and wished death to their unfaithful husbands, my mother instead spoke highly of him to her children and everybody she knew. She remained an ever-loyal wife and mother. This virtue, I know, I learned from her.

Bittermelons and Mimosas

I miss my mother's unassuming and simple way. I miss hearing her lullaby song to my sister Beth. And I feel her presence whenever I sing it to my granddaughter Isa when I rock her to sleep. I miss the aroma of her *dinuguan* (stew of meat simmered in rich, spicy gravy of pig's blood, garlic, chili and vinegar) and *paksiw na bangos* (milkfish cooked in vinegar with ginger root, chili and some vegetables), two of the dishes she learned to cook with perfection and sold at her *sari-sari* store. Ours was a culture where most women knew how to cook. When they chose instead to buy my mother's prepared food, it was recognition of her natural ability and skill. I miss the smell of her *itso* (ground betel nut, *ikmo* leaf and lime chewed and used as stimulant by the older folks), the only relief she had during those many nights of sadness. I miss the comfort that put me to sleep when lightning and thunder played tag during the stormy nights. I miss the small presents she brought me from her market trips when I was in elementary school: the white and yellow tablets of paper where I put down my many juvenile prose and poetry creations. So crispy fresh, I could smell the scent of the tree where it came from. I miss the giant yellow "Mongol" pencils that helped me compose and the small packages of "Crayolas" that brought color and life to many of my youthful dreams.

I miss Inang's advice full of the wisdom she learned from life. I miss everything about her. But most of all, I miss the presence of Inang.

Young as I was, I had no inkling that it would be just a matter of time before we would break up as a family.

Nieves Catahan Villamin

Chapter Nine

Breaking Away

If you dedicate all your efforts
to the process of self-development,
Eventually you can make changes
that you never thought you could!

Dr. Marcelino C. Catahan

The decade of the 1960s rustled into our lives like an autumn breeze, bristling but comforting. Darkness couldn't mute the streets, especially during nights when a raging storm whacked away branches of the acacia trees lining the street between the electric posts. Changes were engulfing the once sleepy barrio. Like the blown-down acacia branches, breaking away for some members of our family became inevitable as the decade rolled in.

The first to fly the coop was Kuya Lino. In early 1959 he was one among a group of talented students enrolled at the best technical school in the province, the Central Luzon School of Arts and Trade (now NEUST). From there, he was recruited for a favorable job at Lirag Textile Mills in Malabon, then a suburb of Manila. Before rice-planting season of 1960 ended, Huling left for Manila with her new jeepney driver husband. In March 1961, Kuya Lino sent for Sanse Conchita. She worked as a laundry woman for Kuya Lino's friend who lived in Tenejeros in Malabon (now city of Malabon and part of metropolitan Manila).

My father kept quiet about our changing circumstances although we were sure he was seething inside because he had to eat his own words about not having his children work away from home. Kuya Lino and Sanse Conchita sent financial help to support the family. This gave my father some financial freedom so he didn't have to do as much physical work anymore. We also stopped borrowing money from loan sharks. The financial support helped, but it didn't heal the wound that was slowly rotting my parents' relationship. The seed of jealousy planted in years past sprouted and started to grow.

With Diko Unti and three of my older sisters married and Sanse Conchita working in Manila, I became the leader of the pack. I assumed the much harder tasks that fell to the oldest of the children still living at home. My mother tried to distribute the household chores evenly among us. Gertrude, whom my father referred to as the "half-hatched egg" in my mother's nest because she was the slowest learner among his eleven children, again carried the water bucket on her head, to my delight, and she also gathered firewood. Asthmatic Mila cleaned the house and yard. I took care of the rest of the household chores in addition to my farming duties on weekends.

Ammie lived temporarily with Aunt Juana and Uncle Gorio (they had no children of their own) because they bribed her with good food and toys. My aunt and uncle earned a respectable living, as vegetable *viajeros* in our barrio and Ammie was their favorite because she was cute as a button. They could more than afford to bribe Ammie, the most *matakaw* or food lover, among the five remaining children at home. Little Beth with her skin so soft and white akin to the inside of a cucumber, and a smile like the morning sunrise, gave the rest of the family something to be happy about. She was the *Bunso*, and we allowed her to play our strings like a mischievous child would. Instead of lashes of *patpat* and *tsinelas* we gave her our love and attention. She made us forget our family dilemma even if it were only temporarily.

᙭ Nieves Catahan Villamin ᙭

IT WAS THE HOLY Week again, in late March 1961. I regained my footing in school and finished third year at the top of my class. My parents had declared a cease-fire early in the year for their children's sake. And they seemed to get along better. It was summer and nature's bounty was all around us. I was feeling good.

High up the ground were trees lined along the riverbank, some with branches laden with ripe fruits just waiting to be reaped. Down below was the waist-deep river with beds and beds of clams and snails. Every day Gertrude and I were up among the trees or down along the river gathering summer's bounties. Holy Week came, and we stayed put. During Sabado de Gloria it was customary for the out-of-town folks to have a picnic and bathe in the river to cleanse their body and soul.

The 1961 Glorious Saturday would turn out very differently from those of previous years. I was washing the dirty pots and dishes in our wash room and getting ready to cook lunch. My ears were tuned in to the transistor radio across the street broadcasting in full volume, trying to call every neighbor's attention to disturbing news about a faith healer and flagellant named Arsenio Añoza who was nailed to a cross. This was the first time ever in Pampanga province that this had been done on Holy Friday. This form of Holy Week penance was unheard of in those days, which is why Arsenio Añoza made the headlines. I was trying to imagine the scene in my head when I heard Inso Lucing calling from her backyard that connected with ours.

"Nieves, Nieves, come down here. There is a man singing and writing your name on the river shore." Inso Lucing saw everything from where she stood. Our backyards were only an earshot from the riverbank.

"What? Who could that troublemaker be?" I asked Inso Lucing.

"There." She pointed to the river.

Indeed. From a distance, there seemed to be a man bathing in the river and singing a love song. At the riverbank the nosy neighbors started to gather.

Didn't I see something like that in the movies before? It was summer. Love must be in the air! I told myself and proceeded en

Bittermelons and Mimosas

route for the river feeling giddy like a typical teenager. Until I saw the *guyabano* tree that stood close to our bedroom window out of the corner of my right eye. The sight brought me to a standstill. Wasn't it just a few nights ago that I had slid down that *guyabano* tree and hid at Diko Unti's house to escape the serenaders from town? And didn't go home until my father dismissed them because I was nowhere to be found? Oh! My God, I am doomed! Two love episodes in one week? How lucky can I get? But damn it! I have to take a chance on this one! So I kept going, but I was shaking like a leaf holding on tight to a twig for safety during a monsoon wind. My parents' voices, "no higher education, you would just marry like your older sisters," chasing after me like Harrison Ford being pursued by a giant boulder in one of those Indiana Jones movies.

The sight of a man carving I LOVE YOU, NIEVES on the shore was visible where I stood. He was still singing a popular Pat Boone song, "Love Letters in the Sand." Proceso, a bachelor in his early twenties from Talavera (whom I met during their town fiesta one day when Zeny, Lety, Eddie, and I cut classes) was enjoying what seemed to be a bad prank. He was among the other picnickers, and they had set up a big makeshift shelter from the sun at the shallow part of the river, getting ready for a swim. Although Proceso was singing out of tune, he managed to gather a cheering squad. Our neighbors who made it their business to know the details of everybody else's life in the barrio swarmed the riverbank rooting for me. Their cheers grew louder when from the other side of the river, Proceso blew a kiss at me.

The open expression of love thrilled spectators. At that moment, I felt special. A grown-up. I didn't get embarrassed. The world went from drab black-and-white to a wild festoon of many colors as the self-proclaimed wallflower started to bloom! A suitor professing his love for me to people I knew buoyed my spirit. I felt like I could walk on water if I tried. I was enjoying the attention and I liked it!

That was until I saw my father's *banca* moving toward the embankment where we stood. My exuberance washed away quickly, resembling the message in the sand wiped out by the wind and rain that came a couple of days later. I ran back to the house to finish my chores and stayed clear of my parents' path.

That evening at supper, Inang and Tatang ignored the dinner in front of them and zeroed in on me. Trying to focus on eating, I felt the chill of their piercing looks shoot through my skin and into my bones. They knew about the message in the sand, and they were not pleased.

"Such a public display of affection is shameful," said Tatang.

"Very bad taste," agreed Inang. "This is entirely your fault, Nieves."

"What have I done?" I tried to make a case.

"Enough!" my father warned me, "Do not let it happen again."

I knew how serious they were. My mother seemed especially upset because she had always been our shock absorber, especially at this point in their troubled marriage. She always got the brunt of Tatang's anger when one of the children got into trouble. I knew they would not hesitate to withhold the college education I cherished so much. I did not argue anymore. Love would just have to wait until I finished college. I was sure by the rate of how things were going that I would be an old maid long before I become a teacher. But happy thoughts from the earlier "opera" won over. I was wearing a smile as Pat Boone lulled me to sleep singing "Love Letters in the Sand" in my head. *On a day like today We passed the time away, writing love letters in the sand...*

In mid-October of the same year, people in our neighborhood were shaking with fear because of an epidemic that was sweeping Manila where children of affluent families from Cabanatuan were studying. Cholera, a potentially deadly intestinal infection caused by ingestion of contaminated food or water, was rampant in the city. Four hundred thirty-two victims, and counting, were hospitalized in San Lazaro General Hospital, the principal infectious disease hospital in the country. Everyone who heard the news spoke as if by just talking about it one could contract the disease. It was like the saying our elders quoted when we were growing up. After we peed on the dirt, we were told, "Jump over your pee so you won't get pregnant." Perhaps some wise being came up with that adage as a way to more-or-less toilet train us.

Kuya Lino and Sanse Conchita visited in November, at the

Bittermelons and Mimosas

height of the cholera epidemic, to celebrate our barrio fiesta with us. I remember my parents strongly suggesting that they not go back to their jobs in Malabon, a neighboring city of Manila. My parents were particularly concerned about Kuya Lino. He had been a sickly boy and almost died of pneumonia during his early teens. However, both assured my parents they were now quite healthy with strong immune systems. (Being exposed to the worst conditions of nature as farmers had its advantages too, later in life.) Additionally, their explanations that most of the sufferers lived in the slums of Manila, where many disease-carrying insects thrived due to poor sanitation, helped lessen my parents' worries. After their return to Malabon, my siblings wrote letters to our parents that put their minds completely at ease. For a while, I felt that dark shadows had been threatening to obscure the star in my galaxy that had started to shine.

As the government health bureau disseminated ways to avoid the epidemic through their local agencies, the news died down by mid-1962. The further spread of cholera was avoided.

As my high school graduation got closer, I became self-reflective. I saw clearly how lucky I was to have been studying in a family-oriented, close-knit school like Liwag College, a private school known in the community for being an advocate of the poor. Its small enrollment consisted mostly of dirt-poor students from the barrio whose parents were typically farmers. We looked like skin and bones loosely put together because we were, of necessity, almost vegetarians. As our parents' foot soldiers in the fields, we were uniformly dark skinned. Some students from neighboring schools labeled us "brain dead and stupid." Timid perhaps, but not stupid, was my opinion.

The college accepted harvest as payments and often was lenient to those unable to pay tuition fees on schedule. That's how I was able to enroll for my junior year sans a scholarship. My mother promised to pay the school administrator all tuition fees after the December harvest. Still, for whatever reason, some mocked the college and its students. We just let the hurtful remarks whiz over our heads. However one thing was certain: the teachers at Liwag College taught me many things – among them, compassion.

Nieves Catahan Villamin

Compassionate administrators and the school's small enrollment provided us with a nurturing environment. We were more like an extended family living under the same roof for four years. All my teachers were the best in their fields. They chose to be there, not for the money I'm sure. It was common knowledge in the city that their wages were always late. They cared about us misfits, the label stamped on our forehead by students from neighboring schools. That's why they stayed around.

The teachers that will always have a special place in my heart for as long as I live are: Ms. Angelina Leonardo, English; Ms. Maria Villanueva, Pilipino and History; Mr. Norberto Magsumbol, Biology; and the most handsome, and every students' crush, Mr. Jorge C. Roque, Math and Algebra; and our Physical Education and occasional Drama teacher, Mr. Amadeo Hernandez. Although we were a small school, we had a special program similar to a summer stock theatre in the United States. No other school offered this kind of program.

During the barrio fiesta every December 8 (for the four years I was in high school), we put on a show for the folks of Concepcion. This is a barrio in the town of Talavera where the school's owner, Susana Liwag, lived as a young girl. Even after I graduated, the tradition continued, until the barrio folks found out the actors were not professional entertainers, just students. The last ensemble of the school's performer wannabes were booed on the stage and heckled on their way home.

As the days on the commencement calendar passed like falling autumn leaves, the seniors started acting as if the invitations had already been sent out and that graduation from high school was an inevitable event. I, for one, became self-absorbed. "What can go wrong? In just a matter of weeks I will be a college student. Our teachers will address us as Miss and Mister. Oh, what a feeling." That's what was in my mind. Until one mid-morning when the juniors mocked us chanting, "Hooky," "Hooky," as they watched half of us bake under the sun for hours as penance for playing hooky during school hours. We had cut afternoon classes the day before so we could watch a movie at a theatre downtown.

Bittermelons and Mimosas

Playing hooky was something I had never done. I decided to experience a "hooky moment" with the others, not thinking of the price I would have to pay if we were caught. I promised myself, also, that this would be my first and last time to play hooky. But like a forbidden fruit, the first bite was followed quickly with a second one. And the second time it was more exciting.

Spending the night at a classmate's house without our parents' permission was a crime punishable by bodily harm because "slumber parties" were not allowed in the culture especially if you were a girl. Our host parents had no idea we were AWOL from our families. We lied through our teeth, perhaps even better than the politicians that had been sworn under oath, that's why they believed us. After dinner, our host parents excused themselves for bed to prepare for a busy schedule the following day. We stayed up and gabbed until almost midnight. Hardly had we prepared for going to bed when the Cabanatuan City police came knocking at the doors with some angry parents in tow. We were like thieves that were caught in the act with no place to go except surrender or maybe try a suicide escape. Either which way we chose could spell doom. Better than paid detectives, some of the parents were able to track us down. My father wasn't home when I was returned by one of the policeman. It was one of those times when my parents argued a lot over their marriage and he wasn't around. Not wanting to deal with another headache, my mother decided to just let it go. I was scot-free but worried sick for days.

The four years at Liwag flew by too quickly, especially our senior year. I graduated at the top of my class, not Johnny. Miss Leonardo, our fourth-year class adviser told me she had to have a copy of my valedictory address one week before graduation. I was more than disappointed when she made it clear that she wasn't happy with the piece I had written.

"It sounds like you are preaching communism here; maybe you should tone it down," she suggested after reviewing my speech. "It is full of hatred."

Hatred for the rich and for landowners like our landlord, those who would see us starve because the return of their investment was all they cared about. Poor people didn't matter to them. I had learned those things from my father. And I witnessed it happening to our family!

Although I promised I would, I didn't change a word. I didn't receive a standing ovation for my address, but I remember feeling exhilarated afterward. I was able to get something off my chest. Now, I felt I was ready to take on any challenge that might come my way. The best Kodak moment, which I kept for many years, was a photograph taken as my father pinned the ribbon of honor on my chest. After the graduation ceremony in March 1962, all of us huddled in the school ground. Heartbreaking as it was, because we had been classmates since our freshman year, we were aware we would fade from each other's lives after saying our goodbyes. Some of us might see each other again during our 25th high school reunion in 1987. But for some, it would be the last time.

I LEFT SUMACAB FOR Manila in April 1962 to take a scholarship test for engineering students at the Technological Institute of the Philippines (TIP). The test, mostly Math and Algebra, promised a four-year full scholarship with monthly stipends. Although Math and Algebra weren't my favorite subjects, I placed third. Then it went downhill from there. I accepted the fact that I wasn't destined to be an engineer and that no monthly stipends for four years were in my charts. I was already staying in Manila when on May 12, 1962, President Diosdado Macapagal, father of the President Gloria Macapagal Arroyo, signed Proclamation No. 28 moving the date of Philippine Independence celebration from July 4 to June 12. This nationalist gesture strengthened the fact that before the infamous Treaty of Paris of 1898, there was an independent Philippine Republic in the wake of the 1896 Revolution that ended Spanish colonial rule.

As school began, so did the preparation for the Independence

Bittermelons and Mimosas

Day celebration. The festivities at Luneta on June 12, 1962, were splendid. Emilio Aguinaldo, the first President of the Philippine Republic, was the guest of honor. I watched the plays with my new friends together with thousands of spectators. These plays, most of whose participants were students, were about the events that happened during the struggle for Independence in 1898.

THE YEAR 1962 WAS the "it" year for me. I left my *kariton* life in Sumacab for Manila, the center of education and fashion in the Philippines during that period. As I had dreamt ever since my elementary school graduation in 1957, a college education now seemed near, not a galaxy away. I had gotten miles toward the south farther away from being a farmer's daughter. I can't help but smile when I think about my future calling.

~ Nieves Catahan Villamin ~

Sophomore high school commanding my platoon during the July 4th 1959 parade in Cabanatuan City. The De Luxe restaurant at the background is still doing business as of today.

Igorot Dance troupe in sophomore high during the school's foundation day. Mr. Jorge C. Roque, advisor, Mr. Norberto Magsumbol, Science teacher, and Mr. Amadeo Hernandez, dance instructor.

✺ Bittermelons and Mimosas ✺

Miss Maria Christina Villanueva officiating her Junior high school officers. I am third from the left.

Freshman high, Inang pinning the first honor medal on my chest.

Senior high, Tatang pinning the high school valedictorian medal on my chest.

❦ Nieves Catahan Villamin ❦

Some of the 1962 Liwag College High School graduates: Sitting left to right: Remedios Nimes, Leonila Mendoza, Leticia Cruz, Miss Angelina Leonardo, Miss Maria Cristina Villanueva, me, and Elmina Adrineda. Standing behind L-R: Ernesto de Lara, Johnny Ulidan, Ferdinand Liwag, Wilson Padiernos, Graciano Valeda, Pilar Galang, and Rita Udanga.

25th High School reunion in 1987: Sitting L-R: Liwanag Galvez, Me, Cornelia Kuam-Poc, Ernesto de Lara, Cornelia Kuam Poc. Standing L-R: Leonila Mendoza, Milagros Padua, Lety Cruz, Marina Abaya, and Wilson Padiernos.

Chapter Ten

Almost There

In every forest there thrives a snake.

A Filipino Proverb

In the school library we were staring at the newspaper that carried a picture of a weeping and bloody *Gabriel Flash Elorde (a boxing champion and a hero to most Filipinos)*. *The photo had been taken* after a riotous melee following a boxing match the previous Saturday, November 17, 1963, that ended with the disqualification of challenger Love Allotey of Ghana. Although our hero retained his title, his fans worried that he might not totally recover from the fight. In a few days, another hero, honored by many nations, made the headlines.

Late in the morning of November 23, 1963, Philippine time, I was riding a Baliwag transit on my way home to Sumacab to attend our yearly November 24 and 25 fiesta celebration. The regular broadcast on the bus's radio was abruptly interrupted by an emergency newsbreak. The thirty-fifth President of the United States, John F. Kennedy, had been fatally shot on Friday, November 22, 1963, in Dallas, Texas, at 12:30 P.M. U.S. Central Standard Time. This took place in Dealey Plaza as he was riding with his wife, Jacqueline, in a Presidential motorcade. I still remember the passengers looking at each other with fear in their eyes, as if a bomb had been dropped on one of the Philippine islands. The way my father interpreted President Kennedy's death (basing his reasoning upon his previous underground activities) was the possibility that the assassination

Nieves Catahan Villamin

could be the forerunner of an attack like the one which took place on December 7, 1941, when an unannounced military strike by the Imperial Japanese Navy against the United States naval base was lodged at Pearl Harbor. This resulted in the United States' entry into World War II.

It had been only a year since the threat of a nuclear confrontation between the Soviet Union and the United States on Cuban soil made headlines throughout the world. Those two countries, which had gained military and economic strength during World War II, had been in a cold war since. Communism was perceived as a great threat to personal freedom, especially with the success of Fidel Castro's Communist-inspired revolt in Cuba, and western and some Asian countries believed its spread should be curbed. In the Philippines, the root of our fears of a communist invasion stemmed from being brainwashed by American-authored books. The Soviet Union was evil and the United States was good. Because we were one of the United States' allies, they could come to us at any time. We feared communism just like we feared cholera. A year after the confrontation, Kennedy was assassinated; in 1964, in the Soviet Union, Khrushchev was removed from office by his party colleagues, and our fears abated.

WITH THE SIGNIFICANT EVENTS happening around the world being accessible to me through newspapers and classroom discussions, I knew I was in the right place to continue my education because Manila, as I thought then, was the center of Philippine civilization. So I became my brother's shadow, following his trail like a detective looking for clues at a crime scene while both of us were trying to find our much-wished-for greener pastures. Kuya Lino, who seemed as popular in Manila as he had been in Cabanatuan, had already made many friends and acquaintances at the Technological Institute

Bittermelons and Mimosas

of the Philippines (TIP), one of them the president of the school. I was particularly proud when Kuya Lino introduced me to some of his friends, most of them women. I felt elated and very blessed when they extended their goodwill to me.

Like Mrs. Susana Liwag, my advocate during high school, TIP President Demetrio Quirino, Jr., believed money should never get in the way of someone's education if he could help it. The school president was a very caring man who made all the people around him feel important, a rare attribute in a person of prominence and with a fine education. He charted the school's future within the walls of our dreams.

A newly established technological school, TIP offered scholarships to many poor, ambitious, and exemplary students from different schools around the country, students who were filled with dreams but lacked the financial means to pursue them. His precept was, "Study and work hard so you can help me build the school. Someday, we will be one big happy family." A dynamic motivator, President Quirino inspired his scholars to push harder and set their sights even higher, and he watched with care as our aspirations transformed into something real.

President Quirino's wife was a mestiza of petite build and a flawless skin. Her face gleamed like the morning sun from a smile that seemed always present, not on call like that of most women of aristocratic bloodlines.

I still remember how we were awed beyond belief when we first met her at a school gathering. We all exclaimed, "What a beautiful woman!" I even heard someone make the comment, "She should be in the movies! She is much more attractive than many movie stars we have now." When she spoke we could tell she had an intellect rivaling her husband's. President Quirino and his wife, the brain and face of TIP, our beloved school, were our heroes during our college days.

I was studying in Manila. My little family away from home, Kuya Lino, Sanse Conchita, and cousin Pining, rented one of the three rooms of an old Spanish house in Blumentritt in the Sampaloc district of the city. Sanse Conchita and cousin Pining worked as seamstresses

Nieves Catahan Villamin

in a Chinese clothing factory in Divisoria. The three of them shared our daily expenses. For the first time in my life, I did not have to work very hard for my school allowance.

It was the first Christmas vacation after our high school graduation. Lety, who had been my best friend in high school, and some other former classmates, teased me when we got together on Christmas Eve.

"Hello, Manileña! Your skin has become fairer, and you don't look like a barrio girl anymore. I bet you a stick of sugar cane, you won't work in the fields anymore."

"What do you mean? I came home to help harvest," I replied. "And as a reminder, I hate sugar cane."

"Oh yeah!" The others joined in with Lety's banter. Their eyes were teasing me. They knew about my "sugar cane misadventure" in high school and remembered it – that's why the repartee.

After the holidays, I returned to Manila more grounded than ever. I felt very happy knowing I was the only one from our high school graduating class pursuing a college education in Manila. The few of them who were able to continue their education were enrolled in schools around Cabanatuan City.

I WAS TWO YEARS along the way toward a college degree when my brother's life made a detour that turned the normal life of our little family upside down.

"I can't believe she didn't stand up to her parents," he cried.

We saw tears fuse with the mucus running from his nose as the pain that went with his anger consumed his whole being. Kuya Lino's fiancée had broken up with him at her parents' insistence. He didn't measure up to the expectations of a family whose colonial upbringing made them worship wealth and pedigree. Kuya Lino was short on all counts.

༺ Bittermelons and Mimosas ༻

However, the most compelling reason was that her parents had learned about my father's womanizing ways. "Apples don't fall far from the tree; like father like son," they concluded. I didn't realize then that the next time my father's infidelities affected his children's lives, I would be the one who was being judged.

Nevertheless, our wounded hero seemed to heal faster than the hourly changing of the guards who watched over the Rizal Monument at Luneta Park. The following year, he married Mimi, an Ilokana mestiza, whose father was mayor of one of the towns in the province of Cagayan. Her affluent family included university-educated aunts and uncles who had immigrated to the United States in the early 1950s. She seemed like a good catch for our favorite brother. I thought the timing wasn't right because I was still studying. However, I was thankful he found a woman who saw him faultless. The idea about our family's financial needs falling solely on her shoulders overwhelmed Sanse Conchita. She cried incessantly like a child recently orphaned. I couldn't eat for days because of my own worries.

Lady Luck seemed to smile within the same year, however, when a permanent job opportunity allowed my sister Huling and her husband, Babad, and their small baby to move back to Manila. Babad was able to return to his former job as a jeepney driver.

Unlike in the province, help in Manila was hard to come by because neighbors were strangers to each other. Huling needed a babysitter when she had to go to the market, which was almost daily. Sanse Conchita and Huling struck a deal. We would all live in one apartment and share rent and utilities. I would baby sit and help clean the house. In return, I would have a place to live and a small allowance. Again, everything seemed to fall into place. For almost two years, everything worked well. The housework was light and didn't interfere with my studies. The extra income certainly helped. I was with family. This seemed to be an ideal situation, and it made me very happy.

"So, you'll leave on Wednesday evening with Sanse Conchita and Nieves, huh?" Huling was confirming their plans with her husband on a Monday morning before she left with the baby to spend the Holy Week in Sumacab.

Nieves Catahan Villamin

It was a tradition. We all planned to spend the Holy Week at home with our families. Home was with our parents until we had children of our own. As usual, on Tuesday morning, Sanse Conchita left for work at seven o'clock to beat the traffic. I got up to do my chores after she left. Although it was mid-morning, Huling's husband had not yet gone to work. He was still asleep on one side of our one-room apartment.

Around ten in the morning, I stepped into the bathroom to take a bath to get ready for school. I locked the bathroom door behind me. Midway through my bath, I was startled by a strong thud, and the door behind me flew open. Huling's husband, my brother-in-law, stood over me. He reached down and put his hands squarely on my back, as if testing to see how I might react to his advances. My initial shock turned to fear. We were all alone in the house. If I resisted, I was afraid he would punch me and knock me down then rape me. Suddenly, my sense of outrage took over, and I got hold of myself and screamed.

"*Putang ina mo!* You S.O.B.! Get away from me." Loudly. As loudly as I possibly could. It was enough to snap him back to reality. He immediately spun around and dashed outside the house without saying a word. I wrapped a towel around myself, grabbed a knife from the kitchen, and ran out the door. My brother-in-law was gone. He went straight to his wife in Sumacab to do some damage control before Conchita and I got there. Huling believed I was also to blame; perhaps I had enticed her husband.

"What? Huling believed what her husband told her?" I was so disgusted I didn't realize I was shouting at Conchita. She was updating me on Huling's decision not to come back to the apartment because of the incident. Her husband would be staying with a relative close to work and go home during the weekend.

"Sanse, look at the wooden door lock!" I pointed.

"I know," she nodded. Sanse believed me.

The only thing that saved me from shame within the family was the telltale, partially split wooden lock dangling from the door, clear proof of a forced entry. For the first time in my life, Kuya Lino didn't

Bittermelons and Mimosas

come to rescue me and offer me shelter. He was already married and starting his own family. His priorities were now different. My mother explained in her own words, "When a daughter marries, you gain a son. When a son marries, you gain lots of heartaches." It would be many years before I understood what my mother's words meant.

Perhaps out of shame, Huling and her husband returned to the province. My sister Conchita, who found me work sewing at a factory, assumed the rent of the small apartment. She was determined to finish the job that Kuya Lino had started.

I never spoke to Babad again after I chased him while holding a knife in my hand.

Chapter Eleven

A Wilted Mimosa Bloomed

First love is dangerous,
only when it is also the last.

Branislav Nusic, Serbian Novelist

Although I had resided in Manila for almost three years, I still considered Sumacab home. I ran to her at every possible opportunity: on holidays, or to do fieldwork, and often just to be with the family. Family was something I couldn't live without when I was younger. And in our family, age or earning status did not exempt anyone from the rules of my father's empire regarding holidays, especially New Year's Eve.

"Home is where you should be at 12 midnight. If you aren't home by that time, you will be cursed and be like restless spirits trying to find their rightful place."

How he knew that was never fully explained, but none of us were in a position to question him. Perhaps it was because of the danger from fireworks or stray bullets being fired from guns at the stroke of midnight by some wild gun owners bidding the old year good-bye and greeting the New Year. He merely wanted us home safe and off the streets before the craziness started.

I had fun watching my mother filling up our sugar, rice, and salt containers filled to the brim on New Year's Eve. She also kept her purse and pockets filled with coins, again, as part of an old tradition. She

Bittermelons and Mimosas

believed that doing these things meant our family would never experience shortage of any kind. I wish I could say it worked every year.

For his part, Tatang always welcomed the New Year loudly. He pounded a big aluminum pot the very first second after the clock struck midnight. He also kept our windows, doors, and drawers wide open to welcome the New Year's blessing.

While the city folks turned to fireworks, tooting horns, and shooting bullets into the air, we fired Diko Unti's homemade bamboo cannons. Staying awake through all these rituals was a struggle for the younger children. What was this supposedly special night meant to bring? There were no new clothes, no newly permed hair, no big feasts, no presents, and no Christmas carols. It was just another day in a different year and my father banging joyfully on an aluminum pot.

Then came what my father called The Year of the Comet. It happened in 1965 at the tail end of a full moon when I was a junior in college. On that New Year's Eve, the almost half-moon was still bright at midnight. He saw something in the sky that made him apprehensive.

"Look," he said, pointing to the darkness. "See that?"

None of us could. We didn't have any idea what he was talking about.

"It's a comet," my father continued. "Can't you see it?"

We still couldn't. Someone asked him if it wasn't just a star.

He shook his head. "No, it's not a star. I saw a comet," he insisted.

My father was visibly upset about seeing a comet. He explained that war or famine could likely happen after a comet appeared in the sky. It would – just like the last time his parents showed him one, Tatang insisted. That bit of information made the rest of us worried and upset since we didn't know what caused our father to make such a dire prediction. We would not find out until mid-year the cause of his fears.

Nieves Catahan Villamin

ATENG MACARIA WAS MY mother's daughter from her first husband, making her the oldest of the eleven children. She spent most of her growing-up years with our grandmother, Benigna, who lived in Aliaga, a town about 18 kilometers from Sumacab. The only hybrid in a bunch of nine blooms and two shoots, she was the most delicate flower in my mother's garden. Her adolescence was filled with unspoken disapproval from people who looked down on second marriages, which in those days could be the "talk of the town." Dressed in her favorite yellow floral dress with her curled hair dangling past her shoulder, she was our Rita Hayworth, Filipino version. She was beyond beautiful.

For the short period that I knew her, I saw her as a gentle and loving soul. Ateng Macaria's love for us was whole, although we were only her half-brothers and sisters. She never expected love from the family to match the love she held for us. Ateng Macaria had to work extra hard to win the approval of our family, especially my father's. She longed so much for his attention. At 17, she married Pedring, one of my father's HUKBALAHAP comrades. Pedring was a much older man. Everyone expected him to offer maturity and wisdom, along with the love and affection that Ateng so desperately yearned for from my father. They married and moved to a neighboring village.

In the beginning, the marriage seemed to be the answer to Ateng Macaria's prayers. Friends and neighbors observed how marriage had changed her, how happy she seemed. She was. During her first pregnancy, she blossomed all the more. Her personality changed as well, creating a young woman who seemed much friendlier and more outgoing.

Not everyone was happy with this transformation. Pedring, perhaps dismayed at what was happening to Ateng Macaria, became suspicious and critical of his wife. To him, his new bride had suddenly become beautiful and appealing, and he was convinced that she would soon be looking for a new husband. A husband humiliated by his wife and another man is called a *pendeho*, a cuckold. In our chauvinistic culture, it was the most humiliating and demeaning tag that could be given to a married man. Filipino men in such a predicament were often driven to commit murder or suicide.

Bittermelons and Mimosas

History was repeating itself in my family. Pedring became increasingly filled with rage and evil thoughts. Sadly, the difference this time was that my sister simply wasn't as strong as my mother had been and she struggled daily.

Hoping against hope because she wanted so much for this marriage to work, Ateng Macaria endured her husband's tirades and the hell they created. The breaking point came when Pedring turned physically abusive and left her emotionally shattered. Enough, she decided. After a fight that left her with a black eye, a cut lip, and bruises on both arms and thighs, Ateng Macaria grabbed Andoy, her baby boy, and they fled the house with nothing but the clothes on their backs. They had nowhere to go, except to come home and seek refuge with us in Sumacab.

We were all surprised to see her walk through the front door, and we were alarmed by the horror stories that gushed out as my sister tried to retain her composure in spite of her injuries. None of us had any idea this was happening in her marriage. Everything seemed so happy and wonderful when they were together with us during the holidays. Now here she stood, looking so weak and pathetic, telling awful stories. It was more than we could abide.

Tatang was especially stunned and upset. This was not the Pedring he knew. Pedring was his trusted comrade from the HUKBALAHAP. I could see the anguish on my father's face as he listened to Ateng Macaria and clenched his fists in angry silence. When Ateng was finished, my father did not yell at her. He did not accuse her. He did not blame her. He had only words of kindness for her, but I knew that Pedring was destined for a far different response.

We could only imagine that Tatang's conscience bothered him. He felt responsible and perhaps thought that his unloving ways toward Ateng had driven her into the arms of a man who caused her much grief. There is no denying that my father cheated on my mother, but he never, ever, hurt my mother physically. What Pedring had done clearly touched a nerve inside him. For reasons he never disclosed, Ateng Macaria's abuse disturbed my father profusely. Pedring had crossed a line and would have to pay.

Nieves Catahan Villamin

My father assembled some friends and relatives and headed out in search of Pedring to make him pay dearly for what he had done. Each person was armed with razor-sharp bolo. The whole Catahan clan (my fathers' three brothers and two sisters' husbands and their older children) cried out for Pedring's blood to heal my sister's bruises and wounded spirit. Fortunately for Pedring, who had been tipped off earlier, the hunters arrived after he had fled to the mountains. The marriage between Pedring and Ateng Macaria was over.

BY THE TIME OF the year of the comet, Ateng Macaria had remarried and her new family had already been relocated in Sumacab for three years. As in the past two years, they celebrated New Year's Day with the rest of the Catahan family. After ten years of blessings from their farm in Bibiclat, drought came. After that farming cycles were disrupted by typhoon after typhoon. These caused massive flooding and destroyed the *palay* crops that were only weeks from being harvested. The nonstop rain turned the rice fields into a big marsh. Eventually, the land became unsuitable for farming. To survive, Ateng Macaria and her husband Tomas borrowed money from loan sharks until the time came when they were forced to sell their two *carabaos* and other animals to buy food. Tomas fished every river and stream nearby and did handicrafts that Macaria peddled in the market. With six mouths to feed, there was not enough money to buy food. Finally, they had to sell the house and lot it stood on. They were not sure what would happen next.

Once again, my father showed concern and intervened. Well aware of what was happening in Bibiclat, he seemed to magically appear on their doorstep one day with a proposition.

"Come home to Sumacab," he urged them. "Try your luck there."

Ateng Macaria was speechless – she felt the invitation was a genuine expression of love from a stepfather she had thought felt nothing in his heart toward her. Initially, Tomas was hesitant to accept the offer and leave his family, but Ateng Macaria persuaded him.

Back in Sumacab, my father gave the couple a small lot on which to build their house and an equally small piece of land to farm. This was to be a new beginning, my father told them. The rest of

Bittermelons and Mimosas

us pitched in wherever possible to help in the transition. That first harvest left them some grain in their *matong* after all the debts were paid, an encouraging sign.

For the first time in years, Ateng Macaria radiated with happiness and acted like the young newlywed of so long ago. As we watched her once again blossom, it seemed to us that Macaria was happy because her dreams were finally coming true – a better life for her family and the cherished love of my father.

Only later did the family discover the truth. Macaria had secretly been seeing her first husband, Pedring. She was still in love with – and loving – the animal who had beaten and abused her. Somehow, he had materialized in a nearby barrio and reconnected with Ateng Macaria, apologizing from his heart and swearing he was still in love with her. They started this ill-fated affair built on mounds of apologies and pronouncements of love. Ateng Macaria knew she was playing a dangerous game; she knew that many people could be hurt. Still she didn't care and the affair continued until that Friday, August 13, 1965, a day of grief that will always be remembered by the Catahan family.

THE RAINY SEASON OF 1965 had been a heavy monsoon season and August promised to be no different. In early August, a typhoon had been looming for several days, threatening at any moment to speed into overdrive and wreak havoc on anything in its path. Nana Didang, our labor contractor, usually scheduled rice planting in our area months in advance. For years, she had accurately predicted the weather by charting the appearance of heavenly bodies.

That week in 1965, she guessed wrongly. Nana Didang had scheduled planting as a typhoon was fast approaching. My father knew about the typhoon because he had heard about it over the radio. He thought that if he delayed the planting for a few days, the rice seedlings would mature beyond their transplanting days. They would be of no value to us, and we would have to start over again, delaying the schedule even more, and spending more money we didn't have to buy additional seeds. Despite the weather, there was little choice. The planting moved on as scheduled.

The morning of August 13 was bleak, wet, and cold. The fact that it was Friday the 13th gave most of the rice planters some misgivings. But Ateng Macaria offered a startling contrast with her extra-cheerful, warm, and affectionate manner. She was singing, joking, and hugging everyone, acting like a cheerleader and making everyone feel comfortable enough to get through the miserable day ahead. It must have made a difference because we stuck to the schedule that day, despite the heavy rain, and did not fall behind. It was zero visibility on our way home because of the heavy downpour.

However, Ateng Macaria would not be deterred. She walked along the road with a group of friends and my sisters Ammie and Mila, each one laughing as they exchanged gossip and jokes. My sisters Clarita, Gertrude, and I had finished our rows ahead of the others, so we left a few minutes early. Part of the walk home involved a three-mile trek along a busy highway. Clarita, Gertrude, and I were already deep into the other side of the rice fields when we heard loud screams and intense cries coming from the highway.

"Come back, come back!" We turned and saw some of the rice planters motioning frantically for us to return.

Ditse Clarita and I dashed back, while Gertrude rushed straight home to call for help. We knew something bad had happened.

As we got closer, I could see some of the planters standing by a ditch, pulling bodies out of the water. Then we got close enough to see. Five bodies were stretched out on the ground. I immediately recognized two of our neighbors. Then, my sister Ammie. My sister Mila. And next to them, Ateng Macaria.

"The jeepney driver blinded by the torrential rain plowed your sisters into the water-filled ditch at the side of the road to avoid head-on collision with the slow-moving tricycle. He couldn't control

Bittermelons and Mimosas

the vehicle so it landed on top of them." This was the story I heard over and over again for many days.

"Where is he?" I asked for the jeepney driver. "We saw him hitch a ride," someone told me. We found out the following day from one of the politicians that visited the hospital that the jeepney driver hitched a ride, went straight to the police station, and surrendered.

I remember that a truck stopped by and the driver quickly leaped from his seat and helped load the injured. When he picked Ammie up, we saw her legs dangling loosely, as if they were lifeless. That's how we found out that her thighs were completely broken.

"Oh, my God, Ammie's legs! What's going to happen to her now?" I shouted in anger, not in grief.

Nana Juana, Clarita, and I accompanied the injured to the hospital. Ditse Clarita consoled Ateng Macaria, who was not saying much. I stroked Mila's swollen head gently to ease her pain. Nana Juana attended to Ammie, who was numbed from her waist down and with blood leaking slowly from her wound. No one comforted the two others who suffered only minor injuries.

Although I was wet and barefooted, a hospital staff member told me to look for blood donors just in case the Cabanatuan Red Cross did not have enough supply in their blood bank.

I called Ditse Clarita who was attending to Ateng Macaria's needs. "Ateng Macaria is giving me her last wishes. She feels she won't live for long." Ditse Clarita was very hesitant to leave her bedside.

"But we have to donate blood," I insisted. Had I known my sister was dying, I would have gone to the Red Cross Office by myself and made them take my blood for the two of us.

At the hospital lobby, we found many relatives and neighbors who had just arrived. It was a perfect time for to ask blood donations. They listened to my plea and proceeded to the Red Cross Office. Ditse Clarita went back to Ateng Macaria, who by that time was almost gone. That's when we found out she was the one who had suffered the most severe injuries.

I was inconsolable because of the tragedy that had struck our family without warning, so Ditse Clarita decided to send me home.

"Get some dry clothes for us and food. It will be a long night," she said.

Ateng Macaria died at the hospital a few hours later, leaving behind six young children, from two to 13 years old. I witnessed the pain and suffering of the injured when Kuya Lino put me in charge. I was the cheerleader and "gofer" during the whole time we were in the hospital. I took a brief break from my duties only to attend to Ateng Macaria's funeral.

GRIEF CONSUMED OUR HOUSE and showed no signs of leaving as the family wrestled with unexpected financial and emotional issues. Money was needed for a proper funeral for Ateng Macaria. Ammie and Mila both had medical expenses that needed to be covered. Relatives, friends, and neighbors stepped forward, donating blood, giving us food, and leaving behind a little money, but there were major expenses to be faced. Ammie needed immediate surgery to protect her bones from further damage. Mila's head injuries were severe enough to require multiple x-rays and other tests. The bills piled up each day, thousands and thousands of pesos. There was no immediate solution, but I knew that my father would think of something. He always did.

In the old days, most politicians had genuine concerns about their constituents' daily plights, especially those who had had a hand in electing them to office. Every politician courted a large and reputable family such as ours for their votes. So for many years, Tatang, the designated head of the Catahan clan, had used his blood relationship to curry politicians' favor. And he had always delivered winning votes. Therefore, we didn't need a *compadre* to accompany us to the mayor's office during our time of need.

Word about the tragedy got around at the provincial hospital and support from some highly respected persons we hardly knew poured in instantly. Mrs. Rose Mora, a social worker (I don't remember if she held office or she just happened to be there), made sure we got all the assistance a public hospital could provide. She was a petite woman with a cute round face and so full of kindness that when she told me about blood transfusion for the injured, I was ready to sprint to the

Bittermelons and Mimosas

Our "angels of mercy." Mrs. Leonila Garcia (then Cabanatuan City mayor's wife), me, and Mrs. Rose Mora, almost 44 years later.

Red Cross Office, barefooted and soaking wet. Dr. Benjamin Morales (I remember him as being so young and handsome), the orthopedic surgeon who operated on Ammie's legs, showed compassion and assured us that she would be able to walk again once the surgery healed because she was fairly young. And most of all, Mayor Mario S. Garcia and his wife Leonila (to my father's delight, I asked her to be one of my *Ninangs* during our 1969 church wedding), helped with our misfortunes. Almost overnight, they arranged the funeral for Macaria and for the majority of the medical expenses to be subsidized by the social welfare agency.

We all understood what was happening. My father was cashing in on his chips by selling his loyalty. And all of us were expected to keep our end of the bargain. Being a large and impoverished family, we had no choice but to accept the "handouts" with big lumps in our throats. For years to come, the routine continued. At election time, my father, true to his word, distributed a list of the political candidates he supported to his children, relatives, and friends. I am certain that if politics exists in the afterlife, his political affiliation would not have changed. A man of intellectual integrity, my father was one of the last mavericks of his generation.

"Tatang, we have to take legal action!" Kuya Lino's voice boomed around the room like the roar of thunder signaling a typhoon. The sight of Ateng Macaria's family crying hysterically during the funeral was still fresh in his mind.

"Ateng has been killed. Ammie and Mila have been seriously injured. None of this was their fault. The driver of the jeepney should be held responsible for our suffering."

The pain was visible in both men's eyes. My father shook his head. The stoop of his shoulders suggested defeat.

"I know a lawyer who can help us," Kuya Lino said. "His name is Melanio Catahan. I saw his name listed in the telephone directory. I have never met him, but I am confident he is a relative."

Perhaps a blood relationship really existed. Melanio agreed to take the case pro bono upon learning the circumstances. We were initially optimistic. In filing a lawsuit, we assumed that justice would be served. Given the tragic facts of that rainy afternoon, how could it not?

Traditionally, justice in the Philippines was known to work in strange ways. Judges, not juries, typically heard cases. Then, it was nearly impossible to obtain a conviction, even if the other party admitted guilt, especially when your political connections did not run high enough. It was sad but true most of the time; someone needed a powerful sponsor to even have a chance in court. The ordinary person off the street had no chance. Tatang had political contacts. They would help us. But the driver who caused the horrible accident had political clout of his own, even more than we did. His friends used their influence on the judge to get delay after delay, postponement after postponement.

This went on for a few months, and my father quickly realized the game that was unfolding. His options were few, and my father feared the driver would eventually be acquitted without any fine.

Against the advice of his attorney, my father agreed to a settlement of 2,500 pesos ($685 in U.S. currency at that time). He wanted to take the money and just try to move forward from that traumatic

Bittermelons and Mimosas

occurrence. None of us really cared about the money. Ateng Macaria was gone and no amount of money could ever bring her back. The terrible tragedy and the injustice that followed made me even more determined to break away from my farming roots, which perhaps would be tougher than trying to escape the sizzling lava of a volcanic eruption chasing me down a mountainside. My college education would be my only way out. It was all I could think of the rest of that year. And the following year. I was taught to have faith, so deep inside I knew that God has something planned for me. Better days would be here soon!

"How can I get a job here at TIP?" I asked my friend Elvie, the bookkeeper at the Technological Institute of the Philippines, one evening. We were standing in the hallway waiting for our eight o'clock class in Commercial Law, the course she needed to take before graduating that semester. She had caught me one time wiping away tears during a class discussion about issues that touched fresh wounds. I told her about my family heartbreak and that I needed a job badly to stay in school. Kuya Lino and his wife were preoccupied with their second child and most of Sanse Conchita's wages as a seamstress were paying for Mila and Ammie's medications. The crops were still three months away from harvest.

"Talk about timing!" I felt the compassion in her voice. "I was offered a job at Purefoods. I can recommend you as my replacement to my boss, Mr. Dioscoro Adto."

Elvie and I knew how the system worked. It was whom you knew.

"What does the job entail?" I asked. I was excited yet scared because I was a neophyte when it came to office jobs.

"Actual bookkeeping is much easier than what we are taught inside the classroom. You won't have any difficulty," she assured me.

Elvie made good on her promise. She trained me as her replacement the following week. Her kindness was the Christmas gift I would remember for life.

Everyone in the family remained traumatized over the accident for a long time. It did help that my brother-in-law relocated his motherless family closer to his parents a few weeks after the funeral.

Nieves Catahan Villamin

Eventually, Mila's headaches became fewer until they completely stopped. Ammie was in her cast for almost a year, but after that, she fully recovered. After using crutches for six months, she eventually walked with only a minor limp. She enrolled as a high school freshman in Cabanatuan the year after the accident. I was settled in my new job.

The unusually bountiful *palay* December harvest that year lifted our spirits a little. Ateng Macaria was watching over us, we thought.

Chapter Twelve

The Charlatan, the Macho, and the Prince

> Love is not written in paper,
> for paper can be erased.
> Nor is it etched in stone,
> for stone can be broken;
> But it is inscribed on a heart,
> and there it forever remains.
>
> *Anonymous*

When the first semester started in 1966, I was feeling proud about myself. School at night and work during the day kept me grounded. I had no time to think or do anything outside my comfort zone. Until that evening in my Spanish class when I sat beside a young man who, I thought, was cute and charming at five-feet-three. I kept glancing at him, trying to make eye contact, but his attention was focused elsewhere. Then, one evening it happened.

"Hello, I am Morales. I know your brother." He turned to me and introduced himself after our professor called the roll.

"Really?" I pretended to doubt him so we might talk longer.

"Yes. I'm a senior student, only missing a couple of Spanish classes to graduate. I am very sorry about your loss."

Of course, you know my brother, I told myself.

I felt lightheaded, like a mimosa plant ready to fold, and then hide, as he smiled at me during our short chat. I was sure he had noticed my delight when our eyes met. However, it didn't take me long to observe that Morales was much friendlier with the pale-skinned city girls in our class, most of them with bright smiles outshining the dimness of their brains.

As days passed, it became obvious to me that my sunburned *probinsiyana* skin would be a cause for disappointment, perhaps even heartbreak. I had to do something if I wanted to be noticed before the semester ended, which would be in about five months. I was developing a huge crush on him.

"Did I see you walking last night?" my cousin Linda asked me over breakfast.

"Where?"

"Down Avenida Rizal, across from the hospital. Was that you?"

"Yes. Yes, you did," I replied. "I walked home. The traffic was bad so it would have taken too long if I had waited for a ride."

Shame hit me the minute the words left my mouth. Linda probably knew it was a lie, but what was I supposed to tell her? That I was walking to save my jeepney fare so I could buy some of Dr. Perez's wonder bleaching soap? The pink round soap helped bleach my deep brown complexion, and I had to pay dearly for each bar. I was already bleaching my skin even though it wasn't an accepted practice then. I kept telling myself on those long walks home that Morales was worth it.

Yes, at five-feet-three, he was short, but he was intelligent and charming. He was also a good writer who was full of dreams and high hopes for a better life, according to my brother when I told him about Morales. Because I wanted to make my interest in him known, I'd smile warmly in his direction. Morales would nod vaguely. It seemed hopeless.

Filipino tradition frowned on any girl expressing her heart too publicly, so I told my feelings only to my closest friend, Delia. When I found out much later that she let the secret out, I was too embarrassed to ask Delia for any feedback.

Bittermelons and Mimosas

"You are joining the field trip this weekend, right?" Delia was trying to pin me down for our Spanish class field trip to Tagaytay City.

"I'm not sure if my sister will let me. She is *masungit*, irritable."

"But you have to," Delia insisted. "I asked Morales to be in our group, and he promised he would."

As a true friend, Delia was looking after my interests. It would be rude of me to let her down. Besides, it was almost the end of the semester, so I decided it was now or never. Luckily, my sister Conchita worked overtime that weekend. She didn't notice I was out the whole day.

Sprawling hills surrounded the city. Those willing to trudge to the top were rewarded with a spectacular view. Delia, our group leader, dutifully shepherded us along the well-worn, winding path up the hill. I marched right behind her; Morales was behind me. He said he wanted to catch us if either one slipped, but I suspected he was more interested in a different kind of view: my legs or Delia's backside.

We hadn't gone far up when I heard Morales laugh so loudly it startled me. I turned my head to see why and saw his eyes looking down fixedly at my legs, staring at the scars, those ugly doodles, which he had noticed even though I was wearing pantyhose under my knee-length skirt. Then he dropped a bomb-like comment that made my head sizzle like a marinated *bangus* cooking in a frying pan.

"Nieves, it looks like a furious hen scratched and left tens of scars on the skin of your legs," Morales said, jokingly. I knew he was teasing me, but I didn't think it was funny.

"I bet you I am the only girl you know in the whole world with tattooed legs." I pitched the joke back at him so I could disguise my real feelings, which were a fusion of embarrassment, anger, and hurt.

How I wished, I could blend them into an "odium shake," a tonic I was confident would turn a tactless man like Morales into a genteel person because the taste would be so bad he would beg for forgiveness from the person who gave it to him. And I would mix a big dose of my odium shake with his favorite soda pop when he wasn't watching. I wanted him so much to know how his remarks made me feel very insecure and unwanted.

"Sorry, Morales, but I am very proud of my scars," I told him.

Yet, I stopped short of telling him that those wide and shallow dimples on my legs were a reminder of joys in my childhood the like of which I was sure he never experienced. Morales didn't deserve to be told about that exciting afternoon when I was a kid, when a group of us were caught red-handed in our neighbor's tree stealing guavas. He would have laughed heartily had he known how we jumped to the ground with our mouths and pockets stuffed with precious guavas. We ran fast for our safety, all the while being chased by a big dog. Perhaps he would have appreciated my guts because I was so focused on not dropping any guavas I jumped over the barbed wire fence (the last hurdle to avoid a dog bite and possible lashing from our parents) without caution. And in my haste, a sharp nail pierced my right leg. The leg bled, but my eyes were dry.

I didn't want to hear Morales' cynical laugh again, which surely I would have had I told him that story. However, his laughter brought back memories about my elementary school days instantly. I could hear my schoolmates as they laughed and called me "ginger toes." Morales' words and the tone of his laughter chased away all hope I had had up to that time. It was clear from his comments that Morales was no different from many other Filipino men who wanted an ornament for a girlfriend. He could not see that beyond the *probinsiyana* ways, dark skin, and polka-dotted legs, there was a gem waiting to be polished. After that field trip, I avoided him as if he had a transmittable disease.

"Someday my prince will come. He will love me unconditionally – scars and all. And he will come to me when the time is right." I told this to myself when I was reminded of Morales' derisive laugh.

Men began to notice me after Morales moved on. I knew it was because I started to smarten up in an effort to impress them. My job at the school also gave me respectability. I ran for office and was elected Secretary of the Student Council. I became sociable and smiled more often. Men found it easier to approach and talk to me now.

OUR COLONIAL TRAITS TAUGHT us rigid moral values and to expect the same from others, which often made us extremely judgmental.

Bittermelons and Mimosas

I should have seen the danger signs coming during my junior year when I started dating Dick, a guy from a Tagalog province. Friends at school warned me that Tagalogs were known to be the most conservative and possessive of all men.

"He is a very good guy and very much in love with you," Andy, my smooth-talking friend, kept telling me this as he tried to convince me to become Dick's girlfriend.

In the overly chauvinistic Filipino society, men were known to be generous to their girlfriends and the girl's family as well. I saw how nicely their boyfriends were treating my female friends. After the rejection from Morales, I thought it would be nice to be fussed over. To a point, that is.

"What are those?" I asked Dick one time when he showed up at the apartment with a sack of rice and other goodies.

"Nothing much. Just something I thought your family would enjoy." I saw the satisfaction in his smile as he watched my housemates dig inside the sack full of goodies.

That was the first of the many gifts with which Dick showered my extended family and me. However, each time after I received a gift, the excitement wore off. I felt awful, then nauseated, and then very angry with myself. I knew I did not love him, that I could never love him. In spite of his generosity, he certainly was not my prince – he would never be.

"Dick, I can't be your girlfriend anymore. I want to concentrate on my studies." I tried to break up with Dick about a year into the relationship. I expected some understanding from him. After all, he seemed to be a nice guy who I didn't think would cause me any trouble.

I got the shock of my life when he responded. "What? After all I have done for you and your family?" Dick quickly turned into my prince of darkness. If looks could kill, I would have been dead in that instant.

"I didn't ask for those," I protested.

"I didn't hear you say 'stop' either." Dick was right. His argument kept me at bay. "Nobody is going to have you. Nobody! Do you understand?" He screamed at me as if I was his kept woman.

✍ Nieves Catahan Villamin ✍

I realized then that he was madder than hell. He was deeply in love with me and very serious about our relationship. After that confrontation, I realized that Dick began carrying a gun, guarding me like his precious property, never letting me out of his sight.

As days passed, any affection I might once have felt for him turned to fear. I felt trapped at a dead end street with no way to turn. A couple of bachelors still courted me, even though they knew about Dick. After Dick threatened them with his gun, however, they quickly disappeared.

I HAVE ALWAYS BELIEVED there is a reason for everything. In late 1966, Kuya Lino, an aspiring writer, entered a writing competition sponsored by a radio station of ABS-CBN, a broadcast television network in Manila. His winning composition was about our family and focused on Ateng Macaria's tragedy, my parents' common-law marriage, and my father's other lovers, which I only knew was only one. To gain more listeners and win the rating games, the radio program accentuated my father's infidelities – not his bravery and courage and love for his country.

Dick's mother heard the radio program. She was shocked and she asked him, "What? Your girlfriend was born out of wedlock. What will people we know think of us?"

What made me see Dick's "horns" was the fact that he had the nerve to tell me that his family saw me as unacceptable. They also thought I would follow my father's ways someday, claiming, "An apple doesn't fall far from the tree." It was an expression I heard for the second time when Dick repeated to me what his family had told him, sneering as if I were dirty.

The disgust written all over his face made me recoil. Perception overtook what only my eyes had seen. He was a devil with a grin that made my blood boil.

"You S.O.B., who do you think you are?" I shouted at Dick, but he only laughed at me.

"Hey, I should be the one to ask you that question," he said, taunting me.

"Do you think people will respect you if they find out you are an

Bittermelons and Mimosas

illegitimate child? Let's see if they don't spit on your face. You should be thankful you have me."

His insults infuriated me. I gritted my teeth and kept quiet so I wouldn't hear more humiliating words from him. I told myself later. Don't worry. One of these days, Dick will get what he deserves.

I couldn't tell my family about the hurtful exchange of words I had had with Dick. I was embarrassed and I also didn't want to bring them the pain they felt when Kuya Lino's fiancée broke up with him. Dick continued to court their favor by constantly bringing them gifts. My family admired his respect and consideration, not knowing the trouble that lay beneath.

My association with TIP would eventually become even more remarkable because President Quirino gave me an unexpected promotion after graduation. In October 1967, I received my bachelor's degree in accounting from the Technological Institute of the Philippines. I got the surprise of my life when the school president called me into his office one afternoon before the holidays.

"Your boss, Mr. Adto, is leaving at the end of the month. How would you like to be our Chief Accountant?" he asked.

I couldn't believe what I had just heard. I looked at him as if I wanted to cry.

"I guess you're okay with it," he laughingly said before I could say yes.

I was too overwhelmed to say anything, but he knew I wanted the job. Never in my wildest imagination had it occurred to me that being the accountant of a rising school was in my future, just fresh from graduation and without yet passing the board exam. I did not expect either that two years of clerical experience could make me a candidate for such a responsible job. Given the fact that I would be supervising a department of five made my luck unbelievable, almost surreal. As an added bonus, I was given a light teaching load that gave me further respect. I was very lucky because I was at the right place at the right time and he chose me.

In retrospect, I feel the turn of events might have been different had I chosen another school, not TIP. And all of these happened because there was a TIP, a school run by someone who believed in dreams and disadvantaged students like me.

"Congratulations, Miss Chief Accountant." Frankie, my friend who worked at the registrar's office, was the first one to congratulate me after the announcement was made to the staff. "You know, I was also offered a promotion, but I turned it down," he said.

"Why?"

"I am going to get married soon. I can't support a family if our salaries continue to be delayed every month." I could feel the sadness in Frankie's voice.

"I know. Once I gain the experience, I will leave this place, too," I said.

There were others. Frankie, Gil, Ped, Magno, Ponso, Tessie, Flor, and I were all working students. President Quirino, being true to his words that he'd make us a part of his family, offered us job promotions after graduation. But most left because not only were our salaries late every month, we were also asked to make stock subscriptions through salary deductions. Many of us rejected this option. We were paid whatever small amount was left when funds became available. We were too young then to see the bigger picture that lay ahead. Although it was either feast or famine because our wages were always late, I at least had something to look forward to. The delayed wages worked to my advantage as they turned into a nest egg. Before the New Year arrived, I was able to put a down payment on the first ever television in our neighborhood.

"What's inside the big box?" our neighbors kept asking my father while he and my cousins were unloading the cargo from a rented vehicle.

Bittermelons and Mimosas

"Wow, a television!" everyone shouted after the box was unwrapped. "Turn it on; turn it on," they chanted in chorus.

"We have to install the antenna first. Come back after supper," my father told the crowd.

That night I felt so proud. The dream I had had since I first saw a television set displayed inside a department store along Cabanatuan's Burgos Avenue in 1960 when I was in junior high had come to fruition. I remember the square table my father built for a television stand. The table served as a ledge to our ground floor window where the TV sat and was viewed by hordes of neighbors, young and old, for many nights. I knew my father felt very proud about the fact that the Catahan family was the first in Sumacab to own a television set.

I WAS WORKING IN professional heaven while struggling in a personal hell. For the first time in my life, the holidays brought me despair instead of joy. As the days rolled over into Valentine's Day, Dick became suspicious and impatient, especially after I turned down his invitation for a Valentine's lunch.

"I'll come over and get you."

"You can do what you want but I'm not having lunch with you," I told him.

He slammed down the phone in my ear. Instead of anger, I felt relief. While most of my friends went out for lunch dates, I sat at my desk, wondering how I could make him understand that I truly didn't love him.

"Nieves, phone call for you. It's your brother." Maruja, our secretary (an Audrey Hepburn look-alike, front and back, without starving herself, and with a heart so chaste any man would have been proud to have her for his wife), interrupted my thoughts.

I rose to get the phone call. I hesitated for a moment, thinking it might be Dick calling again, passing himself off as my brother as he had done in past phone calls. But it could be an emergency call about our family in Sumacab. For all I knew, maybe my mother had been rushed to the hospital again. I hurried to the phone with that in mind.

"Hello? Who is this?" I let contempt triumph over my voice.

"This is Danny." The voice on the other end didn't belong to Dick or either of my two brothers. I felt relieved.

However, before I was able to say another word, the caller continued as if he was in a hurry to catch a plane, and in a commanding way.

"I need a copy of my brother's transcript immediately. He is enrolled in the College of Engineering. Can you help me expedite the release?" Not even a word of "Please."

Already in a bad mood, I became more incensed. "You called Accounting, not the Registrar's Office. This office deals with money, not with school records," I replied curtly to get back at him.

"You are such a snob!" the voice on the other end said laughingly which I interpreted as a sign of rudeness.

I hung up the receiver quickly without replying to his last remark. "*Napakabastos!* What a bastard." I was fuming on my way back to my desk. Nobody had ever called me a snob. Maybe shy, but a snob?

In the weeks that followed, my staff told me about a young, slender man looking in and smiling at me through the glass window on his way to classes. Sometimes he stopped and peeked his head inside the office, not saying a word. I thought nothing of it; Dick was always on my mind. However, it didn't take long before the word spread around.

"Nieves, one of my students has been asking about you. He said he wanted to date you," Ponso said when he stopped by my office to tease me one night. (Teacher and student relationships are common in the Philippines. But in reality, Danny was enrolled at another university as a third-year electrical engineering student and had been employed by the Philippine Long Distance Company (PLDT) as a telephone technician for over three years already. He dropped out of

Bittermelons and Mimosas

the university and enrolled at TIP after seeing me in my office one evening when he visited a TIP student friend.)

"Huh, is that for real?"

"Yes, but I told him he's got no chance because he is just a student. I was also sure your boyfriend would not be pleased to know about him."

Ponso was right. Still I was intrigued.

One night, unable to contain his feelings any longer, Danny finally showed up in our office, first approaching one of my staff, Edna, at her desk.

"What's her name?" he asked Edna, pretending not to know my name.

"Why do you want to know?" Edna decided to play along.

"Because I plan to marry her someday." Danny did not hesitate in his response.

"Fine. Then why don't you go ask her yourself?" Edna was not impressed.

That is exactly what he did, walking straight in my direction as a surprised Edna chased along behind him.

Reaching my desk, he extended his right hand. I was surprised to look down and see a small box of Black Magic chocolate in his other hand.

"Thought you might like this." Before I could say thank you, he took my hand.

As I held his hand, the oddest sensation came over me. My mouth felt dry and I became lightheaded. The office suddenly seemed hot and dazzling with light. Our eyes met and, as corny as it may sound, I knew right away that my prince had finally arrived.

He was just less than six-feet-tall and fair-skinned. He was thin, but his gait and manner both suggested a strong sense of confidence. His crooked smile emphasized his boyish looks. I thought he was very handsome. Then I heard his confession.

"When I first called you, I told you I needed the transcript for my brother. That was a lie. I kept seeing you everyday in the office and you looked so sad. I just wanted to meet you. I thought maybe I could put a smile on your face. Please don't be upset."

I also found out that night that he was the student Ponso had mentioned. Once he walked into my office that evening, Danny confessed later that he knew he had entered a danger zone. He was aware I had a boyfriend because he had often seen him waiting for me outside the building. But that did not stop him from getting to know me. He captivated me, too!

The few times I sneaked out of the office to meet him at a nearby café were exhilarating. I had never felt this way with Dick. Although his dramatic arrival complicated my life even more, I knew Danny was the one. Thinking about Dick's temper, however, kept me awake at night. What if Danny and Dick crossed paths? One of them might be seriously hurt. I decided I had to face the danger myself if I wanted to live a life of love, or one without it, like Aunt Elena for the rest of my life. The day after Danny proposed to me, I packed a pair of shears in my purse before heading to school and then kept them with me always.

Meanwhile, Dick had smelled something fishy because I kept ignoring his daily phone calls at work.

"She left for home already," my officemates would tell Dick every time he came by during the evening and asked for me.

I staggered my office hours to confuse him. When he stopped at our apartment after his classes, I was already asleep. Dick had not seen me being escorted home by another man. Because Danny worked the night shift, he did not know that I was usually seeing Danny during my mid-morning breaks.

It worked for a short while, until Dick got smarter. He came one late morning to surprise me. But instead he got the surprise of his life. I was at the school canteen with my best friend Bel and Danny having a snack. He approached us casually, and then asked me to leave because he wanted to talk.

I said, "No."

He left red faced and very incensed. Dick didn't vanish as I hoped he would. He waited outside the school building the rest of the day, then followed me on my way home around six P.M. I walked to the jeepney stop unescorted. Danny was already at work. Not knowing he was behind me, I boarded a nearly empty jeepney. As I sat down, out of nowhere, Dick jumped inside and sat down next to me and fenced

Bittermelons and Mimosas

me in with his arm extended to the back of the passenger seat in front of us. Once again, he was very determined to talk to me. I told myself, enough, I would have no more of this. It's either now or never.

"Dick," I said, trying my best to remain calm, "I don't want you following me anymore. I'm getting married soon. Look, my boyfriend gave me an engagement ring." I showed him the ring Danny had lovingly slid on my left finger a few days before.

It was then when I became aware that that he might have seen the ring during our morning encounter at the school canteen. I saw the flash of anger in Dick's eyes as my words sank in. Before I knew it, he grabbed my left hand and pulled off my ring. His unexpected action caught me by surprise. He tried to force me out of the jeepney as it began pulling away from the curb.

At that moment, I knew I had to do the inevitable. I pushed him away from me and pulled the shears from inside my purse. I pointed them directly at Dick.

"Don't you ever touch me again!" I yelled louder than the time when "Judas" forced himself into our bathroom when my sister was visiting our parents. Death or a prison sentence? So be it! But no way would I become Dick's wife.

Dick looked at me, then at the shears, then back at me. The other passengers on board began screaming at the sight of the shears. It did not take long for Dick to make up his mind. He jumped off the jeepney nearly as fast as he had jumped on. I never saw him again.

Danny's face turned scarlet red when I told him what had happened, but his anger slowly subsided. "Never mind the ring," he said. "You're safe. That's more important."

Five months after the Valentine month, on July 9, 1968, Danny and I secretly exchanged marriage vows before a minister at the Manila City Hall.

Nieves Catahan Villamin

1968 WAS "THE YEAR of ecstasy" for Danny and me. But in the U.S., our future home, it was "the year of unrest and discontent." The war in Vietnam (1954–1975), a neighboring country of the Philippines, that escalated during President Lyndon Johnson's administration had just suffered a major setback. In January 20, 1968, around 30,000–40,000 North Vietnamese Army forces seized Khe Sanh, a remote hilltop outpost in the NW corner of South Vietnam where 6,000 U.S. Marines and South Vietnamese regulars were based. On the night of 31 January, during the Tet (Lunar New Year) holidays, 84,000 Viet Cong enemy troops attacked seventy-four towns and cities and temporarily seized the U.S. embassy in Saigon. This prompted widespread outrage around the world and reduced further the United States' support at home for the war in Vietnam. In April 1968, Martin Luther King, Jr. was assassinated. The assassination was followed by urban riots nationwide in up to 76 cities. In June 1968, Berkeley mayor Wallace Johnson declared a state of emergency and a three-day curfew to curb the violence as a result of student demonstrations. In November 1968 the San Francisco State University students began a 167-day strike.

The war in Vietnam, being so close to home, caused most Filipinos many sleepless nights. The unrest quickly spilled over into the Philippine academic and political environments. In July 1968, the University of the Philippines Student Council (USC), Philippine Collegian, Pagkakaisa, Katipunang Makabansa, and the Partisans led 14 busloads of students to the Congress building, where they opposed the Second Philippine Civil Action Group bill regarding the involvement of the Philippines in the Vietnam War. On August 16, 1968, at the U.S. Embassy and Malacañang, Metrocom dispersed a UP student–led rally to protest the "Special Relations" between the Philippines and the USA; five of the UP students suffered bruises in the action. Senator Lorenzo Tanada, the head of the Movement for the Advancement of Nationalism (MAN), protested the Americanization of UP in September 1968. In addition, USC started to lead demonstrations against U.S. imperialism, the Vietnam War, Philippine participation in the war, implementation of the retail trade nationalization laws, and oil monopolies.

In November of the same year, Danny showed me a telegram instructing him to report to the recruiting office in Makati immediately for a physical examination. His three years of employment with PLDT as a telephone technician had landed him the telecommunication specialist job for an American Satellite Company that he had applied for a few weeks earlier without my knowledge. If all went well, he would be on his way to Vietnam in a few days to work there for a year. But the Vietnam job was ill timed. We had been preparing for our church wedding that would take place within a couple of months. I knew a similar opportunity would come because he was good at what de did. Without much convincing, he let go of the job offer.

Nieves Catahan Villamin

Officers of the TIP 1965 Supreme Student council. I was elected secretary.

President Quirino congratulates me as secretary of the Student Council.

Bittermelons and Mimosas

TIP R.O.T.C. blood drive, 1965. Me, standing back third from left.

Induction of Kappa Beta Sorority officers. I am fifth from the left. Miss Aurelia Pilar, adviser, in black dress standing at far right end.

Nieves Catahan Villamin

Obligations and Contracts Class: Sitting from left to right: Elvie Fabrigas, Atty Llanes, and me.

Finally...College graduation, October, 1967.

200

꧁ Bittermelons and Mimosas ꧂

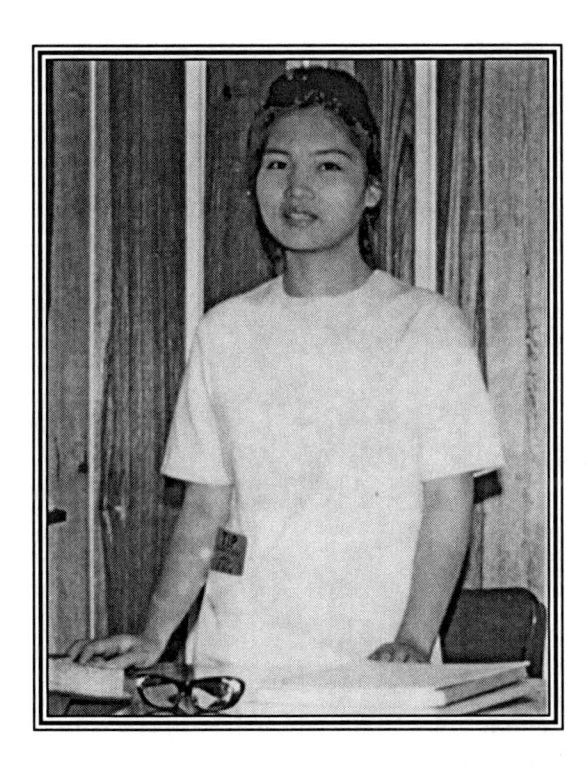

My first day at work as TIP's accountant.

My Accounting staff after performing a native dance during TIP's Christmas party. Third from left to right: Me, Aida, Cora, and Precy.

Chapter Thirteen

The Sukob Fears

Without its posts,
a house will not rise;
Devoid of light,
it will be ghostly dark.

a popular Filipino adage

I thought that was such a cliché until that July 9, 1968, afternoon when I found myself listening to the same words being delivered by Reverend Salvador Payawal, the Minister of the Gospel who officiated at our civil wedding. He used the maxim to describe our roles as husband and wife, which Danny and I had just become.

"Danny, being the husband, you will provide the family with love and comfort until you breathe your last. You are the anchor that will keep your family grounded when happiness abounds, and gather them together as one to fight the pangs of grief. And Nieves, you are the beam of reason that will

January 5, 1969. Danny and I first pose as husband and wife.

Bittermelons and Mimosas

illuminate your family in choosing only righteousness to live inside your home. You will provide your family warmth during the cold days and refuge during the hot summers."

I don't remember crying after the minister finished his sermon like most women did in the movies. I do remember feeling uneasy and scared.

Danny quickly brushed aside my fears by saying, "Don't worry, I'll take care of you." (I should have held him liable for that promise he made.)

A church wedding on January 5, 1969, sealed our civil wedding. The two of us took care of everything, which was uncommon at that time. Our combined savings were enough to pay for our wedding outfits, food, photographs, and other necessary expenses.

We didn't mind that the flower girls and the bridesmaid did not have matching dresses. It was okay for us that there was no open carriage to deliver me to the church. A friend of a friend of a friend loaned us yet another friend's car to take the bridal party to the chapel. No firecrackers in the churchyard announced my arrival. There was not even a band playing.

All I had was an army of friends and relatives whose love took me through a day of excitement that was accompanied with tears of sadness, not joy, because my father had been dilly-dallying about whether or not to attend our wedding ceremony. Had Mrs. Leonila Garcia, one of our female sponsors and the mayor's wife, not interceded God only knows what would have happened.

One part of the ceremony remained very special despite our minimal budget. Waiting for me in front of everyone was my handsome groom. When I saw Danny's smile, I knew we would be together for the rest of our lives. It didn't bother me that my family gave our marriage the cold shoulder because I felt very safe and complete with my husband. My family didn't think much of Danny because he didn't have the credentials I knew they were looking for in a husband, especially for me. Danny was a college dropout who at that time didn't believe a degree was necessary to find a good job, which in his case proved to be true. They were worried about whether he could support a family. He was not like any of my brothers-in-law. How could he get along with the rest?

My family kept telling me, "We don't know where his family came from."

Deep inside, I knew we would be all right. Danny, like my father, was educated by life itself. And I was very much in love with him.

To appease my family, I relinquished ownership of all my material possessions to them before I moved with Danny into our new home. Maintaining my place within the family circle was more important to me than those material things. Within the same year, my sister Ammie started college. I withdrew all my investments at TIP and paid for her four-year college tuition in advance.

At first, Ammie lived with Kuya Lino and his family. However, it didn't work out. Soon, Ammie moved out and joined Danny and me in our small one-bedroom apartment.

OUR FIRST HOME AS husband and wife was one of two bedrooms in an apartment on Aurora Boulevard, Manila, that Danny and I rented for 80 pesos a month. Owned by a Chinese concubine with one child, our building was within walking distance of the tiny apartment I had lived in with my sister Conchita, niece Flora, and cousin Pining during my single years.

The church had only sanctified our marriage in January – Danny and I were still newlyweds. 1969 was supposed to be our year. Yet, my sister Ammie brought home disturbing news when she returned from a visit to our parents. It all began one day in March with a soft knock on the door.

"Mila eloped with Rene," she announced. "Inang and Tatang want you to come home next weekend for the *pamanhikan*."

I could not believe what I was hearing. My sister had decided to

Bittermelons and Mimosas

run off and marry her boyfriend? What were they thinking? Agitated, I bounced out of my chair.

"Why didn't they wait until next year? Don't they know the consequences?" My questions flew around the small room.

Although I wasn't really superstitious, I couldn't help but be a little frightened. A day before our civil wedding in July 1968, Danny's only sister, Dolly, had eloped. Now here were Mila and Rene eloping. This was double *sukob*. *Sukob* is like a curse. According to our beliefs, a double wedding will bring bad luck to the family or one of the couple. Belief or non-belief, I felt I had to pray twice as hard.

By the time Mila and Rene married in May 1969 (two months after they eloped), Danny had left for Vietnam to work for an American satellite communications company. My new husband reapplied for the same job (for an American satellite communications company) he turned down the previous November, and succeeded again. The pay this time was almost twice as better than before. Leaving me, even though I was three months pregnant, seemed reasonable. He left for Vietnam in March 1969.

All I could do was pray each night, "Please, God, don't let any harm come to any of us. Please."

Rene and Mila seemed to be prospering. Rene had taken on a new position as a DDT (a synthetic pesticide) sprayer for the Malaria Control Program, traveling to remote corners of the countryside on a regular basis. (DDT was eventually banned in the United States on December 31, 1972. Perhaps some companies in the United States found outlets in third world countries like the Philippines to strengthen their sales.) Rene and Mila only saw each other on weekends, but Mila understood her husband's work and appreciated the steady paycheck.

"At least, you see him even if it is only during weekends," I sighed to her one Saturday when they visited to check on my pregnancy.

As days turned into weeks, the vacuum left by my husband became larger than our dreams. In one of my letters to him, I begged him to come back even if he had not completed his contract. I felt so downhearted. We were still in the honeymoon stage, yet I would come home every day after work to an empty room, with nobody to share the joys and pains of pregnancy.

It was hardest during the night, as I lay alone on my bed. I missed him so much, his tender hands caressing my face, the warmth of his body as he lay beside me, his boyish smiles and childish jokes that always put a smile on my face. I wanted so much to hear him talk and sing to the baby inside my tummy. To tell him/her how much he/she was loved. My greatest comfort was from reading his letters that arrived almost every other day.

I know my prayers worked. Edna was born, and Danny returned safely. We decided to live in Sumacab. Danny and Tatang built a new house for us, just across the street from where Rene and Mila lived. My husband's safe return, a healthy baby, a new teaching post (thanks to my father's connection), and being close to my relatives made me very happy. *Sukob* or not, it seemed not to matter anymore.

FILIPINOS WORKING OVERSEAS WERE still a part of the future in the 1960s and 1970s; the husband or wife working abroad and causing the separation of families seldom happened. Families either immigrated together or wallowed in poverty collectively. Poor salary is a common problem facing Filipinos. This has also prompted many government officials and politicians to be corrupt; they need the money.

Here I was, a college professor, and my husband was also employed at a telecommunications company in the city. Yet, our combined salaries still weren't enough to meet our daily needs. Not withstanding our happy marriage, the hard reality of life in the Philippines sank in quickly.

Our luck seemed to change with the coming of 1972. In March of that year, after tons of documents and several visits to the U.S. Immigration office, I was finally granted a professional visa for which I had applied in 1968. The same month, I became pregnant with my second child. In June, I received an unanticipated promotion to head the Management department at the university when classes began in July. These blessings coming in succession had altered our plan to immigrate to the United States indefinitely.

Even the talks of an impending declaration of martial law to curb the insurgencies all around the country did not deter our plan to push back our immigration to the United States a couple of years. We were not political activists. There was no immediate reason for us to leave ASAP like some of our friends, or so we thought. However, since we had obtained our visa, my father had been advising us not to delay our immigration any further. He had lived through martial law during his HUK days. He had seen how the military became drunk with power and quick on the draw because they were the law. Because human rights were nil, a jealous neighbor could easily turn our luck into a misfortune. Surely we would miss the "chance of a lifetime," immigrating to the land of opportunity, something we had waited for almost five years.

My father's worries were warranted. On March 29, 1969, Jose Maria Sison's Communist Party of the Philippines (CPP) (a Stalinist-Maoist Political Party) along with the HMB (HUK) faction led by Bernabe Buscayno, organized the New People's Army (NPA). This was the guerilla-military wing of the Party, whose insurgencies around the Philippines, particularly in the northern part of the country, persist to this day. The NPA seeks to wage a peasant-worker revolutionary war in the countryside against landlords and foreign companies. Since my father used to be a HUK, he was afraid that he would be recalled to serve in the movement again.

I remember some headline news before martial law was declared on September 21, 1972. On July 14, 1972, the image of the Santo Niño de Tondo, patron saint of Tondo, Manila, was stolen. A series of typhoons following the one that arrived before the image was stolen came in succession with rains that lasted a biblical 40 days and 40 nights and put Manila and the surrounding area under water. Many Filipinos attributed this flood, which was reminiscent of Noah's, to the theft. The persistent rain ceased when the Santo Niño was returned to Tondo in a procession led by Imelda Marcos on August 2, 1972.

Nieves Catahan Villamin

LIKE THE REST OF the country, Cabanatuan was experiencing a mixed bag of instability and zest. A group of striking bus drivers had been picketing for days, throwing stones at every bus in order to stop the other drivers who crossed the lines. Commuters, many of them students, were on tenterhooks because the opening of school was just a few days away. Although I feared for his safety, I had to send Danny on an early morning trip to Manila to buy my reference books, which weren't available at the local bookstores.

Going by a stream of angry strikers throwing stones at passing buses, my husband was hit on the head. Blood oozed nonstop from Danny's forehead, which had been cut open to the bone. The driver drove my husband to the nearest hospital, which happened to be in the middle of nowhere. The bus then continued on its journey, leaving Danny to fend for himself.

Life in the provinces was wonderful, especially during emergencies. Without the benefit of a telephone or "texting," news traveled fast even from the farthest distance. News of my husband's accident reached me at high speed before midday. How people knew, I still haven't figured out. I dropped everything I was doing and rushed to his side, not thinking about taking any money (which we didn't have anyway as payday was still a few days away).

When I got there, an empty hospital bed greeted me. Danny was nowhere to be found. He had escaped because the hospital was demanding payment from him the minute he woke up.

"I was the victim. Why should I pay? If anything, I should receive *danyos perhuwisyos* or payment for damages. Go after the bus operator," Danny had argued stubbornly with the hospital staff.

My husband's reaction didn't surprise me a bit when I heard the story. I knew him too well. Forget about the consequences. He was a man of principle. He always spoke his mind.

Dazed and still weak from his blood loss and traveling, Danny went to my father upon learning from our neighbors that I had followed him to the hospital.

"Tatang, go after Nieves. They might hold her hostage. I escaped from the hospital because they were trying to make me pay." Danny knew that was exactly what would happen.

The hospital guards who were told about a woman asking for Danny spotted peso signs when they saw me approaching the receptionist area. Before I could say anything else, one grabbed my left arm, forcing me to sit in a corner chair.

"How can I get money to pay you if you make me a hostage?" I shouted at the guard standing close to me.

"Don't worry. They will come for you," he screamed back.

Patients and visitors who heard the loud exchange of words came out to the hospital lobby and watched the spectacle. Upon seeing a white-suited hospital aide guarding me, they must have thought I was either a thief or a crazed patient waiting to be transported to another facility. I didn't try to escape because I knew it would only make matters worse. I sat on the chair and waited for help.

As in the case of my sister Macaria's death, my father again had asked the mayor's office for help because of the complexity of the situation. The mayor sent his representative to settle the matter with the hospital.

The nonexistence of any government health-assisted programs often left us with no choice except to be at the mercy of politicians – politicians who would exploit such an opportunity in exchange for election votes. We learned at an early age that voting was our sacred right, but necessity taught us to sell out such privilege when things worsened. It was a vicious practice.

IT WOULD BE TEN years before we would talk about the "Curse of the *Sukob*" again.

Nieves Catahan Villamin

January 1969 wedding. Tatang walking me to the altar where Danny was waiting.

My sister Ammie as Maid of Honor.

Our wedding female sponsors: TIP President Dr. Teresita U. Quirino and Leonila Garcia.

Chapter Fourteen

Because We Have Each Other

Because we have each other
We are safe, we are secure.
Because we have each other
We can weather any storm.

Anonymous

Hardly had Danny's wound healed completely when President Ferdinand Marcos declared martial law. The Immigration Department advised visa holders to leave immediately or risk having their papers revoked. Filipinos leaving the country were being screened with a fine-toothed comb. We understood that this was a now-or-never situation. Danny and I both knew what had to be done.

But after we worked the numbers, we quickly realized that we simply didn't have enough money to leave and move to the United States. It was opportune when we found out that TWA had this fly now/pay later plan that also paid $75 as a cash advance. The offer was too good to pass up, and we took it as a sign that we should follow our hearts and leave the Philippines. It would be a huge gamble, but Danny seemed confident that he could find a good job within the first week. Edna would have to be left behind for a few months until we had ourselves established in California. Otherwise, having Edna with us early on might be difficult, especially for her. What we really needed was some kind of host family who would take us in, even temporarily, until Danny found a job.

Just days before our scheduled departure, my sister-in-law's husband volunteered his newly married sister in Oakland to be our host. We carried a brief letter of introduction with us in the hope that she would let us stay in their apartment for at least that first week. Neither one of our families could help us financially. We were literally on our own.

On the day before our flight, Danny, Edna, and I left Sumacab for Manila, armed with two crammed suitcases and our dreams. Danny's parents lived in Quezon City, then a suburb of Manila. We would spend the night with them.

At breakfast the next morning, our spirits were high and we were full of hope. Edna seemed restless, as if she could sense what loomed ahead. But Danny and I felt good about our decision. We were going to the United States, and our lives would be better.

Two hours before the flight's departure, Danny called for a taxi and hauled the suitcases outside one at a time. During his second trip down, Dante, my brother-in-law, stopped Danny and asked him for money he had loaned him weeks earlier. Danny had borrowed money to pay for clearances and other fees required for our trip. Dante owned a small grocery store. He needed his money back. The timing, though, was out of sync.

"I don't have the money to pay you back now," Danny told his brother. "But as soon as I get a job in the U.S., I will send you what I owe you."

That was not good enough for Dante. He was adamant about being paid back. Now. I thought he was not being unreasonable. The money Danny borrowed was Dante's revolving capital for his small grocery store. We all knew that without it, he might go bankrupt, perhaps in a week's time. But Dante should have realized it would be like squeezing blood out of a turnip. There was no money to pay him now. He would just have to wait.

The anxiety brought about by the implementation of martial law had started to tear families apart. And it obviously had affected the behavior of both men. Their angry fists were determined to outwit each other's plan. Danny was in a rush to catch a plane that would

Bittermelons and Mimosas

take him and his family to a place where peace and order is the way of life. Dante, a student leader, would soon join his comrades' underground activities and fight for their cause to end Martial Law. Both were in dire need of financial support.

"You can't leave unless you pay me," Dante demanded. "I could go broke."

My mother-in-law overheard the conversation. She felt she had to offer her opinion. "Yes, Danny, you owe your brother some money. You have to pay him back," she said, stoking the fire even more.

The drama got worse. Danny tried to move toward the waiting taxi and Dante physically blocked his path. Incensed, my husband dropped the suitcase and shoved Dante out of the way. Dante retaliated, pushing Danny, and a fight quickly ensued. It was a sight! We were trying to catch a plane to the United States, my husband and brother-in-law were rolling around on the ground fighting like two angry school kids, and my mother-in-law was standing over them, trying to stop them. My mother-in-law finally broke them apart.

Danny struggled to his feet and pointed a finger directly at his brother. "I will pay the money I owe you as soon as I get a job. After that, don't expect any help from me because I will not give you any."

There was no time to argue further. The taxi was waiting. The plane was waiting. We still had not broken the news to Edna. I could not believe what had happened. I was too shocked to say anything, even goodbye. Danny told the cab driver to step on the gas. He drove at full speed, as if he was fleeing from a crime scene. I didn't look back. It was better for me not to look back and wave.

THE THREE OF US sat in the back seat of the taxi, no one saying a word. I felt queasy, which wasn't surprising since I was seven-and-a-half-months pregnant. There was also some anxiety about the 16-hour plane flight that lay ahead, my first such trip. Mostly though, I felt uneasy because at that moment everything seemed overwhelming. I

Nieves Catahan Villamin

still could not believe what we were doing or where we were going, no matter how many times Danny tried to reassure me. I looked at my husband as he stared quietly out the window at the busy Manila streets. Danny wore his simple black suit, the one he had bought for our wedding. I wondered what he was thinking – was he also feeling nervous about today? His reassuring words from the last few weeks drifted through my mind again.

"We're going to America," I could hear Danny say in his typically confident, determined voice. "We are going to make it. Things will be better for us over there. You'll see."

Perhaps.

My greater concern at the moment sat on Danny's lap. Edna, our three-year-old daughter, was excited to be riding in a car, even in the heavy morning traffic. She was wearing her favorite dress, white cotton with small red and yellow flowers, and shiny black shoes and white socks. I always thought she looked so sweet in that dress. She had picked it out herself as a birthday gift the previous September.

There was no way for Edna to understand what was about to happen or why. We hadn't told her our plans. That would come at the airport when there wouldn't be much time to argue. What could I have said to Edna beforehand?

The thought of abandoning our homeland to pursue new lives in America, an unknown territory, sent chills up and down my spine, keeping me awake at night, making me second-guess our plan constantly. We had no savings, just a little available money. Danny carried only $75 in his wallet, money we had borrowed for the trip. We had not left yet, but we were already saddled with debts from TWA. Our host family in America had offered to have us stay until we landed on our feet. But they had just married the week before and treasured their privacy like all newlyweds. We lacked a specific plan of action, making our trip a true leap of faith.

Worrying about all these issues had reduced me to tears more than once. Our Edna could not have possibly understood the difficult decision Danny and I had to make and how she would be affected by it

Bittermelons and Mimosas

in the course of that day. Being stopped at the checkpoint by stern-looking armed soldiers in green uniforms brought me back to reality.

Our burning desire to escape from the poverty ravaging our country intensified when a global oil embargo crisis had hit the Philippines in the early 1970s. The nation's economy was affected tremendously. Prices of prime commodities zoomed. There was massive unemployment. The Philippine peso depreciated. Governmental graft and corruption were rampant, with the worst offenders being President Ferdinand Marcos and his wife Imelda, who used national funds for personal luxuries. The gap between the rich and the poor widened. Crime spread across the country. Law and order was an empty phrase.

Matters only grew worse when the Filipino Muslims in the South tried to secede and the military wing of the Communist Party gained strength. President Marcos had declared martial law in September 1972. Filipino troops were called in to assist local police in keeping the peace. Residents holding visas either had to leave the country forthwith or risk having their papers revoked. The political climate became too unstable to predict. Marcos had already jailed several of his more vocal critics. As the war in Vietnam was coming to an end, we feared that the Philippines would be next. We wanted to be safe. We wanted our freedom. It was now or never. We had to get on that plane. The soldiers waved us through. Now, nothing stood in the way except our own hesitation. The date was Friday, October 13, 1972. I was 27 years old.

THE TWA TERMINAL AT Manila International Airport bristled with people, more departing than arriving. It is traditional in the Philippines that friends and relatives go to the airport to send off their loved ones. There were at least 15 family members who made the journey to see us off at noon. No one knew when we would all be together again. Danny checked us in at the ticket counter while I held Edna, squeezing her extra tight but trying not to alarm her. We

Nieves Catahan Villamin

all walked together, no one saying much, toward the airport lounge. Edna ran on ahead, pointing excitedly to the TWA jet, already parked and waiting to take us to America. Danny and I exchanged nervous glances; both of us were struggling to fight back tears as we realized it was time. We had to break the news to our daughter, our little baby, whom we loved more than anyone else on the planet.

My husband knelt down and called Edna over. I held her hand as Danny started speaking. I couldn't control my sobs. The memory was still fresh. It was not too long ago that Danny had said goodbye to me at the same airport as he was bound for Vietnam to work for an American satellite company. He left our home for a good-paying job in a war-torn country at a time when I needed him the most. Nevertheless, I couldn't fault the man who had been dreaming of building his wife a house since learning I was pregnant with Edna. Danny took the job in spite of the possibility that he could come back to his family inside a plastic body bag. This time, it was we who were leaving. Danny's voice interrupted my thoughts.

"Edna, see that airplane outside? Mommy and I will be riding on it to go to America." He paused, forcing out the next sentence. "But you are not going with us. You are going to stay with Aunt Mila and Uncle Rene in our house in Sumacab. Temporarily." All I could do was quietly nod as I squeezed Edna's hand tightly. A mother should never have to leave her daughter behind, but we had no choice. With no money and no jobs waiting for us, there was no guarantee of a better life for Edna. She would be better off here with my family until we could send for her.

"Temporarily only," Danny repeated for emphasis. "Daddy will come and get you as soon as I get a job and have enough money. I promise."

Edna said nothing, staring blankly at us. Then she leaned over and wrapped her arms tightly around Danny, a sorrowful expression on her face. She understood that Dad was leaving her. No words were needed. Danny returned the hug. We both knew that this was the right thing to do under the circumstances, but that didn't make it any easier.

My husband tried to give Edna to my sister Mila. Then the crying

Bittermelons and Mimosas

started. She resisted fiercely, shouting, "No! No! I don't like! I don't like!" It took both of us to put her in my sister's arms.

"Daddy! Mommy!" she cried, tears streaming down her face. "I am going with you! I am going with you!"

My entire family was reduced to tears while trying their best to calm her down. Mila took Edna and waved us toward the Immigration counter.

"Go. Go!" she urged.

"Do not worry." Danny tugged gently at my hand, guiding me toward Immigration. We could hear Edna sobbing behind us. "Please don't look back," my husband said, his voice cracking. "Please don't look back."

Hard as it was, I didn't look back. It will only be for a few months. This is for the best, I kept on telling myself, following Danny through Immigration and the boarding area, then outside onto the tarmac. My family had gathered on the other side of the chain-link fence, waving goodbye. Edna was still crying, jerking the chain-link fence hard and trying her best to climb it.

Danny again told me not to look back, and I turned my head toward the plane. We kept walking, looking ahead. "We're going to America," Danny said firmly as we approached the plane. "We are going to make it because we have each other."

Each step closer to the plane took me farther away, not only from Edna, but also from my beloved Sumacab and all that had come before this day. A new life was about to begin, but as I walked up the steps to the plane, I knew that the old life would not be easy to leave behind. There were too many memories.

Once we were up in the air and the seat belts light had gone off, I took our slim photo album out of the carry-on luggage. Not thinking about Edna was impossible – already I had to see her face again. With every family photograph, other memories came flooding back. I closed my eyes. Part of me felt excitement about what awaited us in America. The other part wished I were not leaving my beloved Sumacab.

Our route was Manila–Taipei–Hawaii–San Francisco. The flight to Taipei took us more than two hours. Except for a slight headache and motion sickness, I felt fine.

Nieves Catahan Villamin

Taipei's new surroundings helped me forget the drama we had left behind. We weren't in the States yet, but I had already discovered some benefits of our journey: real orange juice and vending machines. The orange juice my husband got from a vending machine at the Taipei airport tasted better than Royal Tru-Orange, a favorite soft drink of many Filipinos. The taste made me realize that Royal Tru-Orange was only part orange, mostly combined with other citrus fruits grown locally. We did not farm orange orchards in the Philippines, only *kalamansi* and *dalanghita*, small citrus fruits that have a juicy taste comparable to that of the popular California navel oranges.

When we were children, my mother told us that Royal was the best cure for common colds. I believed her. During the Christmas season, nights were colder than usual, and the sudden temperature changes gave most children a fever with a hacking cough. I can remember us children catching colds on purpose so we could drink the thirst-quenching "medicinal" Royal Tru-Orange.

I had never been to an international airport before arriving at Taiwan, so orange juice wasn't the only thing new to me. I had never seen a vending machine, even when I spent almost ten years in Manila. I'm sure many commercial places in the business districts had vending machines installed all around their offices, but perhaps they were not as big and colorful as the ones I saw in Taipei. I was amazed to see juice flowing into the small cup that nestled comfortably on a small opening carved in the vending machine's body. I even tried figuring out where the juice was coming from, but couldn't. The varieties of snacks inside the vending machine left me speechless. How had they gotten there? I thought it was a modern marvel. No way could this be compared to the small candy and cookie jars lining the bamboo shelves of my mother's *sari-sari* store in Sumacab.

To tide me over until the next meal, Danny bought me a soda and some cookies for the next leg of our flight. "Just in case you get hungry," he said. We spent ten of our $75 pocket money. Then we sat down and waited for boarding.

The eight-hour trip to Hawaii seemed to take forever. And when I had my first glimpse of the Hawaiian coastline, I was not even happy

Bittermelons and Mimosas

at seeing it. It was not what I imagined it to be. Leaving Edna behind in Manila continued to tug at my heart, and the long trip had completely drained me.

Danny kept massaging my swollen legs and feet that had become two sizes bigger than my shoes, trying his best to comfort me. "Those shoes are ugly anyway." He tried to be funny. "I will buy you a new pair of shoes that fit like a glove as soon as I get a job!" I looked lovingly at him and put my head on his shoulder. I was still very upset, yet delighted because I saw the image of a better life flash through the sparkle of his eyes. We comforted each other for several hours.

Finding our way in a big airport was not difficult because signs were posted everywhere, but the line leading to the immigration area seemed endless. Finally, an immigration officer took us to his office, where we were asked routine questions. The travel agent had prepared us well, and we breezed through the interview. There I met my first challenge.

The immigration officer paused shortly before he called my name after looking at my passport. "Neevs Villamin?"

"No, sir. It's N-I-E-V-E-S. Nieves."

"Oops. Sorry. Nee-veys."

I had no idea there would be many more monikers (the best one yet is Nervous Vitamin) waiting for me to discover after the immigration officer had butchered my name.

Sobbing silently, I painted the picture of why we left behind our families, including a precious three-year-old daughter. The immigration officer looked at me sympathetically but said very little. When he was finally satisfied, he smiled and handed each of us a plastic bag and his congratulations. That plastic bag might as well have been brimming with gold. We knew we had finally arrived in America.

Inside each bag were our passports, health records, and other immigration documents, official confirmation of our new status as resident aliens of the United States. We had spent four years trying to get to this point, and I could not believe it was finally happening.

Another four-hour plane ride took us to San Francisco, our final destination. The city by the Bay, I said to myself, thinking of Tony Bennett, my favorite balladeer. We arrived at San Francisco

Nieves Catahan Villamin

International at around ten that Friday evening. The shimmering lights of the city below seemed so impressive – almost enough to make me temporarily forget my sadness and discomfort. Danny hugged me as the plane taxied down the tarmac.

"Don't worry," he again assured me. "We will make it here."

"Okay," was all I could say. I was very tired and sleepy.

The door leading to the arrival area spewed out travelers waving to friends or relatives waiting for them with big smiles on their faces. Nobody waved at us. But we weren't worried because we had had a plan before we left Manila. Danny had a letter safely tucked inside his jacket that would introduce us to a couple we would meet that night for the very first time.

We had landed finally in the land of opportunity. Danny would find a job soon, and we would get settled. We thought that his first paycheck and our meager reserves would be enough to set up our own apartment. A week or two of charity was all we needed from our host. And a month after the baby was born, I could start working so we could repay the money we had borrowed, plus buy clothes and toys to send back to Edna. I didn't want our precious daughter to think we had forgotten her.

"What time is it, sir?" Danny's voice brought me back to my new surroundings.

The Filipino porter who was helping pull our suitcases from the carousel glanced at his wristwatch. "It's almost 11 P.M."

"Can you please tell me where the nearest phone is?" Danny asked.

The porter pointed to the phones mounted in stalls along the wall.

"Who is he calling?" The porter was curious as Danny rushed to a phone booth.

"Our ride," I answered. An exchange of a few more questions and answers between us took place before Danny came back with a big smile on his face. He had reached Rita and Jimmy, the couple who would host us temporarily, and they were on their way. I felt as if a heavy load had been lifted off my shoulders. I touched my stomach lightly and whispered. "Thank you, Elaine, for not giving me any discomfort."

For the next 45 minutes, the porter stayed with us at the place where Jimmy and Rita had told us to wait. "In case they don't show

҈ Bittermelons and Mimosas ҈

up, you can stay with my family tonight," he offered kindly.

We didn't have to wait much longer after the porter left to return to his job. A handsome couple in their mid-twenties both grinning from ear-to-ear waved at us. The woman was wearing the latest style of boots and a gray wool coat, and the well-groomed man was wearing a brown tailored jacket.

Rita and Jimmy Yalung

Once inside their green Mustang, I asked them how they were able to recognize us instantly among the crowd.

"Well, you were the only pregnant woman wearing a flowery dress among the crowd. And your husband is exceptionally tall compared to a typical Filipino," replied Rita. A total give-away!

We arrived at the apartment way past midnight, so they insisted we go to bed right away. They didn't have to tell us twice. We could fill them in the next day. As I crawled into the bed and closed my eyes I saw Edna's face before me.

That was the very first night I could not put my arms around my darling daughter so she could fall asleep. Even so, I held back my tears. I needed a good night's rest.

My husband, a stranger in a foreign land, knocked on every business door along East 14th Street in Oakland the following Monday. It did not surprise me when he came back Tuesday afternoon having already found a woodworking job. His new job paid $2.65 an hour, but we felt rich after converting the dollars into pesos, which at that time were four to one. However, he complained that his feet hurt. The leather of the Ang Tibay shoes he had worn during our wedding and our trip were not meant for working and were very uncomfortable.

Two days after, calluses appeared on Danny's small toes. I asked Rita for some band-aids and plastered them on top of the calluses.

"How much of the $65 is left?" I asked Danny after applying first aid to his aching feet.

"Not much," he said. "I bought lunch Monday and Tuesday."

"I tell you what. Let's take the bus to the downtown so you can buy a comfortable pair of shoes. Do leftovers and lots of Ritz crackers and giant bananas (twice the size of Philippine bananas) sound good for lunch the next three days?" We both laughed at my suggestion.

There it was. Our first U.S. purchase was a $10 pair of brown moccasin shoes shaped like sailboats that we bought at a discount shoe store in downtown Oakland. We got what we paid for. After a couple of weeks Danny had to keep gluing the cheap shoes to keep the soles from falling off every time they got wet during the October rains. We had arrived in the United States Friday night. By Tuesday, Danny found a job, and on Friday we celebrated with his first paycheck by buying some fried chicken at Swan's. We mailed a money order to Dante and closed that chapter behind us.

"When is your baby due?" Rita asked me the second Saturday morning (exactly eight days after we arrived in the U.S.), while we were in the basement of their apartment building.

She was showing me how to operate a washer and a dryer. Rita had never asked me to do any household chores, much less their laundry, because she could see how big my stomach was. However, since Danny had gone to work, I found myself always thinking about our daughter. To keep my thoughts away from Edna, I busied myself by doing exactly the opposite of what I was told, including washing their clothes by hand using the bathtub as my *banyera*. Earlier that Saturday morning before going down to the basement, Rita saw me squatted on the bathroom floor with my two legs wide apart because of my big tummy. I was almost finished laundering clothes in the tub.

She was horrified. "That's it. Whether you like it or not, you'll learn how to use the elevator, and the washer and dryer in the basement. It's for your own good, and for the baby's sake." (These are not her exact words, but the message was there. I appreciated her concerns very much.)

"End of November." I had calculated that since Edna was born the first of the month, the next baby would be around the same day.

"Have you thought about the hospital where your baby will be delivered?" she asked.

Bittermelons and Mimosas

"No, I don't really know what to do." I felt the urgency of my situation now that we were discussing it.

"I will give you phone numbers to call on Monday to ask for information. If the person you reach doesn't have the information, you will be referred to somebody who does." She explained to me with diligence how the American way works.

When we came back up to the apartment, Rita thumbed through the phone book, wrote down a few numbers and gave me the list. "You know how to use the phone, right? She wasn't insulting me; she was just making sure I knew what to do.

Before Monday, I made a short list of the questions I wanted to ask. I had to ensure I wouldn't forget any, especially the most important ones.

By the next weekend I had all the information about delivering a baby at Highland Hospital even without health insurance. I also had an appointment to see a social worker on Friday. I don't recall who accompanied me because my appointment was on a workday. Maybe I took a bus. That couldn't have been surprising, as I wanted to learn my way around.

I still remember Rita and Jimmy diligently explaining to me how the system works before my appointment. They also assured me that Highland Hospital would take good care of me. They were right. Before my appointment was over, I had my first ever pregnancy check-up. It was followed by a couple more before Elaine was born. When I had Edna, I saw a doctor at the maternity clinic only after my water broke. A few days after her birth at the clinic, I took her home. It was that easy, nothing complicated.

Our good fortune allowed us to move into our own apartment the third week after our arrival. It was in a six-story apartment building on 12th Street for low-income families, where newcomers like us were accepted without much hassle. This was our first official residence in the United States. The few Filipinos we met at the elevator were very friendly and extra helpful to us, especially because they saw that I was very pregnant.

A couple of weeks later, Elaine was born.

Chapter Fifteen

Postcards From the United States

Homesickness is like bereavement.

Anonymous

Elaine was born at Highland Hospital, a day after the first Thanksgiving which we had celebrated shortly after settling in Oakland. Almost a month after her birth, we received a bill from Highland Hospital. "Thank God! It's only $748.00," Danny sounded relieved. Because we didn't have any health insurance he had been qualified to apply for a sliding fee scale. Otherwise the hospital bill would have been over a thousand dollars. (Before we moved into the Berkeley house, we paid Highland Hospital.)

"Rita said we could apply for free medical assistance even though we have just immigrated because you don't make enough income. We might need it for the baby's check-up." I mentioned this to him the day after he took me home from the hospital.

"I don't feel good about getting handouts. I will work overtime or find a second job. I just don't think it's right for us to receive dole-outs." Danny's pride was bigger than our potential financial need.

Thank God Elaine was a healthy baby. Danny's health insurance coverage from work came after three months. We were able to breathe more easily.

Outside our small studio apartment on 12th Street, the northern California climate was changing rapidly, and the brisk cold of autumn hung in the air. The chilly weather and closed windows were

Bittermelons and Mimosas

a dramatic change from the hot tropical climate and open surroundings of Sumacab. Fearing that the baby or I might get sick from the change in the weather, we stayed close to home. The unregulated indoor heat sometimes became warm and stifling. The lack of constant fresh air and being alone with an infant often made me anxious.

However, I had to think of Elaine first. Shirley Temple movies on TV kept us company, and somehow I got through those early months and my first change of seasons in the new country.

Admittedly, there was not much to this first apartment. We took it because it was all we could afford. Additionally, it was just a few steps from the bus stop. Since we could not afford a car, the bus was critical to our daily mobility. I came to enjoy the easy access. That more than made up for the loud ruckus caused by the drunks stumbling off the bus in the middle of the night.

Inside the apartment, space was at a premium. The simple living room was transformed into a bedroom at night, affording us enough space for a full bed, a table lamp, and a crib for Elaine. The combination kitchen/dining area was larger than anything I had experienced in Sumacab.

One of our earliest joys came in discovering that the markets in Chinatown often stocked Filipino food items. The weekend before I gave birth to Elaine, Rita and Jimmy gave us a tour of Chinatown, riding in the Granny Smith apple–colored Mustang, which was their pride and joy, and which I thought was a very cool car. We bought our first twenty-five pound sack of Jasmine rice (the variety that only rich people in the Philippines could afford) from Sam Yick Grocery at 8th and Franklin Streets in Oakland.

In the beginning, Danny and I stuck to traditional food, meaning frequent dishes of fried *tuyo* or dried fish and squid in the morning, and meat and vegetables cooked with *bagoong* for lunch and dinner. The strong odors usually escaped our apartment and filled the hallway. We received nasty looks from our neighbors before we finally discovered air fresheners. Our appetite for traditional dishes faded, especially once we discovered the neighborhood Kwikway, a fast-food chain on Telegraph Street specializing in succulent, fall-off-the-bone

Nieves Catahan Villamin

fried chicken. Some nights it was just easier to go out than to stay home and cook.

There were other things we loved about our new lives. We had a working tub with real hot water – no more baths in the river. There was toilet paper (the first time I saw a roll I didn't want to use it the way it was intended to be used) in the bathroom, not a *tabo*. Off in the Mustang during spring weekends, Jimmy and Rita helped us find some luxuries that became our first "necessities" (a toaster, an electric clock radio, a tea kettle, a working vacuum cleaner – no more brooms) during our many journeys to the flea markets stretching from Oakland to San Jose.

IT DID NOT TAKE me long to learn that bluntness and compassion were traits of the American culture. From my experience, I have to say that social service here in the United States is the best in the world, even though I can only compare it with that in the Philippines. A couple of weeks after Elaine was born, a Highland Hospital social worker began making follow-up visits to make sure I was being cared for both physically and emotionally. Lorie, the social worker, knew from my hospital records that we didn't have any family or friends close by because we had recently immigrated to the States. I will never forget her genuine concern for my baby and me. For the next three months, she was my doctor, friend, confidant, and psychiatrist.

I knew her concern was genuine, although I must admit she was also crazy about my home-cooked Filipino dish of spring rolls and noodles. I had never experienced that kind of public service before. In the Philippines, efficient and fast public service always came at a price. Try to get a copy of any official document, and the first thing you heard was, "*Pare, ang lagay ba, eh.* Grease money, *Pare.*" Pesos talk. Only then will public servants work. Bribery was a way of life there.

Bittermelons and Mimosas

Most Americans affably welcomed Filipinos and treated us with warmth. Danny and I experienced that with Lorie, the social worker. and with Danny's boss from Gall Furniture. He offered Danny a salary advance (Danny refused and instead worked overtime on weekends to earn extra money) so he could buy a washing machine for Elaine's laundry. There was also the apartment manager who let Danny forego part of the second month's rent so he could buy me a used television set.

Straightforwardness was another trait of the American culture that was strange to me at first. Most Americans wouldn't think twice about expressing an opinion, and some opinions could be brutally frank. Notwithstanding, after a heated debate or discussion where they called each other names, they would act as if nothing had happened.

In the beginning, I found this hard to understand. It was as if they were hiding what they truly felt about each other. In our culture, we called such behavior being pretentious. Here in the United States, it meant teamwork, or getting the job done, whatever it took. One had to learn to get along, even if it meant engaging in office politics in order not to be perceived as a troublemaker.

In Christmas of 1973, Danny brought home a washer he had purchased on credit from Sears using his first credit card ever. My husband was tired of having to launder the baby's diapers at the apartment's washing machine or sometimes at the local laundromat. His daughter deserved the best, he decided.

But the first machine had been the one that we really, really needed. Owning a car was seen as the first sign of success for people living in a foreign country. In our case, this was no mere prize. Having a car was a necessity, and our limited budget meant we had to find the best deal available. I watched TV commercials closely and scanned the newspaper ads. While we waited at the bus stop Danny and I

Nieves Catahan Villamin

pointed to passing cars we thought would be good to own. In no time at all, we became car experts, knowing exactly what we wanted, what we were willing to pay, and where we would go to buy. It was just a matter of time, we agreed.

On a cold December morning, Danny, Elaine, and I huddled at the bus stop, waiting for a ride to take us to Highland Hospital for the baby's first check-up. Danny glanced down at Elaine and became concerned. Despite being bundled up to her ears like an Eskimo child, her cheeks were bright red from the winter cold. That was all her father needed to see.

"I am buying a car before our next hospital appointment," he declared on our way home.

"But you've never driven a car before," I protested. Danny didn't even have a driver's license; thus, he had no car insurance. Nevertheless, he was determined to own a car because of the baby. He would not listen to my concerns.

"I've seen other people drive," he assured me. "I've seen them drive on TV. Learning to drive will not be that difficult."

I was in the midst of cooking dinner on Thursday evening of that week when he called. "I am at the car dealership right now. Watch for me in the parking lot around six o'clock. Look for a green Rambler." He sounded more excited than he had been on our fifth day in the United States when he came home telling me he had landed a job.

"What?" I had heard him. I just could not believe what he had said. We had moved to our second apartment at 14th Street and San Pablo. The building was across from Rhodes Department Store, where the well-lit parking lot was always full during the shopping rush hours.

From the kitchen window, I saw Danny wait for a car to pull out so he could park his new purchase. "I put a $100 down payment on it. I'll pay the balance in two installments within a month," he explained to me as I greeted him at the door. My accountant's brain started to compute.

"At $2.65 an hour and with a small baby, that will be hard," I complained.

Bittermelons and Mimosas

"Don't worry about it," he said. "I'll just have to work a lot of overtime." As usual, he had everything figured out.

After dinner, we left Elaine with a Filipino neighbor and went down to inspect the car. It was a 1960 green, four-door Rambler with a stick shift, complete with cigarette burns on the back seat and a big dent on the shiny bumper. It was big enough for three people and ideal for our tight budget.

"What's with the dent?" I asked. While I knew nothing about cars, I could tell it was a fresh dent.

"Oh, the stupid salesman. He parked the car in reverse after our test drive. When I stepped on the gas, it lurched backwards and into the concrete fence." He was smiling as he talked.

He was very proud of himself. He had just bought a car without a driver's license or car insurance. When he signed the sales agreement, he didn't even know the car had a clutch! And wasn't automatic. He had not been in the country long and he had beaten the system already!

"Did you have somebody with you when you drove it home?" I started to sense something fishy. The smile quickly disappeared from his face and he became impatient.

"No. And unless you have a better idea, don't ask any more questions."

"I wasn't nagging. I'm just scared for you," I said as I tried to comfort him.

Beneath my concern, I was very proud of my husband. By the time Danny reached our apartment after he left the car dealership, he had figured out the difference between the clutch, the gas pedal, and the brake.

For more than a week, my husband left for work an hour earlier than his usual time to avoid the traffic, which at 5:30 in the morning was very light. He also drove his car with only the parking lights on to ward off unnecessary attention from other drivers or patrolling policemen. What he didn't know was he was driving illegally because it was still pitch dark.

"What's a car for if I can't drive it? I'll go take the driving test today after work." Danny decided he had waited long enough for a neighbor who had promised to teach him the way around Oakland in his Rambler.

I didn't have a better idea so I left him alone. If he landed in jail, I figured, he wouldn't keep his mouth shut. We would be featured in the news and some rich couple would help us after reading our story. I could see the newspaper caption: "FOR MY BABY'S SAKE."

My husband was determined to drive his baby to her next hospital appointment because, unless you were a duck, a winter commute in Oakland's wet weather was no fun. With a baby in your arms, trips around town were even more frustrating. The driving instructors from the Department of Motor Vehicles (DMV) were the ones who taught my husband how to drive. After he failed his first driving test, he went into the next DMV office and took the road test again. Soon, sympathetic DMV employees figured out what he was doing and began helping him master the basics of driving safely. He finally got his driving license after the fourth try.

Our first joy ride around Oakland happened one afternoon after Danny received his license in the mail. We waited for the real license to come because he did not want to chance getting a driving citation while using a temporary permit. He had sweated bullets for his driving permit and it was not worth the risk, he said.

However, as fate would have it, a police car pulled us over after Danny turned left at an intersection on our way home from our first drive. He had tried to beat the yellow light that changed quickly to red before his turn was completed. As the police officer approached our car, I was coaching Danny.

"Pretend you don't speak English very well. He might feel sorry for you."

Danny didn't have to pretend. The first encounter with a law enforcement officer made him so uneasy that he stuttered a bit (although he would never admit it). We knew that helped. After seeing Danny's new driver's license, the police officer gave him an earful of advice instead of a citation.

As the police car drove away, we looked at each other. "Wow, welcome to the American way of life," we said to each other. We both

Bittermelons and Mimosas

sighed in relief. We knew we had been given a break. We also realized that breaks like that do not come in pairs. We became observant of traffic rules since.

"Are you sure she will be okay?" I asked Danny for the fourth time as I dressed a half-awake Elaine in flannel pajamas and wool coat with a furry hood, for her 6 A.M. trip. Monday, January 15, 1973, was a first day for both Elaine and me; she for the babysitter who lived at 27th Street, and me for my first job on Broadway Street (both in Oakland) as an accounting clerk. Elaine was only 53 days old. Showers on an early winter morning compounded my worries.

"My poor baby. She might catch a cold."

"Don't worry; this is just temporary. I will find us a babysitter who lives in the same apartment building even if it means we have to move again," Danny reassured me.

However, we had not lived in our building that long, and I knew moving to another place so soon was unrealistic. He was only trying to calm my fears. I followed as he went downstairs, carrying a well-bundled Elaine in his arms. After he drove away, I went up and got ready for my first day of work in America.

Mrs. Johnson, the tall, blonde, blue-eyed personnel manager, warmly welcomed me to her office at 8 A.M. She handed me new employee forms and a ballpoint pen after I sat down.

"Fill these out so you can get paid at the end of the month," she instructed.

Our first meeting a couple of weeks ago had seemed more like a friendly chat between former acquaintances, not a job interview. Her face had lit up when I told her that I was Filipino. She and her Army husband had lived in the Philippines for some time after World War II.

"Oh, the sweet mangoes, chicos, *atis*, papayas, and watermelons

Nieves Catahan Villamin

of different colors and sizes!" she exclaimed. "What was the name of that fruit stand on Blumentritt where my driver used to take me after Sunday mass?"

I mumbled some name as if I really knew the place that she described.

"And the fresh fish, shrimp, and vegetables my maid used to cook, and the *lechon*. I loved most Filipino foods, except *balut* (boiled fertilized egg) and *dinuguan* (chocolate pork). Yuukkkk."

She made a face as if she was going to throw up. That moment, when she shared her memories with me, I knew I had a good chance of getting the job. After the interview, she complimented me on my good command of the English language.

"Thanks to my American friends," I quickly responded. Talk about pandering!

In the spring, Danny's reassurance proved true. There were a pair of newly hired apartment managers, a retired Filipino couple who did babysitting as a side job. Elaine didn't have to make those cold early-morning trips anymore. Work was only a few steps away, so I often lunched at home and stopped by the babysitter to check on Elaine on my way back to work.

One afternoon, Jenny, our secretary, asked, "So, Nieves, you go home for lunch almost every day, huh?"

"Yes," I replied.

"We have a name for people like you," she continued. The twinkle in her eyes cautioned me that I was in for a joke. I just didn't know what it would be.

"And what is that?" I asked.

"Nooner," she replied. She hardly contained her giggles while repeating this in a singsong voice on her way back to her desk: "Nieves is a nooner. Nieves is a nooner."

"Well, I guess I am a nooner then, because I go home for lunch," I admitted. Everybody in the office laughed. What could be so funny about that? I asked myself. Maybe they were laughing at my accent, which sometimes my co-workers did in a friendly way.

My supervisor, who heard the laughter, joined in the conversation. "Nieves, do you know what a nooner is?" he asked.

Bittermelons and Mimosas

"Somebody who goes home for lunch?"

"Not close. For your information, it is somebody who goes home at noon for S-E-X." He couldn't say the word. So he spelled it out for me.

"Oh, my God, no!" I cried out. I was so embarrassed. My generation never talked about S-E-X in the Philippines. I was a greenhorn, not used to dirty jokes.

"I guess I learned a new word today," I told everybody.

I didn't want to be called a party pooper. It was in my interest to develop a thick skin and get along. I had a lot to learn. This was only the beginning.

ALMOST A YEAR HAD gone by. Elaine had started to walk. Our adventures with Rita and Jimmy in the Mustang in the summer took us to San Jose to the south, San Francisco to the west, and Sacramento to the north. Jimmy's car had more legroom than our tiny Rambler. When the wind became crisp then cold again, I felt homesick and missed Edna even more.

The trees along Broadway Street in Oakland were starting to shed their leaves like the first fall when we had arrived. In the Philippines, martial law was still in effect. News about missing people and the arrest and prosecution of Marcos' enemies there were not openly discussed, especially among Filipinos with ongoing petitions like Edna's. We avoided discussing politics during overseas phone conversations with relatives. We were told the phones were being tapped. With all the negative news being fed to us, we couldn't help but feel that our family reunion might never happen.

Our anxiety rose to a new level one Saturday afternoon in early October. After reading my mother-in-law's letter, I felt sick to my stomach.

Nieves Catahan Villamin

"Tatay Pilo's application for a tourist visa was disapproved. What are we going to do?" I asked Danny as I handed him the letter.

Edna already had a visa. We were all waiting for my father-in-law's tourist visa to be granted so he could accompany our daughter to the States.

"I wish I knew." As if it were yesterday, I still see the worry on Danny's face. Like me, he could not see Edna traveling alone for 16 hours, even though most of it would be airtime.

"After dinner, I'll call Nestor in Manila," Danny finally said firmly. "It will be late morning there. He'll know what our next step should be." Danny's confident demeanor calmed me.

Nestor was our travel agent friend who had helped us with our immigration process to the United States. I knew if anybody could find another way for Edna to travel with a companion, he would be the one. Our long-distance conversations with Nestor became frequent in the days that followed. I added up the dollars every time we hung up at the end of every phone call. We were still paying off several loans. It would be still another loan for Edna's airfare, but it didn't matter. Danny could always get a second job, my back-up solution for any monetary shortage. The second week of October, Nestor called us with the news we had been waiting for.

"I have a passenger flying to San Francisco this week," he said. "For a small fee, she will chaperone Edna during the flight. I will call you with all the details before their departure."

Danny repeated the conversation to me after he hung up. What he told me buoyed my spirits like the times when I heard the bells ringing at the City Cathedral after a midnight mass on Christmas Eve when I was growing up and in the fields guarding our harvest. I bent down and kissed my almost one-year-old Elaine, who was peacefully asleep in her crib close by.

"You'll meet your older sister soon," I whispered softly. "And our family finally will be complete." I knew she heard me. She moved her legs, opened her eyes and smiled, then went back to sleep.

The day we had waited for over a year finally came. Edna's flight was scheduled to arrive at 6:30 P.M. We left for the airport early to

Bittermelons and Mimosas

avoid the late afternoon traffic. We wanted to be there early just in case the plane arrived ahead of schedule. The chaperone was a stranger. What if we missed her? Only the Lord knew what could happen to my baby. I shook off the negative thoughts trying to creep into my mind.

We sat in the airport lounge close to the immigration area with Elaine on Danny's lap and waited. I was busy feeding a restless Elaine, who was very excited at seeing that many people for the first time. Then the doors flew open. Passengers came bursting out, pushing carts filled with suitcases and boxes stacked to the top, some higher than the person pushing the cart. My back was turned away from the door when Edna and her chaperone appeared, the elderly woman holding her hand tightly.

"Here they come!" Danny exclaimed.

Unlike in the movies, Edna didn't come running the minute she saw me. I searched her face and eyes to find a connection. I knew we were both lost.

Friends and relatives bade goodbye to Edna at the airport. Tatay Pilo wearing glasses, Nestor Dizon holding her travel papers, Dolly holding a handkerchief, Vergel next to Dolly, Dante at the back, Ammie holding Edna on her shoulder, Liza next to Edna, Nanay Dely next to Liza, Rene in front of Liza, and pregnant Mila.

Nieves Catahan Villamin

She was very stylishly dressed from head to toe in a red cowboy outfit complete with a red hat and white boots. Just a year and my baby had grown so much. She was taller; her baby fat was almost gone. Her timid smile showed a developing maturity, not innocence, on the face I had longed so much to see and touch again.

Confused, Edna stared at the baby in my arms with a look only a mother and daughter would understand. She was the little girl in the Philippines who would not stop talking and was so full of energy. How come she wasn't excited to see me? Was she angry because we had left her and thought we might even have replaced her? Or was she feeling pain because she had been uprooted? I could only imagine what was going on inside her. I held out Elaine's hands for her to touch.

"This is your sister, the one inside my tummy when we left, remember?" I knew she understood what I said, but she didn't say anything. She remained quiet and shy during the whole introduction.

After the exchange of few words, with Edna hardly answering our questions, the elderly woman left to catch her flight to Los Angeles, her final destination.

"Are you hungry? Would you like some hot chocolate and some apple pie?" Danny asked her as soon as we found a corner to sit. "*Opo, tsokoleyt and apol pay.* Yes sir, chocolate and apple pie." She repeated her Daddy's words, sounding a little more cheerful.

Edna's first night in a foreign environment was not peaceful. She tossed and turned. When daylight came, she told us she wanted to go home. This is home, we told her. Edna remained quiet and withdrawn during the days that followed, sometimes in tears. She said she missed the people she left behind. I didn't get jealous. I understood. I knew that was exactly how I had felt the first few days and nights after we left the Philippines over a year ago.

⁂ Bittermelons and Mimosas ⁂

OUR APARTMENT BUILDING IN downtown Oakland was like a semi-residential homecare facility of today. The tenants hardly left their rooms except to buy alcohol and groceries and run errands. Most of the tenants were retirees who couldn't care less about children.

"Shut her up, she's loud." As expected, complaints about a baby crying on weekends became frequent.

However, moving to a better apartment was not an alternative for us. We hardly had any money left after buying necessities and making payments on our loans and the Highland Hospital bill every month. Still, for the children's sake, we had to do something. Danny decided to move us, not into a bigger apartment, but into a small house, even if it meant a second job for him to afford the monthly mortgage.

"What do you think about this one?" Danny asked me.

It was the fourth house we had seen in a week and I was getting impatient. Before we left, the apartment manager had told us over the phone that the tenant in Room 304, the room above us, had brought up complaints about the children's noises again. With that at the back of my mind, I made my way up to the porch and sat on the bench placed next to the house's front door. Facing the manicured gardens on both sides of the street, with bunches of flowering plants in a rainbow of colors, on that spring weekend made me feel very blissful. Being there felt right.

"This is it," I told Danny. It was a small, two-bedroom, fixer-upper treasure in Berkeley, with a yard at the back twice the size of the house itself. The house was in a marginal neighborhood, but the $17,500 price tag was hard to resist. The huge yard space boasted a small workshop, a vegetable garden, and the perfect spot for a swing.

Peter Klatt, our realtor and financial advisor, taught us the art of creative financing. A $500 tax refund, together with a personal loan from Household Finance, covered the 20 percent down payment on the house that became ours in the spring of 1975. (Peter was Danny's boss from MB Designs. He and his wife, Joannie, became our lifelong friends.)

Berkeley was a far cry from the frenetic pace of Oakland where anything could (and often did) happen. Unlike Oakland, which went through a dramatic revitalization in the early 1970s, Berkeley's growth was relatively subtle because of rent control. However, both cities prided themselves on a diverse population and culture. It was a comfortable area for us to have our home. We found a babysitter who lived only three houses down the street. Edna was bused to her pre-school with schoolmates who lived close by. Sometimes, I drove home for lunch because my place of work was near. And traffic was not yet a problem any time of the day.

The next two years breezed by quickly, and Edna became much like her old self. After two years of living with us, Edna seemed happy again and seldom thought about the family she had left behind.

However, Elaine was exactly the opposite. She was exceptionally quiet and didn't talk much. She made occasional sounds as if she was carrying on a conversation, but the only word we really understood from her was "No." When we directed Elaine to do tasks for her age, she understood and followed. We thought all the while she was well behaved and that was why she didn't say much.

This continued until one summer night when Elaine was wailing in pain. She could not sit or stand still. With great concern, we bundled her up and took her to Kaiser Hospital.

"What's the matter?" The doctor tried to talk to her after taking her temperature.

"No, No, Aahhhaahhh..." was Elaine's reply.

"What did you feed her for dinner?" the doctor asked me after feeling Elaine's stomach.

"The usual, but she ate a lot more than normal," I answered.

"Sometimes you have to provide restraint," the doctor told me with a smile, as if she were telling me I should know Elaine's limits better than Elaine.

"Here, have this prescription filled." She turned to Danny and handed him the prescription and a card. "Give it to her as directed. Is she really almost three years old?" she asked us after looking at Elaine's chart the second time.

"Yes." I thought it was somewhat strange that she doubted the information recorded on the chart.

"Well, she should have been speaking in whole sentences by now."

Bittermelons and Mimosas

I never expected to hear those words from anybody.

"Make an appointment with that psychologist and have your daughter evaluated," she suggested after handing Danny a business card.

"Is she retarded?" I asked. My brother had two "special children." I was aware of the sacrifices his family had gone through and the uncertainty of the future of both his children. I felt anxious and my palms started to sweat.

"No, she's not. It's just a case of delayed speech." The doctor's assurance was very comforting.

On our way home, it became as clear as if we were viewing our lives through a magnifying lens that our busy schedules had taken precedence over our family duties. Monitoring our children's well-being, particularly Elaine's, had become secondary. Also, maybe we didn't know any better. I have never yet met any parents who intentionally neglect their children's health for any reason. Even in the Philippines, families sold everything they owned when a family member's health was threatened.

The psychologist told us what we prayed we would hear. Elaine passed all the tests administered to her. She was not mentally handicapped. Then the psychologist asked us a question.

"How many babysitters has she had during the past three years?" We never thought the answer would be the reason for her much delayed speech.

"Elaine has had her share of babysitters over the last three years," I said. "There was a Kapampangan, an Ilokano, and a Bisaya. None of them spoke Tagalog, the language Elaine hears at home. Then there were Cuban and Mexican babysitters with many different Spanish words."

Apparently, Elaine was confused from the many languages she had heard from the string of babysitters. The psychologist told us to enroll Elaine at a pre-school where only one language, English, would be spoken, and told us we should speak the same at home.

The next school year Elaine attended a nursery school at the corner of our street, while Edna went to Thousand Oaks for her preschool. Hard as it was for us, Danny and I hardly spoke any Tagalog in front of the children for a while. For Elaine's sake, English became the spoken language at our home. It was well worth it. After six months, Elaine began to talk in complete sentences. The girl who was once so quiet could not stop talking, especially when she and her dad were engaged in a heated discussion.

IN 1976, I NEEDED a change in my prescription lenses. With the prescription in my purse, I went to GEMCO, a cooperative store in San Lorenzo that offered discounts for all their members' purchase. Most of the wire-framed eyeglasses on the glass shelves looked outdated to me. So I concentrated on the more stylish and up-to-date big plastic frames displayed on the opposite wall. I found a few pairs that I liked. Since I wear them everyday, I might as well wear a pair that I am happy with, I told myself.

However, there was one big problem. The plastic frames didn't have nose pads like the wire frames had. They kept sliding off my face every time I tried them on.

"Do any of these plastic frames come with nose pads?" I asked the saleslady.

"Yes, but they wouldn't look right on your face." She grabbed a pair from inside the display case and handed them to me. "Here try one of these and see for yourself.

She was right. The nose pads held the plastic frame way above the tiny bridge of my nose. They made me look like a clown, but at least they stayed put.

"God," I cried, "if only I didn't have such a small nose."

"No, you don't have a small nose," the sales lady contested. I thought she was empathizing with the inadequacy of my nose. Until she dropped the killer words.

"YOUR NOSE IS FLAT," she stated without batting an eyelash.

꧁ Bittermelons and Mimosas ꧂

"You ugly lady, you just lost a customer," I mumbled as I rushed out of the store.

I was still fuming mad when I got home.

"I want to have a nose lift," I told Danny as we were lying in bed. Danny was engrossed with his favorite TV program, *Hawaii Five-O*. When it was on, even an earthquake wouldn't get his eyes off the screen.

"Why?" he asked, but his eyes were still on the TV. Although he may have wanted to, he couldn't dismiss me because I was lying on my side next to him.

I told him the story. His gaze still glued to the TV, he said, "Don't pay attention to that woman. She should not be in sales."

"She was telling the truth," I insisted. "I'm getting tired of being teased about my nose. Also, I think a more prominent nose will improve my looks." I was breathing in his ear.

"What's wrong with the way you look?" He turned around and faced me.

This time, he looked irritated because I was keeping him from watching his favorite program. Danny knew that sometimes I became obsessed about my nose. I often joked that in my next life I'd be tall and skinny with a nose like Catherine Deneuve's, the French actress who I thought had the most striking nose among all the actresses of her time.

"Why do you want to be beautiful?" I wasn't getting any sympathy from him and I was becoming very upset. "Beautiful women are only for display. Had I wanted to marry a beautiful woman, I would not have picked you."

Lord! I felt as if lightning had struck me twice during the same day. As expected, our conversation went downhill from there.

"You mean I'm ugly?" I asked. I was so annoyed I felt ready to shoot had I had a gun in my hand, which luckily I didn't.

"No, you're not. That's not what I meant." Now he was getting defensive and very irritated.

"Then what do you mean?" I was almost in tears.

"How did I get myself into this mess?" Danny realized what was coming. Before he dug himself a deeper hole, he hugged me and apologized. "That's not really what I meant. You are beautiful inside and out. You are a very good mom, an excellent cook, and you make me laugh. Most of all, you put up with me."

Nieves Catahan Villamin

I knew he meant what he said. My husband seldom articulates his compliments. After all, he is a man of action, not words. He didn't tell me what I wanted to hear, but I felt the sincerity in his voice. I calmed down and fall asleep.

WALLY, A HIGH SCHOOL teacher and Danny's first American friend, invited us to dinner at their house one summer in 1977. Wally and my husband became friends when the high school teacher moonlighted as a consultant at the construction company where Danny was employed. Since I was at that time thinking about going back to school to get a teaching credential, Danny had thought that his new friend could be my guidance counselor. Our only other real social contact with Americans had been at company picnics or birthday parties. Obviously, we were curious about what an American family was like. With a mixture of excitement and apprehension we looked forward to our first dinner invitation from a non-Filipino family. So the children were briefed about the do's and don'ts a few days before the occasion. "Absolutely no Filipino time. Let's show our appreciation and respect by being there on time."

And on the day before we left for our dinner date, "Don't forget to remind the children about their table manners. How they behave will reflect on us. And children, try your best not to embarrass us, okay?" The children couldn't help but roll their eyes as soon as Danny turned his back. They had heard his cue for the umpteenth time.

"We're just having dinner with an American family, we are not going to see the Pope," I reasoned. It was a quiet ride from Berkeley to Oakland.

The house that overlooked the Bay Area spoke well of our hosts' achievements and status in the community. From an open stained-glass double door, our hosts emerged and greeted us warmly. They introduced us to their son and daughter ages twelve and six respectively. The entire family seemed friendly and genuinely happy to have us in their beautiful

Bittermelons and Mimosas

home, which, Wally had proudly let us know, had been designed and decorated by his wife Bertha. With architecture in her lineage, Bertha was one of the most successful architects in the Bay Area. After a tour of the house, we had drinks at the bar and chatted, while the children played board games nearby.

"So impressive! Why, you guys speak very good English," Bertha remarked before stepping to the dining area to finish setting the table that was only a few yards away from the bar.

"It was our medium of instruction in school." It was a repeat of my conversation with Mrs. Johnson, the lady who interviewed me for my first job a few years back. But I didn't flatter Bertha, like what I had done to Mrs. Johnson.

"Tell us something about the Philippines," Wally inquired. "I only knew what I had read in history books, which wasn't much."

"Then you know a lot more than us," Danny said jokingly.

"Well, actually, the Philippines is only a small country, about 116,000 square land miles. Slightly larger than the state of Nevada, but populous. The last time I researched the statistics for my Economics class, our total population as of 1970 was approximately 38.6 million," I explained.

"Dinner is ready, let's talk more as we eat," Bertha called out from the dining room. We took our assigned seats and then we started dinner.

We hardly had a few bites of the green salad when the phone rang. Wally excused himself and stood up to get the phone, which was only a few feet away from the dining table, and we heard the one-sided conversation.

"Hello, yes, Greg. No, sorry, not today. We are having company. I will call you back tomorrow."

"What was that call about?" Bertha asked as Wally returned to his place at the table.

"Greg and Ricky, they want to stop over for a drink. I told them not tonight, we are having company."

"But we are not company. It's fine with us, really," Danny interjected. I thought he was out of place for butting in the conversation without being asked. I felt a bit embarrassed.

Both of us had not yet adjusted well to the American culture. I knew Danny was thinking about back in the Philippines when friends or relatives dropped in unexpectedly during dinner (we didn't have telephones then), and there would always be a plate for them. If they were out-of-town guests, the family would cook even if it was their last chicken, goose, or duck to feed the unexpected guest.

"Greg and Ricky, they are a ridiculous couple. You are our guests tonight. They could come any time."

Wally's description about his friends being a ridiculous couple stirred my imagination.

Hmm...a couple, and they were both males, I repeated to myself.

I looked at Danny, who sat across the dining table from me. Our eyes locked. We read each other's thoughts. We were both tongue-tied and doubting Thomases at that moment. And Wally had read our minds.

"Yes, they are gay, and have been living together for quite some time," he further revealed.

What an eye opener for us! I grew up in the Philippines where gays were laughed at and ostracized by society and the church. Living together as a couple? That was a "first" for both Danny and me.

As I became engrossed in Ricky and Greg's story, a flashback of my high school friends Frank and Kit suddenly appeared in vivid colors. Frank and Kit's close and unusual friendship gave the Catholic bees in my barrio something to buzz about, more so because Kit was gay but Frank wasn't. But instead of honey, the buzz created tragedy. Frank's love for Kit was pure. But Kit's love for Frank was sinful. The vicious chatter that had gotten louder as time went on bothered Frank's conscience. One day he severed his ties and stayed away from Kit completely. Fragile Kit became inconsolable after the breakup. Eventually he killed himself by taking rat poison. Frank mourned the death of his friend for many years. He married late, well into his forties, and had kids.

Silence was golden, especially if it was timely. And the moment was fitting. I kept the story to myself.

Our minds had hardly absorbed Greg and Ricky's story when another culture shock came halfway through dinner.

"Wally, pass the bread, please," Heather, the daughter, asked her dad.

Did I hear what I heard? I was talking to myself again.

"Here," Wally handed her the basket of dinner rolls.

"Thank you, Wally," Heather said nicely to her dad.

By that time I had figured out that Heather had addressed her dad by his first name. After being raised in the Philippines, I had a hard enough time calling my supervisor at work by his first name, no matter how insistent he was about it. Now, here was this girl behaving so casually toward her father. It was the '70s. I deduced perhaps what I had witnessed was the influence of the hippie culture that swept the U.S. during the previous decade.

I pretended to check on my children's plates to mask my uneasiness. I was so thankful when Wally started to ask about our immigration to the United States.

"It was a very long process. I had applied for a professional visa in 1968 before I married Danny."

"How long did it take you before you were able to immigrate?"

"A little more than four years. Although my application for a professional visa was approved within six months after it was mailed, the visa processing took almost four years."

"Long wait, wasn't it?" Wally was in agreement.

"Yeah, but we almost missed our chance had it not been for some divine intervention."

"What do you mean?" Bertha was now all ears.

"Well, in 1969 we moved from Manila to Sumacab. We had filed for an address change at the U.S. embassy, but the barrio postman didn't recognize my new last name. For months our letters sat in the Post Office's dead letter file. Luckily, one of my students at the university who was working there recognized my name on the list of letters to be returned to senders. The envelope that had the U.S. embassy return address also had the word FINAL stamped on it. He sensed the importance of the letter, so he took it upon himself to hand deliver it to me." It was a long explanation but I sure held their interest.

"Good for you and your student," Wally quipped.

"Actually, yes and no."

"Oh?"

"He hardly had attended any of the classes during the semester; naturally, he failed most of his exams. So I flunked him. I couldn't pass him even if he had done me a great favor. It was against my grain to give students grades that they didn't deserve." I heaved a sigh after my last word and for the first time since, I wondered what had happened to him.

"What would have happened if that letter had been returned to the

Nieves Catahan Villamin

U.S. embassy?" Wally now couldn't wait for the next word to come out from my lips.

"I could only imagine. The letter required us to provide the U.S. embassy a qualified affidavit of support to prove that we would not be a liability to the U.S. government. In doing so, we had to update our tax records and property title. We had to conserve our money for more important expenses, so we didn't heed the advice of many to grease the wheels of our government service so it would turn faster. As expected, the completion of our required documents took much longer than usual."

"But you weren't asking them a personal favor," Wally was genuinely surprised to hear about that part of my story.

"We also had to go through a thorough medical examination to ensure we would not be carrying any disease into the United States. And finally, that nerve-racking interview where we were cross-examined about our place of destination because I was in the early stage of my pregnancy. I thought we wouldn't make it. By the time we were awarded the actual visa in early September 1972, I happened to be seven months' pregnant."

"Really? Wasn't it dangerous to fly at that stage of your pregnancy?" Bertha's face expressed astonishment.

"Probably. But even if I had been nine months' pregnant then, we would still have flown. We were very determined and we didn't know any better." My last statements elicited a hearty laughter.

The long table conversation had made the children bored and restless in their chairs, especially Heather. Her mother had tried to calm her down and agreed that she could leave the table after dessert, but the young girl was in no mood to listen. Instead she responded with a scream loud enough to be heard in Manila. Followed by another. And another. Danny and I felt uncomfortable, but we did not interfere.

"Enough. You are going to bed now." Her mother excused herself and took the girl to her room, leaving her there to watch television. There was no attempt at discipline. The mother merely had calmed her down and promised a toy-shopping spree in the morning. As we watched all this unfold, my mind had traveled back to Sumacab. I knew how Tatang would have dealt with that young girl. Belt or slippers? No television. No promises of toys. That was for sure.

Before the 70's decade was over, Danny and I had been fully integrated into the American way of life. Our whole family was nicely

Bittermelons and Mimosas

dressed, lived in a small but comfortable house with the latest home appliances, drove our own cars, visited nice places on weekends and holidays, and almost every Friday had lunch at an "all-you-can eat" seafood restaurant on Fruitvale Avenue in San Leandro. (The all-you-can eat crab planted the bed where cholesterol thrived and gave us problems twenty years later.) With the indoctrination came a new version of a song from the animated movie *Snow White and the Seven Dwarfs* that we hummed everyday with smiles on our faces on our way to work; "I owe..., I owe..., off to work I go."

I STILL REMEMBER OUR neighbor Esteban, a transplant from the Ilocos province, whose naive imagination kept us amused for many years. Esteban had a couple of uncles that immigrated to the United States in the mid '50s. When Esteban visited his Ilocano folks during the holidays, he had always brought back to his children *pasalubong* or gifts such as chocolate candies and colorful cotton shirts labeled "made in the U.S.A." He also had often flaunted a couple of bills in his wallet which he said came from his immigrant uncle. We repeatedly watched his children eat their chocolate candies wearing their new and "stateside" shirts from our window. "*Ilokano kasi,* that's why they never shared," said our elders. Esteban had told us after his Ilocos' visits, "in the U.S. money grew on trees and my relatives are pickers." Not exactly his words, but that's how we interpreted them. With the bills and goodies he brought back from Ilocos, we grew up believing that notion.

Having chased hunger as far as we could remember, we children dreamt of becoming "money tree pickers" someday also. Some of us even told our parents that maybe they too could grow a similar tree in their backyards. But my idealist farmer father had dismissed the idea and told us, "perhaps there is such a tree in the U.S., but a tree would not yield any fruit if you hadn't planted it right and cared for it properly. And depending on Mother Nature's many moods, harvest could either be bounty or dearth." My father was right. One day we found out (I don't remember the circumstance), from Esteban also, that his relatives worked as apple pickers in the Washington state area.

I would understand Esteban's active imagination to a greater extent after we had immigrated to the U.S. and started the vineyard/winery many years later. Yes, in the U.S. money does grow on trees, in our case, vines. We grow, pick, and make wine from our grapes to sell. Our back-breaking work is often rewarded with award-winning vintages produced from our vines. (Thinking about it now, I wouldn't be surprised if the "money tree" dance as part of a Filipino wedding reception, where guests pinned money on the bride and groom's clothes during their first dance, had been concocted by Esteban's Ilocano folks' active imagination.)

When Danny started his woodworking business in July, 1978, I thought that having the appropriate skill and being in the right time and place was better than planting a tree and waiting for a harvest of gold and silver that may never crop up. For two decades, the bustling construction industry in the Bay Area had kept Danny busier than the morning traffic on Hesperian Boulevard in Hayward during rush hour. His custom-made cabinets were featured in a number of houses constructed by the Blackhawk Development and Broadmoor corporations, two of Danville's best. He built conference desks for Cisco and Xerox corporations, and teller counters for a number of start-up banks around the Bay Area. His business had prospered so quickly that on weekends, my two girls (in exchange for the "all-you-can-eat" steak, sometimes with lobster, at Black Angus, and ice cream sundaes at Baskin Robbins on Hesperian Boulevard) and I helped him build the cabinets. To keep up with the demands of his growing business, Danny tooled his one-man shop with modern equipment and machineries.

In May 1981, I accompanied Danny to Germany where he made his biggest purchase, an edge bonder, directly from the factory in Frankfurt. While I toured the city, he attended a two-day

Bittermelons and Mimosas

woodworking and machinery workshop to learn the proper use of the equipment as service calls could be very expensive. After Germany, as a treat for ourselves, we explored parts of Western Europe outfitted with a big canvas bag, a Minolta camera, and the mighty Eurail Pass. Mostly by train, we started our trip in Germany on May 23 and ended it in London on June 20, 1981, 39 days before the royal wedding of Prince Charles and Princess Diana. We covered 14 cities (Amsterdam, Holland; Brussels, Belgium; Paris, France; Madrid and Barcelona, Spain; Geneva, Switzerland; Monte Carlo; San Remo, Rome, Venice, Pompeii, and Sorrento, Italy; London, England) by train, sometimes sleeping at the railroad stations.

The sidewalk cafés in Paris and the gondolas in Venice were sights to behold. The blessing by the Pope from his balcony in Rome after being serenaded by an Italian inside a bus on our way to Sorrento and being warned about pickpockets in the area was very spiritual. Walking on the ruins in Pompeii brought us back to the times of Emperor Titus of Rome before Mt. Vesuvius erupted in AD 79. The miles and miles of blue water and clean beaches along the French Riviera that surrounded the principality of Monaco (we stopped in Monte Carlo and gambled a little) awed us. But to our chagrin the Madrid leg of our trip turned out to be a shame. I still remember the conversation we had with the taxi driver on our way to a first-class hotel in Madrid, where we decided to spend a day to catch up with our sleep and do laundry.

After looking at the piece of paper where we wrote the hotel's address, the taxi driver asked in his broken English, "This right address? First class hotel, eh?"

"Yes. We got that from the information booth at the train station."

"Okay we go."

The taxi sped up. Danny and I started feeding our eyes with history.

"Maybe you make mistake?" The taxi driver couldn't help himself.

"No, why?" We were getting impatient with the questioning.

"This is very expensive hotel. You domestic helpers, right?" He was eyeing us through the rearview mirror.

Nieves Catahan Villamin

Monte Carlo, Monaco. Danny and I gambled and lost.

Anne Frank's building in Amsterdam, Holland.

The B&B in London where we stayed for a few days.

Ticket for the 2-day seminar.

Vatican City, Rome. Blessings from the Pope through the window.

Bittermelons and Mimosas

"No, we are tourists, American citizens."

"What?"

The taxi driver assumed we were domestic helpers, a job common among Filipino immigrants in Spain. That, in addition to the Philippines being a Spanish colony for over three hundred years, perhaps made him think that way about us.

Our four-week trip was very gratifying considering we had only been in the U.S. for nine years, and in business for two. But the photographs Danny took always reminded us that we made the journey. We were deep in debt after the trip, but hey, business was great so we weren't worried. However, it would be the first and maybe the only pleasure trip that Danny and I would enjoy together outside the United States (except the Philippines), perhaps for the rest of our lives. As the children grew up and went to college, our priorities had changed dramatically.

IN MARCH 1983, I got a surprise call from my friend Nene Joson, who was then living in San Francisco. She informed me that Mrs. Susana Liwag (my high school advocate) and her husband Manuel have been in the U.S. visiting their children and would like to see me.

I had last seen Mrs. Liwag in 1965, a few days after the vehicular accident that snatched away my sister Macaria's young life. Feeling nostalgic about my school, which I passed on my way to the hospital, I had decided to stop on my way back to check on former friends who might still work there. I chanced upon Mrs. Liwag instead, who now owned and managed a rural bank in addition to her vocational and academic schools. A barrio girl who made good, she was respected and admired by the whole community because of her natural business and administrative savvy. She helped pioneer rural banking and used the industry to launch agricultural reforms such as giving loans to farmers during the planting season. This protected farmers from falling victim to usurious practices common at that time. The exact opposite of being a banker, Mrs. Liwag was a strict disciplinarian as a school administrator. She was every pupil's nightmare, known for leaving her students under the sun for hours as penance for making *bulakbol*

Nieves Catahan Villamin

(playing hooky) during school hours. This she did in the name of love, as she wanted her students to succeed and have a better life just as she did. She was a high flier and never had a problem juggling work and family, day in and out.

Mrs. Liwag had heard about the accident, for it had been on the radio for a couple of days. I remember seeing her loving and tender side for the very first time. She offered me her condolences and, to my surprise, a job at the school library even though three years had passed since I had attended the school. I thanked her politely, then updated her about my studies in Manila, and left. Whatever unpleasant memories I had of her from my high school days were replaced swiftly with tender ones.

"We are here to appeal to you for financial support for our poor students." Mrs. Liwag stopped my trip down memory lane. We had just finished lunch and were sitting on lounge chairs in the backyard enjoying the breeze. Mrs. Liwag still looked like she did during my

L- R: Pete Joson, Mrs. Susana Liwag, me, Nene Joson, and Bert Pajar.

high school days, as elegant as a queen, and pristine like the white-pinkish roses blooming in my garden.

"You know how scholarship grants helped you in high school." Her husband Mr. Liwag (still the mestizo and good-looking man that he had always been) helped plead the cause.

Bittermelons and Mimosas

His reminder took me back to the time after my college graduation when I made a pledge to myself that I would help others if I made it, a promise I had set aside because I wasn't ready yet to share what I had with others. They left with happy hearts as I had agreed to start a scholarship program in 1985. Our collaboration lasted only five years. My old school was reduced to rubble by a strong earthquake in August 1990. Shortly after, Mrs. Liwag followed the school's demise. The school was never rebuilt after her death in 1992.

WHEN THE CHILDREN WERE toddlers, we had taken them to Sunset Beach in San Francisco and watched firework displays one Fourth of July. This never happened again because the almost four-hour non-stop traffic from the beach to the Bay Bridge, with the children complaining they needed to pee, made my husband swear he'd never take us back there again as long as he lived. He made good on his promise. Many years later, on a day in July of the year 2000, Edna and I discussed over the phone my 55th birthday that was fast approaching.

"Mom, do you like fireworks?" she asked.

Are you kidding? Of course I do. Fireworks remind me of home," I told her.

"Then it's settled, you and Dad will fly here on July 3. The next day we will shoot fireworks on the street and drink wine coolers with the neighbors."

"Aren't fireworks illegal?" I asked her.

"Not in Portland," she answered.

Portland had been home for Edna and her husband for the past few years. Except for the wine coolers, it was like being a kid again because fireworks were a happy part of my Sumacab childhood. Therefore, I was thrilled when she decided the best gift she could give me for such a significant milestone in my life was to recreate that part of my childhood, which she knew I cherished.

Edna had brought Mocchi along when she fetched us from the

Nieves Catahan Villamin

Portland airport on July 3, 2000. As they walked toward us, Edna kept a firm but gentle grasp on the dog's leash. I remember it was the same way she held her first chocolate ice cream cone when we had walked to a Baskin Robbins in downtown Oakland. I had to admit, Mocchi and my daughter looked cute together, like one of those calendar pictures.

"What a strange-looking face and unusual body. What kind of a dog was that?" I had mumbled, just loudly enough for my husband to hear.

Mocchi was a basset–German shepherd mix. Her big body that rested on four short legs wiggled like Jell-O when she walked. Edna had found the dog meandering at a camp outside Portland looking dehydrated and sickly. She took the sickly dog home and nursed it back to health. She named her Mocchi, after her favorite Japanese glutinous rice dessert.

"Sshhh. Hold your tongue. You know how sensitive Edna can be," my husband whispered back.

It wasn't love at first sight among the three of us when we were introduced. Still, we decided to play along to avoid ruffling Edna's feathers.

"Mocchi," my daughter tugged Mocchi's collar gently, "meet Grandpa Danny."

Danny stooped down and shook Mocchi's paw. "How do you do, Mocchi?"

"Wwurrpp, uurrppp," Mocchi barked. Her tail wagged faster than a helicopter propeller. I could only guess that in Mocchi's language that meant, "Nice to meet you, too."

"And this is Grandma Nieves," Edna said, turning toward me.

"Hello there, beautiful *adobo* (meat cooked with vinegar, soy sauce, garlic, peppercorn, bay leaf, and vinegar) dog," I said, with a teasing smile on my face. It was perhaps like in the middle of a London blitz when her angry outburst went on.

"Mom, how could you describe Mocchi as food? Did you really eat dogs like what the white people thought? Bad enough I had been called 'fish head' when I was in high school because my parents liked eating fried dried fish! It's worse that white people also teased me about Filipinos eating dogs!" I saw anger overtaken by hurt expressed in her eyes because of my insensitivity.

"I'm sorry, *anak*, I am just joking," I apologized. She was right. Thinking about food when I saw Mocchi – how could I do that? Easy. My husband and I were raised in a culture where dogs were not a man's best friend. They were hardly considered pets, especially among the majority of the poor, who barely had food to cook in their pots at supper.

During our stay in Portland, however, I saw how my daughter pampered Mocchi. The dog's signature brand food was always fresh and warm and served in a disinfectant-cleaned ceramic bowl. The dog drank filtered water from the faucet also. Edna had even bought her an antique round chair upholstered in exquisite velvet fabric for her daybed. A red antique chair – I would never buy such an item just for a dog to curl up on.

Danny and I left Portland with our attitudes toward animals a lot better than when we came. We have had several pets since then. Like Mocchi, all the other pets that have left us (Greta, Bantay, Jack, Ian, Snowy, and Satchmo) were honored with tears of affection and memorial of prayers, songs, and love poems after they had been buried down the hill in our vineyard.

Chapter Sixteen

The Sukob Years

Who else would know but you?
Of your mysteries God Almighty,
All passages on this earth,
Happen with your blessings.

Anonymous

Ten years had passed since the year of the *sukob* in the Catahan and Villamin families. I didn't remember anything happening that could be construed as a result of the curse of the *sukob*. I was beginning to think it was all a concoction of our elders' active imaginations. In December 1977, five years after we immigrated to the United States, we returned to visit Sumacab. Danny, the children, and I spent Christmas and New Year's Day in our old house, which by now was occupied by Mila, Rene, and their four children.

It was glorious to see them, and our house was in mint condition, looking better than when we left. Rene knew carpentry and he had made many improvements to the house since they moved into it. The family seemed to be enjoying a good life because Rene had a regular job as a jeepney driver in Sumacab. He made good daily wages and never had to be away from my sister and his children for days as he had when we were still neighbors.

We didn't see any sign that Rene was sick during our stay. And if he ever was sick, my sister never mentioned a word to us. I refused to think that they hid his illness because he didn't want to spoil the vacation we had anticipated for six years.

✣ Bittermelons and Mimosas ✤

An opportunity arose for us during our vacation in Sumacab. A parcel of the Cajucom farm was offered to us for sale. It was the same area where once the mighty *balete* tree stood. The tree that was the home of the mystical *kapre*, whose lit cigar provided light to Tatang and his HUK friends during their family visits to the lowlands.

Danny and I didn't think twice about buying it with Mila and Rene in mind since we knew couldn't farm the land ourselves. The yield would provide my sister and her family with additional income. Their lives could only become better. And to make sure the plants would get watered regularly, Danny had a well built at the heart of the farm before we left.

We returned to the United States feeling good about what we had accomplished during our short visit. The flavor and aroma of the traditional food Rene and Mila fed us during the holidays had barely left my palate, yet I already felt homesick for Sumacab.

The girls were in school, their first day since we got back. Danny was opening our three-week-old mail spread across the entire glass top of our dining table when a knock sounded on the door. I was in the kitchen preparing lunch and I heard him mumble about a registered letter the postman had just delivered.

"Oh, was that the postman knocking?" I asked.

"Yes. What the heck do you think this is?" He was holding a five-by-seven manila envelope in one hand.

"Where's it from?" I asked.

"My employer, MB Designs. It must be important because it's registered." I could see he was worried.

"Open it so you will find out," I urged him. I felt as if the world caved in when Danny read the letter to me. He was fired from his job because he hadn't come back on time. The company had lost bids on new contracts. (Many years later, Danny and I had come to realize that being fired from his job was the one of the best things that had happened to him. He started his own woodworking business within that week and never looked back.) We hardly had recovered from the shock of Danny's termination when word came from Sumacab that Rene was very sick. At first, everyone dismissed it as a bad case of flu. After several tests, the recurring chills and fevers were explained by something far more serious – large tumors on his lungs. Hoping for a miracle, Rene had surgery, even though the doctors feared it would accelerate the growth of the cancerous tumors. After a few days, the surgery seemed successful and Rene gained back his strength. Then a relapse occurred and Rene died just before his 33rd birthday in May 1978. We were with him January that year. In May the same year he was gone!

Overwhelmed by her sudden loss and the burden of feeding four children, the youngest barely a year old, Mila plunged into a deep depression. To buoy her grieving spirits, I sent her back to school the following year for her bachelor's degree. The rest of our family provided for their daily subsistence. Later that same year, I also started a petition for her to immigrate to the U.S. as she had become eligible by being a widow. She was my sister and took care of Edna for a year when we left for the United States. It was my turn to help her. After almost ten years of waiting, Mila was granted an immigrant visa.

With a bachelor's degree behind her, she felt optimistic about her immigrating to the States. I bought two tickets for her and her oldest son. The other three children would be petitioned after she found a stable job. We anticipated their arrival the day after Christmas in 1987. When the phone rang the day before their scheduled flight, I expected the call to be about their flight number and time of arrival. Beth, my nurse sister, instead said that Mila and her son would have to fly after New Year's Day because Mila had a fever. We thought the difficulty of leaving her three children behind had made her ill. I could well understand, having been in that position myself.

New Year's Day came and went, and Mila remained sick. Her condition worsened in spite of the up-to-date treatments she got. By mid-January, doctors at the hospital broke the grim news to my family: Mila was very ill and might die soon. I decided to fly immediately to see her before it was too late.

For the very first time, my cultural values were questioned and put to the test. My supervisor rejected my request for a one-month leave of absence, but I left anyway. I told myself I could always find another job, but no one could put a value on the few days I would spend with my dying sister.

On February 1, 1988, a few months short of her 39th birthday, Mila died of pancreatic cancer. The cold reception I got when I came

Bittermelons and Mimosas

back to work was a sign of big trouble looming. Depressed and angry, I left my job before my supervisor could destroy my career and dignity.

The untimely deaths of both Rene and Mila made me think back to those early days with Danny in Sumacab. Eight families in our neighborhood shared one water pump and we all used that water for washing and cooking. Death had taken someone from each family either by cancer or abdominal problems within the decade that followed. My own family had used that water for three years, and my two children were affected as well. (Both are fine today, but how do I explain what happened to them?) Were all these trials the curse of the *sukob*, or was it just happenstance?

Mila and Rene are gone. (Of course, some of the experts might point to Rene and his work with DDT.) I do not claim to have the answers. Yet, to this day, I wish that Mila and Rene had waited to marry. With all the challenges we had overcome, I can only imagine what kind of life we would have had if we hadn't left the Philippines.

Chapter Seventeen

The Rest of the 20th Century

What God has joined together
let no man put asunder.

Matthew 19:6

The "baggage" we unknowingly carried with us from the Philippines was a good enough reason to consider education a "holy word" in our household for many years. On hundreds of occasions we stressed the importance to our children of possessing a college diploma. We did this every chance we got, especially when they shifted their focus more to Nintendo games and sports rather than school. My husband lectured the children every so often; his continued sermon wore the children out, because it sounded like a litany of prayers at the sound of the church bells at six every evening.

The new MTV–Reebok–Big Mac world handed us a slight culture shock. This so-called open society and lax attitude between parents and children we saw often bordered on the repulsive and horrific. Danny and I decided that our ways and customs were better, so from the time Edna and Elaine could speak, we began our Filipino training. All was well in the beginning, but as the children were in their teens, they happened to question, and to challenge. It was bad enough that their American schoolmates teased the girls over their ethnic appearance, but soon our daughters wanted to know why they were not being given the same freedom. There were many times when Danny felt tested by the challenge of raising children in an open society, but he never neglected his duties as father – he was bonded to Edna and

Bittermelons and Mimosas

Elaine with unconditional love, but found it very difficult to put into practice. Different upbringings like day and night were bound to clash.

Parenting is tough, but we had a particular challenge as two native Filipinos trying to raise two first-generation Filipino-American daughters in a completely different culture. Our old-fashioned parenting techniques conflicted with what our children's friends were receiving, resulting in family arguments time and again. Edna and Elaine would argue and plead and whine and beg and threaten – it did not matter. No matter how hard they tried, they ended up losing the argument. They were only our children, we'd explain like our parents did to us. They had no right to go against our mandates. Admittedly, we were often baffled to see life the way we did when we were their age. We never questioned our parents. We were not about to let our children question us.

Growing up with a workaholic father, my children were trained to appreciate the value of time especially during the holidays. My husband did not see the logic of buying them surprise presents that might end up being returned. He saw returning presents after Christmas Day as foolish, and a waste of precious time. When the children grew old enough to choose their own Christmas presents, Santa Claus received a pink slip from us. However, although our holidays in the U.S. were more commercialized and less spiritual than the ones I celebrated with my family in Sumacab, I looked forward to their arrival every year because of the children. But since they left home, our Christmas celebration became unexciting and lifeless. Sometimes I do not even put up a Christmas tree or décor anymore. When the children were younger, Christmas meant buying the prettiest tree on the lot and decorating it with the best ornaments, going to church on Christmas Day, and partying with friends until midnight. We always stayed as a solid family before. As my children grew older and wiser, however, they chose their own parties and friends to go with. Consequently, the big dinners after mass were replaced with Christmas brunches at Hilton Hotel. Year after year, our Christmas celebration became less and less traditional.

Nieves Catahan Villamin

OUR DETERMINATION TO LEAVE a legacy of which future generations could be proud was rather intense – admittedly, Danny and I were concerned about how others would perceive us if our children should become failures. We demanded nothing less than the best from our children, deliberately setting very high standards, just as our parents had done with us. They were to be better and to excel at all costs, so we took total and complete control of those critical early stages of childhood. As a mother, the worst situation you can find yourself in is having to choose sides between your spouse and your child.

My husband, bless his stubborn heart, did not want to listen to what I had to say. "They're only kids, Danny. They don't know any better. Please..." My husband would shout back, his eyes popping out in anger, his Adam's apple running double time up and down. "Give them more credit, they are as smart as you are. Don't undermine what I am doing! They are testing how far they can go without being disciplined." He was right of course. Maybe he knew what he was doing, or perhaps we just got lucky; our strict, but loving approach to discipline worked in raising our daughters. I shudder to think of the alternative scenarios with Edna and Elaine running away from home, ending up in a juvenile hall, or even dead. But now that they're older, our children understand what we did, and why we did it. I wonder how they will be with their own children.

In the fall of 1987 many years later, with us comfortably settled in our second and much bigger house in one of the nice neighborhoods in San Lorenzo, my older daughter left for college for her Graphic Communication Degree. She chose Cal Poly State in San Luis Obispo, a university that is only a three-hour drive from home. She wanted to branch out, yet she did not want to be far from the comfort of home, where Mommy and Daddy could come to rescue her faster when she needed help. A couple of years later the younger one enrolled in the University of California in Berkeley, some forty minutes' drive from our house. With Elaine following her sister's footprints, the moment she moved into her own house in spite of the close distance, I knew my children's priorities had changed and my crowning glory as Queen Mother had ended. I also realized they had found their desired niche that would require much of their time and that they would only see Mommy and Daddy during breaks from their busy schedules. Their transformation from happy-go-lucky children to responsible mature adults my husband and I witnessed with beaming pride during those precious visits. Soon our big house was empty. The pitter-patter of small feet was replaced by Audrey's (our Persian Himalayan cat) huffing noise trying to catch her breath in excitement through her flat nose as she ran through the hallway while playing with her fuzzy ball. It wasn't too long before my husband and I couldn't take the silence and memories anymore.

In 1990, we decided to relocate to Creston, San Luis Obispo County. Although we told the children the place was in preparation for our retirement, it was in all honesty a tacit move to get closer to at least one of them. To my heart's delight, our first daughter moved back with us in the new house shortly after. But soon she missed terribly the independence she had already gotten used to and decided to move out of the house the last time. The company of birds and wild animals, and the beauty of nature that surrounded us, helped ease our longing for the children's visits, which became fewer as days went by. Our big house was empty once more and we were right back where we started, just my husband and me, again an unfamiliar land.

In June 1993, Edna received her Graphic Communication Degree at Cal Poly State, San Luis Obispo. She got married the same year. In 1997, Elaine graduated from the University of California, Berkeley, with a degree in Liberal Arts, major in Sociology. Danny and I could not be happier. My children broke the cycle. They were armed and ready to make a name for themselves.

And unlike us, they would reap their worth.

IN 1993, I WENT home to attend my mother's funeral. To my surprise, she wasn't the only one who would be mourned in our neighborhood. Her one-time foe, and later best friend, had died the night before. The morning after my mother died, a commotion accompanied by unearthly cries emanating from the house across the street awakened us.

Nieves Catahan Villamin

"Aunt Ruping, Aunt Ruping. Oh, my God! She's stiff! She's not breathing!" Lolita, one of Ruping's nieces and her neighbor, was crying hysterically.

Beth was the first one to dash out our bedroom door to investigate the noise. I was right behind her. But she stopped me because she first wanted to be sure what was happening. For all we knew, it could have been a bloody fight. So I returned to my bed.

This was the story she told us when she came back upstairs. Lolita, who had been bothered by the sound of water overflowing from the drum, entered the bathroom to shut off the faucet. Inside she found Ruping's stiff body still sitting on the cement floor as if she were taking a bath. She had apparently died from a heart attack a few hours earlier.

The peace between Ruping and my mother that came only during the final months of my mother's life was very sacred. Ruping knew Inang was dying. Perhaps she felt guilty; perhaps she felt the need to make up for lost time. Whatever the reason, Ruping became my mother's constant companion, nursing and entertaining her, even though Inang could hardly recognize her.

"I'd like to dress her," Ruping was insistent in preparing my mother for her last rites.

At first, my sisters objected, but the old woman persisted, arguing that it was very important for her to complete this last act. They finally relented, ignoring the long-established tradition that only close family members could dress a sacred dead body. That first night of the wake, Ruping sat on a chair beside my mother's coffin until her eyelids became very heavy. When the clock struck twelve, she arose and prepared to leave.

"I'll be back tomorrow morning before eight," she promised. She said her good-byes and closed the door behind her and would never return.

Two houses across the street from one another displayed black cloths hanging outside their windows as signs of mourning. Ruping was buried a day before my mother. Everyone thought she was a friend through and through. She made good on her promise because she didn't let my mother walk alone to her final destination. Tatang attended Inang's funeral. My mother's tomb was the last one he erected.

Bittermelons and Mimosas

PART OF THE REASON for my visits over the years after Inang's death involved Tatang, who lived to be 89. Outliving everyone in his family, he grew into a proud old warrior, blessed with a large family and a genuine sense of accomplishment. Even in those final years of his life, he managed to walk short distances around the neighborhood with the use of his cane.

The last time I saw him walking with his cane was on September 9, 2001. I had taken another group of Fil-Am students to the Philippines for a cultural and educational visit. Our group stopped by Sumacab on our way to Baguio City.

I told him before we left for Baguio, "Tatang, I will come back on September 12 and stay for three days so we can talk more. Maybe you can read some chapters of the book I am writing." He nodded.

I didn't make good on my promise. 9/11 happened. The uncertainty of everything, and our families calling and telling us to come home, forced us to cut our trip short. Our group flew back to the United States on the next available flight.

Then Beth's phone call came in January 2002. Tatang was very sick and dying. I took the earliest flight available to the Philippines.

After my luggage inspection at the Manila International airport, we drove directly to the hospital in Cabanatuan. There I would see my father, whom I loved because of his intelligence and valor and misunderstood because of his complexity. Deep inside I felt compassion for him, for not being able for the last time to see and touch the face of the woman he loved.

Chapter Eighteen

Sinners or Saints

Like the measles,
love is most dangerous,
when it comes late in life.

An English Proverb

"There you are! We have been looking for you for hours. We thought you'd been kidnapped," Beth had found me in the hospital's chapel and her loud voice brought me back to my surroundings. Concern was written all over her face.

"Be careful; don't walk alone." My husband Danny had verbalized the same concern to me at the San Francisco International Airport. Kidnappings for ransom by the Abu Sayyaf, a terrorist group in Mindanao, had given the Philippine National Police major headaches over the last few years.

I felt exhausted as if I had just completed a marathon. "I'm sorry I caused so much concern. Let's go get some food. I'm starved," I said. Beth liked my idea because it was about food. Her face lit up brighter than the "forever" Christmas lights draped around our roof.

Except for baths, we hardly left Tatang's side for the next two weeks. The time for me to return to the United States came all too soon. Our goodbyes at the Ninoy Aquino International Airport were shorter than usual. I told them no tears. We could save those for later.

"Please pray he lives a little longer, so we can watch the May

Bittermelons and Mimosas

Arakyo with him, even if it is for the last time." After eighteen hours I was back with my husband in America.

Beth updated me about Tatang's condition by phone almost daily after I returned home. By mid-February 2002, Tatang had actually made progress. He went home from the hospital, and I felt some relief. Still, my phone calls didn't stop. The few times I talked to Tatang over the phone, he asked when I'd be back to visit him.

"In May, so we can watch Arakyo together," I said. "I have not seen Arakyo since I immigrated in 1972."

"I don't think I will live that long." I felt the restlessness in his voice.

Days came and went quickly. It was around 9:30 A.M. on Friday, April 12. In Philippine time, it was 1:30 A.M., Saturday, April 13. I took a day off that Friday to help paint the extension Danny had built to shelter the farm equipment from the coming summer heat. I could see birds and butterflies of rainbow colors dancing around us celebrating the nice weather just as we were. Suddenly, a butterfly flew over and perched on the ledge of the wall I was painting. It was a big orange-gold Monarch. Its wings were spread like a king's cape. The butterfly's sudden appearance gave me goose bumps. Right at that moment, I knew that Tatang had passed on. In our culture, the sudden presence of a butterfly is a form of communication from the dead.

I called out to Danny who was at the other side of the shop, "Bring me your camera. I have to take pictures of Tatang."

"What the heck are you talking about?" He was a little bit disturbed when he handed me the camera. He thought I was seeing things, which on occasion I was known to do because I didn't want to help him work at the shop.

The Monarch butterfly appeared around the same time my father died.

～ Nieves Catahan Villamin ～

"There." I pointed at the insect whose wings seemed glued to the wooden ledge.

Danny was wordless when he saw the colorful butterfly. He didn't laugh when I started to talk to the beautiful creature. He would have done so under normal circumstances. I clicked the camera, then tried to shoo away the butterfly. It sat unmoving.

I was cooking dinner around 6 P.M. that same day when Beth called and gave us the news. Tatang had passed earlier that morning at almost the same time the butterfly visited me! His body would be home soon.

"I already knew it." I told her about the butterfly. We exchanged sobs over the phone.

TATANG'S FUNERAL WAS EXTRAVAGANT. Our barriomates agreed that he was one of Sumacab's great heroes and he should have a big send-off. On the day of his burial, the weather was unbelievably mild, even though it was in one of the hottest summer months. His Arakyo cast and friends, dressed in their colorful costumes, led the procession to the cemetery that included a stop at the church for his last rites. Many, including schoolteachers, relatives, and friends, walked behind the limousine, and a brass band played his favorite tunes during the hour march to the cemetery. Two flatbed trucks hauled the flowers sent by politicians and family friends.

As the casket entered the church for his memorial service, the pallbearers (mostly his grandsons) carried his casket under an arch of swords as if he was one of the military's greats. The church was jam-packed with mourners listening to Kuya Lino's eulogy about Tatang's wisdom. He shared the incident that before breathing his last, Tatang asked all the grandchildren to gather around him to hear his last sermon.

"How do you build a fire in the middle of a rain?" Tatang asked them.

The children looked at each other thinking he was hallucinating because they knew there was no way a fire could thrive in the middle of a rain. But the elders knew that Tatang's mind was clearer than one of the summer skies in April. He had always talked like a philosopher,

Bittermelons and Mimosas

so that question didn't surprise them at all. How I wished I had been there so I could have responded to Tatang's question.

I knew he was talking about his children's determination to succeed in spite of the odds. I knew he was very proud of that, and that he had always talked about our accomplishments to anybody who would listen.

"How would you put inside a drinking glass the contents of a water jar without a drop of water spilling over?" Again, the children looked at each other, confused at what they were hearing from the old man.

Hearing the children recount the incidents, however, made me feel as though my father was telling us that he understood our anger and that he was asking for our forgiveness for all the hurt he had caused our family. It would have made his last hours glorious had we vocalized our appreciation for his guiding us during our struggles instead of showing anger because he abandoned our mother at the time she needed him most. I knew he had been proud of us because Tatang's parting words were even more truth seeking. Tatang was the *tapayan,* the "bigger man."

After the church services, the procession continued to the cemetery. The thought of Tatang being gone forever finally hit me when I saw other people, not my father, preparing the grave for burial. In my younger days, I had seen Tatang as a tomb builder, not an occupant. As I looked around, I saw the little monuments he had built with the help of the barrio people for those young and old – neighbors, friends, his brothers and sisters, his HUK comrades, his children (Ateng Macaria, Rene, Mila), and finally, Inang. I could not stop my tears. I could see his legacy everywhere. Our neighbors' houses, the school, the church, the cemetery graves – they had all had been constructed with the help of his skilled hands.

An era was gone. A legend had passed on. What made him such a complex man? I know I will never find the answer to that question. Of one thing I am certain. I am very proud to be one of his daughters. My love for him keeps me motivated to preserve his memory. I want to make sure the people in Sumacab remember him for many years to come.

My dear parents, whom we loved because we owed them our lives. Were they sinners or saints? God would place them on their rightful thrones.

Chapter Nineteen

Breaking the Cycle

Mighty oaks from little acorns grow.

An English Proverb

I once left my daughter behind for over a year in order to pursue a dream in a new land, and I had to leave my beloved Sumacab permanently to find a better life for my family and myself. As difficult as those choices were, I know both were the right decisions. It is remarkable how things sometimes turn out. I traveled thousands of miles away to search for a different life, only to come back to the agricultural roots I had rejected so many years ago.

After our two girls finished college and left home, my husband and I moved to Creston on the Central Coast of California in August 1990 and became farmers/vintners (not my choice), a vocation he first referred to as a hobby. Most friends who visit call our current residence located halfway between Los Angeles and San Francisco "a paradise." Unlike in Sumacab however, farmers here own their land and make their own wine.

Sitting on our porch on a weekend spring morning, I visualize familiar scenes as I look down the flatlands. Instead of Bill, our neighbor, working on his 20-acre blueberry farm, I see my brother, Diko Unti, and Kalakian, our family's loyal *carabao*, plodding through the rice fields. At a distance, Bill's tractor reminds me of Kalakian pulling the plow with Diko Unti coaxing behind. I hear Diko Unti's voice soothe a tired Kalakian after hours of work and not Bill swearing at his tractor

Nieves Catahan Villamin

because it won't start. Bill's crew, paid by the hour, stand around waiting for instructions; and Bill's frustration grows by the minute.

For a moment, I hear, "Tsk, tsk, tsk. Good job, my friend, good job." Diko Unti whispers to Kalakian as he tethers the *carabao*'s rope to a tree for pasture during their lunch break. Kalakian wags his tail happily and bends his head to feed on the grass.

Then I realize it's my neighbor's voice. "What is the matter with you, Tractor? Why can't you be reliable?" A frustrated Bill screams, grunts, and then kicks the big machine.

"When was the last time you oiled my engine, Bill?" the tractor seems to holler back. "Last month? Or some time last year?"

Creston, my Sumacab in the States, reminds me very much of the place where I grew up. I am surrounded with familiar things. The vineyard substitutes for our vegetable farm. The cattle, especially the ones with horns, are as big as Kalakian. The hot weather and cool evening breeze, the blue skies, the company of birds and wild animals, the fresh air and clear water from the deep well, the spring flowers that crowd the hill slopes, the pristine surrounding. These all make me feel at home and connected with almost everything around me.

IT TOOK ALMOST THREE years for Danny to relocate his woodworking business at our new address as everything moved slowly in San Luis Obispo County because of the building moratorium due to the drought. From getting permitted to the actual construction (that included flattening two hills as the first one didn't work out) with the help of a local contractor and my daughter Edna, Danny's cabinet shop became operational in fall 1993. He operated his business in the Bay Area on weekdays so I lived alone at that white house on top of the hill. With our front gate always locked especially during the period of construction the neighbors stayed away. Once his business was moved completely, he

Bittermelons and Mimosas

was able to focus on securing and improving the property. By fall 1995, we were settled finally. We were ecstatic because his business was doing well in spite of the change in location.

It was during those trips to the Bay Area to deliver jobs when he discovered the enjoyment of watching vineyards come to life in the agricultural areas where we lived. However, I had misgivings when the vines caught Danny's fancy and he began to dream of planting some, disguising his idea as a newfound hobby. The "hobby" took life in December 1995, when our neighbor Kate, an Irish widow, hosted a Christmas party at her big house on her 350-acre ranch, just as she had done religiously in the past. (We received invitations the previous years but had never gone.) She invited all the neighbors within a 20-mile radius.

We had been living in Creston for almost five years already, yet we have not met most of the neighbors before. That night, we made the acquaintance of most of them. When Danny shook hands with Bob and Doris and heard what they did for a living, his face lit up. Bob and Doris were experts in operating vineyards. They farmed 20 of their 160-acre spread with grapes. Danny didn't waste any time and started to badger Bob for lessons in planting grapes. Hardly having gained his acquaintance, my husband was already pestering Bob to teach him about grapes.

"Growing grapes seems logical because I have the land," he told Bob. "I'm challenged and intrigued by the business."

"That's not good enough to be a vintner. And besides, between the vineyard and a full-time job, I hardly have time for anything else, much less to time teach," Bob said.

"Maybe I could start it as a hobby."

"It would be a very expensive hobby," Doris joined in the conversation and also tried to discourage Danny.

However, Danny didn't stop his "inquisition." He followed Bob like a hound dog around the table, as Bob filled his plate with food.

"What part of 'No' don't you understand?" Bob blurted out to Danny at one point. He was now irritated and he showed it.

Danny got the message and came back to where I was sitting and enjoying my food. Although he had been rebuffed, he still looked like a boy who was just handed a new toy. Something was wrong here! Danny was just turned down and was still all smiles? I started to panic.

Furious was an understatement. I was raving mad by the time we got home from the party. "What do you think you are doing? I thought we came to the United States to break new grounds, not to plow old ones!" I shouted at Danny.

But Danny was unmoved. He ignored my anger and went to bed without saying a word. I could swear he slept with "that" smile on his face.

A vineyard, like any other kind of farming, is a risky venture. I knew that too well. I moved far away from Sumacab as far as the United States to avoid being a farmer's wife! I wanted nothing to do with grapes. What made it chancier was that Danny was urban bred and had never even planted a tomato plant in his whole life. In my mind, that put the equation more out of balance. As when we immigrated to this country in 1972, all he had were guts and a lot of faith.

Danny would not be dissuaded. In early February 1996, we drove to Napa Valley and the neighboring areas to find out how hillside vineyards were being crafted. Just as a trumpet announces the start of a race, that trip signaled the beginning of his adventure in growing what some farmers called "green gold."

A week after the Napa Valley trip, Danny bought an antique Caterpillar tractor and started tearing up the hillside in our backyard. He frequently worked from before dawn to almost midnight. Sans moonlight, he used a Coleman lantern to provide light as he mapped out his dream vineyard. From down the hill as I waited for him to come home, I could see him and his Coleman-lighted tractor from the window of our "mud room." It had the appearance of a giant, alien firefly slowly making its way through the darkness to return to its mother ship. Danny's persistence in creating a vineyard made our neighbors call him "the crazy Filipino that lives up the hill" behind his back. At the time, I wholeheartedly agreed that the phrase truly suited him.

Bittermelons and Mimosas

Eden Canyon Vineyards

Danny, me, my friend Pura Dumandan and award-winning artist Don Dumandan. Don would have painted the landscape had he lived longer.

Nieves Catahan Villamin

By late fall of 1996, he was ready to plant with or without help from anybody, although still he occasionally bugged Bob for advice. One day in mid-spring, Bob relented and agreed to help Danny start his vineyard. Danny was overjoyed. As the first sign of new life sprung from the vines, our respect for Bob and Doris also sprung forth. Up to this day it has not ceased.

Eventually Danny's legs refused to walk up and down the hill, and he added an ATV, which he named "Horse," to his fleet. To this day it makes me laugh when I think about his telling me "Horse" was for me so I wouldn't step on snakes on my walk up the hill when I helped him in the vineyard. Ha, like the sound of the engine would chase snakes away from my path. But maybe I could drive fast and run them over. Yukkk! I told myself. Deep inside, I knew it was his tacit way of telling me he needed my help to get his so called "hobby" going.

For the next five months Danny worked like there was no tomorrow. He toiled at the cabinet shop a few days each week to finance his "hobby." And for the rest of whatever time he had left, he was at his vineyard placing stakes in the ground beside each vine and putting in a drip system. At the dining table each night, after a double dose of intense physical labor from both jobs he hardly sat still and enjoyed his food. But he never complained; he was always very happy at what he was accomplishing. When his body hit the bed around midnight, nothing, literally nothing, could wake him up. Sometimes I wanted to yell "Fire, Fire" to test if he'd rouse from his bed. But I had to control myself because there was this Filipino proverb, *"lokohin mo na ang lasing, huag ang bagoong gising* (you can tease a drunk but never someone who has just woken up)." I guessed an interrupted sleep could make someone crazy enough to commit an unthinkable act. And I was the only one with him at the house. So I chose to be extra careful.

I helped him mostly on weekends. That's all I could do because I had a full-time job. It was necessary for one of us to be a benefited employee so that we had health insurance coverage in case we needed it. (And the need came in October 2000 in a way we never imagined.)

The afternoon in late spring after we planted the last rootstock,

Bittermelons and Mimosas

Danny was over the moon. As we retired that night, I felt like a pancake being tossed and turned, as I lay awake in bed, tired and anxious. All the bad memories about my childhood experiences came rushing back and made me fearful. As he had immersed himself more deeply in the pursuit of an established vineyard, aka hobby, I became more frightened for both of us. Whhhaatt iiifff???? The "if" happened during a few days in August 1996 when some of the tendrils were starting to race down the wire trellis.

The Highway 58 fire started small, but the Santa Ana wind nurtured it, and the fire grew huge and almost unstoppable. When the fire was finally put out, it had devoured without mercy thousands of acres, including our vineyard. The stakes made of steel and smoke from the burned rubber drip irrigation system were all we could see remaining on the hillside. Undeterred by this disaster, Danny wanted to replant immediately.

"This is it. I'm out of here." To preserve my sanity, I considered leaving him.

I knew my husband too well. He was and always had been a very determined person. He often joked, "Don't get in my way because I will run over you." Joking or not, I didn't want to stick around to find out if there would always be a first time!

Still, I guess I truly am my father's daughter. The idea that someone else, not me, might sip the juice of our labor of love made me reevaluate my plan. Therefore, I decided to jump on his tractor, and I prepared myself for the bumpy ride ahead of us. By the time he replanted in 1997, I was with him all the way. After 18 months, we had our first real harvest in the fall of 1998. The vines, growing in soil made richer from the embers, thrived and bore quality fruit. I was very happy for my husband because a local winery paid a premium price for our grapes.

"Hhhmm, he wasn't a lunatic after all," I told myself.

As Danny completed the first phase of being a vintner, I began my volunteer job as the advisor of the Filipino-American club at Cal Poly University. I worked on campus as an administrative analyst at Campus Dining, one of the university's auxiliaries. It was a revelation for me when I learned from some of the students that their ancestors were farmers recruited by the Dole Pineapple Company to work in the Hawaii plantations during the early 1900s. Their ancestors' children had moved in the mainland and also worked in many fields (like us in the Philippines, most didn't own the farm they toiled in) of California and other states after the Hawaii migration had stopped. As a result of the backbreaking work they had endured to put food on the table, the second-generation farmers decided to send their children to school to break the chain, so to speak.

"Wow...same story, different times, different places." I often told myself. I knew Danny's heart was in it as I repeated the stories that I heard from the students to him.

I was happy with work and my volunteer job and Danny's cabinet shop and his vineyard were both flourishing. So, I thought we're going to make it just fine. I began looking forward to the weekends when I could be with the grapes. Seeing the pampered healthy vines made me feel so good. Sometimes I found it hard to leave the vineyard even though dusk had began creeping over the hillsides as I made my way down to our house.

From the beginning, I knew the person I married was not an ordinary man. In the same vein of belief, I accept that miracles do happen, some as what we call coincidences. On October 17, 2000, my husband handed me another challenge. This would be the most difficult of all.

"Mom, I just talked to Dad on the phone. He wasn't making any sense. I think he's very sick. Go home and take him to the doctor." It was our daughter Edna's very worried voice on the answering machine in my office. I had just come from a brief meeting with my supervisor and had missed her call by only five minutes. I made a quick call to Danny to find out. He was talking nonsense as if his screws were loose and he was ready to fall apart. After telling my supervisor about the situation, I ran out of my office, terribly worried.

Danny had had a stroke, and we caught it just in time!

Several days earlier, Danny had asked Edna to buy some sweatshirts from Nike, her employer at that time. Edna had called him to

Bittermelons and Mimosas

confirm sizes and colors. Why did my daughter call that Tuesday morning instead of the day before, or the night before? I don't even want to think what could have happened had my daughter not called him that morning. My husband, who was surrounded by heavy-duty power machines, had worked alone in that big shop since he moved his business to Creston. It was one of those miracles in the form of a coincidence. I knew that is what it was!

I knew how he had arrived at that point. But he wouldn't admit he was always stressed out, overworked, and not eating right because he was always in a hurry.

"Nonsense," he said. "I have just been dealt some bad luck. You'll see, I'll be up and working in no time." He adamantly refused to be sidelined by anything, even a stroke.

The next few weeks were a revelation of how miserable our life could have become if Danny hadn't fully recovered. For a while, he couldn't remember many things, even simple addition and subtraction. Ask him a question and had I clocked his answer, it would have run 120 miles per hour. His tongue worked faster than his brain. I thought we would be in that bleak situation for the long haul.

I thank God because He made Danny understand and accept his situation. But Danny would not be Danny had he allowed himself to be sidelined by his condition. He fought back with a vengeance. He attended a couple of sessions on speech and occupational therapy to learn the basics. Then, everyday, he practiced inside his big shop: talking, singing, and even occasionally debating with himself. He astounded his doctors with his full recovery. He was back on his feet after six months, feeling mightier than before. (I took a leave of absence for a few weeks so I witnessed what he had done to get better quickly.)

Danny, my ever-optimistic husband, decided we would crush our own grapes in spring of 2002. He had this notion (I have no idea who planted it in his brain) that his grapes would produce award-winning wines. Danny also said he was bored, again, and needed a new challenge. "We'll just try to see if our grapes can stand on their own inside a bottle," he said, wearing a mischievous smile on his face. I hated that particular smile because I knew it indicated he had something cooking. He talked also about "breaking the cycle" as he was planning his next move.

"Oh, you want your freedom now that you found your true calling?" I tried to derail him with this accusation.

"What a dingbat you are," he said laughingly.

It would be futile to try and stop him. "Here we go again," I thought to myself, but I never verbalized it. We refinanced the property for the second time, the first when we replanted in 1997, to finance the building of a winery. We extended the cabinet shop squarely by another three thousand feet. One end was the lab and the other end was the warehouse. The barrel room in the middle occupied the largest square footage of the winery.

In 2004, our younger daughter, Elaine, quit her six-figure paying job in the city and joined her father full-time in running our wine business. We regard her as the face of our wine label.

Now in my golden years I am settled to the life I had despised in my youth. "How could I let this happen?" I have asked myself a million times since we bottled in December 2004, the date when Danny's hobby came full cycle. However, our family's collective adventure made history we never dreamed about. Eden Canyon Vineyards is said to be the first Filipino-American estate winery in the United States. That was what Danny meant when he told me, "he wanted to break the cycle." He wanted to go beyond where other early Filipino farmers in the United States had gone before. And he accomplished it. We may not reap the financial rewards of our endeavors during our lifetime. However, we are pleased just the same knowing we shall leave our two girls a legacy they can be proud of.

In my head, I can hear Tatang's remarks made many moons ago: "Once a farmer, always a farmer." He knew I would miss our simple life and humble beginnings and eventually would try to recreate them because I would come to realize they meant the world to me.

I traveled half the world to escape being a farmer's wife, only to find out later that it was my destiny. Deep inside, I was happy to be one.

Bittermelons and Mimosas

Planting grapes is now more fun,
Pruning vines 'till set of sun,
Light green blooms then purple fruit so fine,
Juice from these grapes becomes ambrosial wine.

A Letter From My Father

~ Nieves Catahan Villamin ~

<Tagalog>

August 29, 1997

Nieves,

Natanggap ko ang sulat mo at ikinararangal kong kayo ay maguing bahagui nang mataas na karunungan sa daigdig na ito kung kaya at hahalawin ko ang ilang bahagui nang aking nalalaman ukol saiyong kahilingan. Sisimulan ko ang kasaysayan nang Catahan Family ang aking ama Brigida Catahan ama nang Brigido, Pedro at Valintina Badiola ina. Ang aking ina Catalina Sebastian ama nang Catalina Melencia at Sebastian at Juana Cabrera ang ina at ito ay pawang taga Sumacab. Ang Catahan family ay nabuhay nang hindi masyadong mahirap nguni at salat sa karunungan kung kaya at nang sko ay lumaki at maaari nang magaral ay pinangarap kong magaral at matuto sapagkat noong panahong iyon ay pitong grado lang ay maari nang magturo. Kaya't siyam na taon na nang ko ay makapag aral dahil malayo ang eskuelahan halos may tatlong kilo metro ang layo at ito ay nilalakad lang namin. Naguing mainam naman ang sking marka at nang ako ay ika lima nang grado ay sa Cabanatuan na nag aaral nguni at July pa lamang ay natiguil na ako at nagkasakit ang aking ama at wala nang makapag-sasaka kaya natiguil na ako ng pagaaral. Kaya at ito ang aking pangarap nasiya kong naguing batayan kung kaya at kahit na lang ako ay isang mahirap na magsasaka ay hindi ko inagaw ang panahon nang aking mag anak upang sila ay matuto at hinihiling ko natulungan ang hindi nakatatapos at nag-tagumpay ako. Hindi ko guinawa ang tulad nang ibang magulang na kapag ang anak ay maaari ng pakinabanagan ay hindi pagaaralin at kakatulungin na lamag sa trabaho at ang iba nanam ay ipina aalila sa pinagkakautangan at kung may trabaho na ay kinukuha pa rin ang bahagui nito kahit na lang may familia na ang anak. Ito ang katangian nang ating familia. Isang mahirap na magsasaka na halos marami ang nakatapos sa pagaaral sa pamamagitan nang sipag at talino.

Bittermelons and Mimosas

<English Translation>

August 29, 1997

Nieves,

I received your letter and I am proud that you will be a part of the higher education of this world so I will try to select some parts of my life that I know per your request. I will start when the Catahan family, my father Brigido Catahan, father Pedro Catahan and mother Valintina Badiola. My mother Catalina Sebastian, father Melencio Sebastian and mother Juana Cabrera were all from Sumacab. The Catahan family lived not very poor but lacked formal education, so when I was growing up I dreamt of going to school to learn because at that time, a seventh grade graduate could already teach. So I was nine years old when I studied because the school was about three kilometers far and we only walked. My grades were good and when I was in the fifth grade I studied in Cabanatuan but I stopped in July after my father got sick and nobody could farm. Since then it was my dream and my mantra that even though I am just a farmer I would not deprive my children the time to learn and requested them later to help the ones who hadn't finished school and I succeeded. I didn't do what other parents did, such as when their children was able enough they forced their children to get a paying job, and the other children did servitude to the people who lent them money and even if the children had a family of their own, the parents still took a share from their children's earnings. This was one distinction of our family. A poor farmer with children that had acquired higher education through industry and talent.

Nieves Catahan Villamin

<Tagalog>

SA PANAHON NG HAPON

Nang dumating ang hapon kinukuha ang kabuhayan marami ang pinapatay at pati nang ating kababaihan ay pinagsamantalahan kung kaya at nagtinding ang bayan una ay itinatag ang UNITED FRONT. Pagkakaisang hanay laban sa hapon sa bawat barrio ay may isang balangay na ito ay may pang bayang balangay may pang lalawigan at may pang bansa. Sa bawat balangay kukuha nang mga boluntaryong sundalo upang pagsamasamahin sa isang kompanya nakung na kung tawagin ay JOINED FORCES at ito ang kung tawaguin ay HUKBALAHAP at ang nagdadala rito ay ang Pagkakaisang hanay o ang bayan kung kaya at sa guitnang Luzon ito ang unang guerilya na lumaban sa hapon. Ang mga ibang guerilya ay nakatago at kung kaya lamang lumitaw ay noong pumapasok na ang Hukbong Amerikano at sila ang sumalubong at sa wakas ay sila pa ang naguing kalaban ng HUKBALAHAP at iilan lamang ang kinilala nang pamahalaan sa mga sundalo nang HUKBALAHAP dahil sila man ay wala rin noong namiminsala ang mga hapon. At ang pinakamsaklap pa nito sinimulang durugin ang HUKBALAHAP at ang mga organisasyong nagdadala rito at guinawang ilegal ang PKM o ang pangbansang kalipunan nang mga magbubukid sa Pilipinas ako noon ay pangulo ng PKM sa Sumacab nang aking mga kasamahan dahil umiiral na noon ang pulitika kayo inamin kong ako ay PKM nguni at tinalikuran kong hindi ako ang pangulo kung nakapagbibigay man ako nang bigas dahil sa takot dahil ilang na lugar ang Sumacab. Palibhasa ay may uri nang pulitika kaya at nang wala silang mabigat na ebidensia para sa akin ay hinango ako ni Andring Quimson na koncehal noon sa paniniwalang makukuha na nila ako nguni at nagkamali sila dahil sinunod ko rin ang gusto ko.

ARAKYO

Ang Arakyo ay mula sa pangalan nang tao na kung tawagin ay HERARKYO na Bantay sa kabundukan sang ayon sa among orihinal. Ang aming guinamit dito ay pawang paniniwalang Katoliko

⳽ Bittermelons and Mimosas ⳽

<English Translation>

DURING THE JAPANESE OCCUPATION

When the Japanese came they confiscated our harvest and killed people and raped our women so the town organized the UNITED FRONT. Unity against the Japanese in every barrio, then town, then provincial, and finally country level. Volunteers from every level had banded together and called themselves JOINED FORCES and became the so-called HUKBALAHAP under the UNITED FRONT and in Central Luzon they were the first guerillas who battled with the Japanese. The other kind of guerillas that came out from hiding and welcomed the American forces became enemies of the HUKBALAHAPs which weren't recognized because the American forces didn't see them fight the Japanese forces. And the most bitter part was when they tried to suppress the HUKBALAHAP organization and made it illegal, also PKM (PAMBANSANG KALIPUNAN NANG MGA MAGBUBUKID, or NATIONAL ORGANIZATION OF FARMERS) which I am the president in Sumacab, because of politics I did not admit to being the leader and if I had given my share of rice was because of fear because Sumacab then was sparsely populated and an open field. Because of politics though lack of evidence I was imprisoned and was helped to get out by Councilman Andring Quimzon believing I would take their side but they were wrong because I followed my own conviction.

ARAKYO

ARAKYO originated from the name HERARKYO, who was a guard of the mountain according to our original script. We used the Catholic teachings of the cross where Jesus

Nieves Catahan Villamin

<Tagalog>

kung paanong ang Kruz na kinamatayan ni Kristo ay makita ni Elena dahil ito ay tinabunan at guinawang bundok ng mga Hudio at sa ibabaw nito ay tinayuan nang Simbahan na ang pangalan ay Venus ito ay binabantayan ni Herakyo at may mga sundalo siyang *kasama* at siya ang pinaka puno nito dito ko hinango ang kasaysayang ito na aming guinagamit na orihinal hinango sa iabt ibang orihinal at hinango sa banal na kasulatan at maguing sa passion man ay si Elena ang nakakita sa pinag baunan nang kruz ni Kristo sisimulan ko kay Elena si Elena ay anak ng Haring Romulo nang Roma namatay ang hindi naisalin ang korona kung kayat sa pamamaguitan nang hunta nang konseho ay isinalin kay Elena ang korona kahit ito ay isang babae napangasawa si Elena nang Haring Costasio na hari sa Constantinopla naisip ni Costasio na guyerahin ang Jerusalem na ang hari ay si Masensio na ito ay moro nguni at kinapos palad si Costasio at napatsy nang mga moro si Elena naman ay kabuntisan kay Constantino. Kung kayat nang namatay na lamang si Costasio ay ipinagbilin kay Heneral Lusero na kung lumaki ang anak nila ni Elena ay isalin dito ang korona kaya at nang lumaki si Kostantino na anak ni Elena ay isinalin ang korona ni Costasio at guiniyera ni Constantino ang Jerusalem at napatay si Masensio na Emperador nang Jerusalem kayat nabihag ito ni Constantino at si Elena naman pinagsabihan sa pamamagitan nang isang boses nang angel nang Dios upang hanapin ang Kruz na kinamatayan ni Kristo. Kaya guinamit ni Elena ang kanyang mga soldado nilupig nila si Herakyo at sampuo nang kanyang mga sundalo na Bantay sa kabundukan hinawan nang mga sundalo ni Elena ang bundok guiniba ang simbahan hinukay ang bundok at dito nakita ang krus ni Kristo.

Sa wakas ay maraming kumusta na lang sainyong lahat. Kulang pa ang sulat kong ito. Kaya sumulat kang muli kung ano pa ang Kailangan.

Tatang Margarito Catahan

Bittermelons and Mimosas

<English Translation>

Christ was nailed and after being found by Saint Helena was buried and the site was made into a mountain of the Jews and a church named Venus was erected on top of it, guarded by soldiers led by Herarkyo as the basis of the script, and also from different writings based from the Holy Testament and from the Pasyon Saint Helena was the one who discovered the cross. Saint Helena was the daughter of King Romulus of Rome and when King Romulus died Helena became the ruler even if she was a woman and later married Costasio, who later became the King of Constantinople who fought a war with King Masensio of Jerusalem who was a Muslim and Costasio died and left Helena pregnant with Constantine who when he became king avenged his father's death and conquered Masencio and in her dreams Helena heard the voice of an angel telling her to look for the cross where Jesus Christ was nailed to his death. So Helena took many soldiers fought and defeated Herakyo and his guards and they cleaned the mountain took down the church and dug the mountain where they found the cross of Christ.

In closing I am extending my regards to all of you. I don't have everything here. So write again for whatever you need still.

Father Margarito Catahan

Chapter Twenty

Epilogue

Once there were green fields, kissed by the sun.
Once there were valleys, where rivers used to run.

The Brothers Four

The Sumacab of my youth is now only a shadow of its former self, having been transformed from the rice-roots up as the next generation became educated and prosperous, branching out into different endeavors. People from other provinces, uprooted by the recent volcanic eruptions from Pampanga and floods, took permanent residence in Sumacab with their relatives. Furthermore, most children of Sumacab's baby boomers never left home even though they married someone from out of town. The population grew so

Pampanga River and its surroundings have been transformed.
This is how it looks now after a flood.

much that Sumacab had to be divided into three barrio districts: Sumacab Norte, Sumacab Sur, and Sumacab Este.

The river and its surroundings have also been transformed. The once mighty river now seems small and humble, its course altered, the vegetation almost decimated, and the surrounding landscape permanently changed. The acacia, *kamatsile*, and *sampalok* trees are no longer standing along the riverbanks, all casualties of time and progress.

The amount of land assigned for vegetable farms and rice fields has shrunk tremendously with new concrete houses rising out of the fields, and a landfill has claimed part of the yellow winding brook. The hectares of farmland that stretched beyond the river still produce turnips, watermelon, eggplants, tomatoes, yams, and string beans, but none is as big or as healthy or in as many shapes and colors, as when I was growing up. The cornfield that was once a part of our homestead was destroyed by land erosion.

Once a month, the magnificent full moon and a galaxy of twinkling stars still adorn the sky, though I doubt they dazzle young people of today the way they awed me when I was young. In my memory, the moon and the stars illuminated the entire barrio. Today, however, the barrio is equipped with electricity, and the streets are flooded with the harsh glare until early morning hours. Karaoke machines and noisy voices replace the traditional serenades on the guitars.

The *dulang*, where our family shared meals while my mother talked to us about good Christian virtues and family solidarity, and which was once the focal point of every family's supper, has been replaced with a carved narra dining table with matching upholstered chairs. Today, the modern narra dining table and its matching upholstered chairs merely serve as décor. Modern family members have no time to discuss life during meals. They have individual suppers in front of televisions. The tenet that in Christian teaching says, "The family that prays together, stays together," is now rapidly fading as well. Today, very few families say their rosaries together.

Gone are the days of solidarity. Filipino families do not stay together anymore. Even the Sumacab bachelors have changed completely. They still gather during the evenings, not for the purpose of discussing their problems on the farms or serenading their maidens, but to drown their loneliness and frustration in many bottles of San Miguel beer while idly playing cards or mahjong. The honorable moral code followed by the bachelors of years past has disintegrated, and bachelors of today have replaced it with gambling, drug addiction, and other forms of pleasure-seeking, in great contrast to their predecessors.

With water irrigation, machinery, and cultured seeds, the farmers are able to cope with the erratic weather. The improved farming brought additional harvests and increased income to farmers. However, this new method also polluted and killed many natural species in the brooks, rivers, and rice fields. Most significantly, it killed the tradition that brought families together and the work that united them. Gone is the ideal spirit of *bayanihan*, where once upon a time the entire village would work as one solid family.

Today, each family tends to its own business, and sometimes neighbors do not even know each other. Gone is the *patanim*, the practice where mostly *dalaga* and *binata*, unmarried women and men, of the barrio, planted rice. Today, individual farmers do the rice planting mostly by sowing the *palay* seeds.

Gone is the virtue of *utang-na-loob* (indebtedness). Once, if someone asked your help, you were happy to oblige because your parents taught you it was the godly thing to do. I recall Tatang telling us repeatedly when we were growing up, "It's better to give than to receive, and remember, you're worse than a snake if you bite the hands that feed you." Tatang lived by this example when he invited his HUK friend Kanor (a.k.a Razon) to move their house close to ours so that his "cousin civilian guard protection" would be extended to them. This was his way of showing gratitude to Pascual, who had once saved Tatang's life. Pascual and Kanor are relatives. People are indifferent nowadays. Their memories are short in regard to integrity but long in regard to deceit. Any mention of earlier favors might set them off and have them accuse you of keeping scores, and sometimes even to the point of repudiating your good intentions.

Gone is the *gapasan*, a practice where cutting ripened *palay* was done voluntarily through *batarisan* or *bayanihan*. Today, mostly family

Bittermelons and Mimosas

members with the aid of some machinery do harvesting *palay*. Gone are the friends and neighbors piling up the harvested *palay* into large mandalas for the huge mechanical rice thresher. The harvested *palay* is no longer piled into mandalas, and threshing *palay* is done by small and mobile threshing machines.

Gone is the traditional *pipigan*, where the *binata* and *dalaga* pounded rice flakes. The rice flakes were then toasted and added to a native delicacy cooked with coconut milk. Today, the barrio people rarely prepare native delicacies. They have abandoned this treat for pizza and hamburgers. The *halo-halo* booths that lined the street in front of the church during fiestas and Holy Week are all gone, replaced by modern small cafés and mini-stores.

Gone is the place where we harvested and roasted corn on an open fire beneath the acacia trees. Gone are the small treehouses we built using twigs and branches from the acacia trees. Gone are the fish and shellfish that were once abundant, as pollution has muddied the once clear and pure river.

Gone are the beautiful and special people who influenced my childhood and taught me common sense: my parents, Mila and Rene, Ateng Macaria, Aunt Senang, Aunt Didang, Aunt Elena, next-door neighbor Ruping, Spinster Sena, Kanor, Jolly Purok, Eccentric Agaton, Uncle Lope, Uncle Melchor, and two of my childhood friends, Nora and Naty. Their absence always tempers the joy I feel today when I visit Sumacab. I miss these beautiful and special people whenever I go home. I miss them all so very much.

Perhaps in my next life, I will be reunited with the extraordinary people and places whose influences on me radiate far beyond the boundaries of my daily life. Hopefully, I will again witness Sumacab's dazzling full moon and hear young men singing love songs to their maidens throughout the night. Once more, I will be energized by December's perfect weather and lulled to sleep by the heavenly music of birds in symphony with the gentle wind made fragrant by wild flowers.

It is encouraging, however, that despite being divided into three sections, the barrio becomes united again during the holidays. The changing tastes and times have caused deviations from the traditional holiday celebrations. Although they have become a showcase of who has what, the festivities still focus around our Catholic religious practices. Every Easter, all three districts dutifully observe Holy Week, although shorter now in version.

The Catahan family still religiously oversees the yearly production of Arakyo every May 6 and 7, just as it has since the late 1950s.

The barrio fiesta on November 24 and 25 honoring Saint Catalina, our patron saint, is still the most celebrated holiday. Every family still spends lavishly on food like there will be no tomorrow, and new parents still present their children to be christened at the barrio church after the morning high mass on fiesta day. Children still tail the marching band as we did in the old days, in spite of their mothers' warnings of the dangers from motorists.

The candlelight procession before sundown, when we chanted Latin songs and prayers with the *manangs*, has become shorter and has mostly teenage participants. The *zarzuela* that was filled with rich values and traditions, the one I used to watch with my friends until early morning, has been replaced with modern variety shows that corrupt the minds of the people.

Just remembering the nonstop cascade of firecrackers and the roar of homemade bamboo cannons on New Year's Eve makes my heart beat faster. I feel like a kid again.

Like the changing of the course of my friend, the Pampanga River, the customs and traditions I grew up with have evolved with the passage of time. Every time I visit Sumacab, I think about ways of reviving the old traditions. However, I know deep in my heart that it is only a matter of time before the culture I have roots in will be hardly recognizable.

Dear Sumacab, my Sumacab. I will love you until the end of time.

✧ Bittermelons and Mimosas ✧

THE TWO WORDS THAT best describe my family are hardworking and passionate. The hardships our family endured during my father's HUK days gave us an unwavering passion to improve our lives no matter what it took. Our parents were the best parents anybody could have. It adds to the equation that most of us were supportive of each other's dreams. None of my education would have been possible without Kuya Lino. He spared me from a thankless life in the fields, and I will always be grateful to him. Like the domino effect, a succession of educational quests by the second-generation Catahans followed. The third generation is on its way up the ladder as the older and successful ones help them.

Kuya Lino put his own education to good use. He taught social science at De La Salle University in Manila for many years after earning a Ph.D. in educational administration from Pacific Western University in Los Angeles. Prior to teaching, he spent 20 years abroad as a human resources developer, one of roughly ten million Filipinos whom the government calls OFWs (Overseas Filipino Workers). OFWs are scattered around the world, many of them in good-paying jobs. OFWs send much of their salaries home to family. At one point, more than half of the national income of the Philippines was derived from people like my brother sending money home.[1]

In 1973, Sanse Conchita immigrated to Canada as a seamstress

---

[1] The immigration history and socio-economic development of the Philippines have been closely linked to the United States after it was ceded by Spain in 1898. The Philippines later gained their independence in 1946. In the early 1900s thousands of young Filipino men were recruited for the thriving agricultural industry in Hawaii and the West Coast. They arrived as laborers, mostly in agriculture and domestic service, and as students. Between 1907 and 1931, nearly 130,000 Filipinos, mostly males, came to the United States. As of 2011, an estimated 9.4 million or 10% of the Philippine population made up the Overseas Filipino Workers (OFW) count. Their remittances, a major generator of foreign exchange, have been instrumental in helping the Philippine economy offset foreign exchange outflows. OFWs' remittances, which have grown rapidly throughout the years, helped turn the negative GDP into a positive GNP. As a tribute to them, President Gloria Macapagal changed their title to Overseas Filipino Investors (OFWI).

Nieves Catahan Villamin

My father walked my sister Beth during her graduation ceremonies. The first to receive a Nursing diploma, Beth was the first nurse in our neighborhood.

Kuya Lino, a.k.a. Dr. Marcelino Catahan, Ph.D. in educational administration.

Sanse Conchita

My sister Mila

Bittermelons and Mimosas

and filed a petition for Luisito, her fiancé. It was granted and they were married in Winnipeg in 1975. Already in their 40s, they never had children. They filed a petition for Ammie, our sister whose legs had been broken during the 1965 accident.

Five years after her arrival in Canada, Ammie married Art, her architect boyfriend, and moved to Edmonton. They have two children, Lora and Mark. Ammie later petitioned Huling's daughter Emily as their nanny. A few years later, Emily petitioned her fiancée and, with her sister Elvira's help, petitioned their parents and three other unmarried brothers.

Conchita and Luisito first adopted Diko Unti's daughter Ligaya, Mila's oldest daughter Liza, and Huling's daughter Elvira. After Mila's death they also adopted my late sister Mila's three other children. My sister and her husband have not stopped helping relatives immigrate to Canada to better their lives. Forty Catahans and Lestones to date have benefited from Conchita's immigration to Canada, with still more coming.

"Not bad for a woman who can only say 'Yes, sir; very good, sir,'" Kuya Lino teased her often during our *balikbayan* visits.

Conchita speaks English very well, even though she only finished high school. That was his way of telling Conchita, "You go, Sanse. I am very proud of you."

Just as Kuya Lino and Sanse Conchita supported my education, I continued the tradition by helping Mila and Ammie when my turn came. Ammie, in turn, helped Beth, our youngest sister.

Through Beth I saw my parents' proudest moments during the two most rewarding events in the Catahan household. The first was during her graduation with a nursing degree. (Only rich people could afford a nursing degree back then.) My father wept with joy after Beth handed him the diploma for which she had worked for more than four years, with Sanse Conchita and Ammie's financial assistance. The second and ultimate one was during the ceremonial nailing of her plaque as a registered nurse on the outside wall of our house after she passed the board exam. Beth's nursing degree was a significant milestone for the whole family.

Nieves Catahan Villamin

Three of Diko Unti's eight children immigrated to Canada, and four of Ditse Clarita's six children had chosen Canada to be their homes also. Most of them immigrated to Canada with their professional visas. Their parents had worked long hours in the fields to ensure their children a good education. And succeed they did indeed.

Led by Kuya Lino, our family's "Moses," the Catahan younger generation's exodus from the barrio life continues through education and immigration to other countries to this very day. A lawyer, a CPA, two teachers, four engineers, a couple of computer science majors, and many more that immigrated to Canada through professional petitions and adoptions are testimonials to the "movement" my brother spearheaded.

To my gratification, a few from the younger generation chose to stay in Sumacab rather than leave their loved ones for the possibility of a better life in a foreign country. "There is money to be made here also." They are the few of the many who I trust will continue Tatang's legacy in Sumacab after we children are all gone.

Bittermelons and Mimosas

Natatanging Anak ng Cabanatuan Award. L-R: Mayor Jay Vergara, Senator Richard Gordon, me, and my sister Beth Sarmiento.

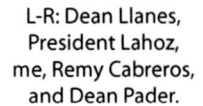

L-R: Dean Llanes, President Lahoz, me, Remy Cabreros, and Dean Pader.

TIP Commencement Speaker, April 10, 2008.

Nieves Catahan Villamin

My high school scholars during the early 1990s.

My Sumacab college scholars early 2000. Standing L-R: Lito and Leonie Ramos, Monica and Armando Catahan, Remy and Boy Francisco, Mr. and Mrs. Temboy Sagun, Ellen and Mely Catahan. Scholars sitting L-R: Angelito Jr., Edith, Jeremy, Everlyn, and Elmer.

My high school scholars during the mid 80"s. Second row third from right: Mrs. Susana Liwag and me.

WOMAN OF THE YEAR

Students included in honor

By Spencer Marley
MUSTANG DAILY STAFF WRITER

Students will be able to receive the Woman of the Year honor for the first time since its conception in 1995. Nominations are now being accepted for the award that features student, faculty and staff selections.

Coordinator for the Pride Alliance center Maya Andlig oversees the event that will culminate with a ceremony on March 8.

"We are trying to honor women who go above and beyond their professional responsibilities on campus," Andlig said.

Administrative analyst Nieves Villamin received last year's staff award. Villamin's role as the Filipino Cultural Exchange adviser combined with her humanitarian efforts made her an ideal recipient. She organized and aided in the construction of school facilities in the Philippines.

This year's awards will also feature a luncheon and silent auction. All proceeds from the event will support women's programs and sexual assault prevention programming.

Business senior Jessica Cardinale organized this year's Woman of the Year award and luncheon.

"It's a good opportunity to recognize all women who have made a difference on this campus," Cardinale said.

Sister Mary Pat White from the Newman Catholic Center will be recognized in a new community category.

"We haven't had the chance to recognize members of the community, and Sister Mary Pat will be a first," Andlig said.

Nomination forms are located in all residence halls, University Union, Kennedy Library and the Women's Center. All forms must be received by today. Nominations can also be e-mailed to cpwomensprograms@yahoo.com. They must include the name of nominee, category and a one-page essay on the woman's contributions.

> **Woman of the Year**
> • Award was first introduced in 1995
> • This year students will be eligible for nomination
> • All forms are due TODAY

2003 Cal Poly Woman of the Year Award article.

Addressing guests during a Fil-Am History celebration at Cal Poly. At the back: PCE President Ken Aquino, and FANHS Secretary Rose Sagisi.

A Reflection on Historical Contexts and Themes in Villamin's *Bittermelons and Mimosas*

Those of us born or raised in the United States probably do not fully understand the immigrant experience. Even those of us with family members who immigrated may not be able to appreciate the challenges. At least, it has always been difficult for me—as a second generation Asian American—to imagine what my parents must have felt or thought when they left behind everything that was familiar and comforting, motivated by what Nieves Villamin described to my students as "hunger." As an immigrant memoir, Villamin's *Bittermelons and Mimosas* provides an individual and intimate perspective of what is often rendered impersonally in the popular American imagination—for example, when immigrants are likened to a "flood" or "horde" crashing the gates of the United States. Villamin's memoir adds complexity to a hackneyed concept like "the American Dream." It describes in detail the personal motivations and the external pressures for immigration. It renders for us what is gained and lost in coming to America. Moreover, *Bittermelons and Mimosas* provides a meaningful reflection on family, home, nation, and other communities of belonging from the perspective of a woman and a migrant and within the context of American imperialism's continuing legacy for Filipinos in the U.S. and in the Philippines.

Villamin is the picture of the immigrant success story. Resourceful

Bittermelons and Mimosas

and tenacious, Villamin goes from being a poor farmer's daughter to owning and operating, along with her husband and daughters, a vineyard and estate winery on California's Central Coast. That this achievement was possible in the U.S. stands in stark contrast to what is possible in the rural Philippines that Villamin describes. There, tenant farmers like her father are subject to the peonage systems of colonial and neocolonial Philippines and cannot enjoy the fruits of their own labor. Against gender and class norms, Villamin doggedly pursues education in the Philippines so that in 1972 she was prepared to take advantage of the newly created pathway to immigrate to the United States. Villamin secures a professional visa shortly after the United States Congress, as a part of a package of Civil Rights acts, finally lifted restrictive quotas against those immigrating from Asia. She also happens to get this visa just as Ferdinand Marcos declares martial law in the Philippines. Villamin and her husband came with only a pocketful of borrowed money and a drive to find a better life for themselves, free from the political and economic turmoil of the Philippines.

Villamin, however, complicates the meaning of success and of American exceptionalism in her reflections on the meaning of home. One might note that the memoir spends the bulk of its pages describing the author's life in the Philippines. Thus, to read this as a typical immigrant memoir—a story of "becoming American" or "making it in America"—would be to overlook what is unique about Villamin's approach and, moreover, what is unique about the Filipino American immigrant experience. As one reads the memoir, one might ask: Who are the imagined readers? What compels Villamin to focus on her cultural, political, and economic experiences of her home in Sumacab rather than her life in the U.S.? How does her representation of Sumacab and its people actually help frame an understanding of Filipino experiences and identity in the United States? Finally, how does the memoir imagine "home" less as a fixed geographic place and more as feeling that is transnational and mobile?

Scholars of Filipino American Studies point out how a unique form of historical amnesia about U.S. imperialism plagues Americans, resulting in a failure to understand Filipinos or the Philippines. Colonization of the Philippines included bloody pacification campaigns (1899-1902) to subjugate the islands to U.S. rule. But because the U.S. was established on the principle of self-governance, the hypocrisy of colonization had to not appear like crass imperialism but a moral necessity—to protect Filipinos from their own supposed savagery. Thus, the colonization of the Philippines required another kind of forgetting: the colonial project would succeed not only by military might but also through an American policy of the "benevolent assimilation" of Filipinos whereby native practices, values, and languages were displaced by American ones. Though the geopolitical battles of the U.S. have evolved (for example, from its fight against Spanish imperialism to its post-WWII fight against communism), the U.S. rise to world power has indelibly, even violently, marked the political, economic, and cultural landscape of the Philippines. Long after Philippine independence in 1946, American military, trade, and cultural and educational institutions shaped Filipino perceptions of themselves and of Americans. Even before setting foot in the U.S., Filipinos already were assimilating into American culture and being severed from their history and their heritage.

The emphasis in Villamin's memoir on the life and people of Sumacab can be read as a challenge to this loss of Filipino history and culture and to the assimilating force of America in the lives of Filipinos both in the Philippines and in the United States. Perhaps this emphasis on the community and cultural life of Sumacab is a way to compensate for what Villamin felt she had to give up coming to America. The memoir portrays her life in the Philippines as one where she is acutely aware of the rich cultural traditions of rural Sumacab. In contrast, it depicts how she leaves this life behind for the exigencies of economic survival in and assimilation to the U.S. as a new immigrant. As Villamin writes, "we learned to bow our heads in silence, socialized a little, and concentrated on our jobs. Most of us immigrated to the United States to find the mighty dollar, not to impose our cultural and political convictions on anyone. We were so focused on being financially sound that teaching our children about our history and our past society was never given any importance." The American dream, then, is pragmatic. But this passage also suggests that this dream simultaneously entails forgetting and loss: not only of one's roots but also, as I am suggesting, of the imperialist legacy that carved out the routes linking the Philippines and the United States.

These conditions, which send Filipinos all over the world seeking opportunities or leave them struggling in the Philippines, affect Filipinas like Villamin on the most intimate level. The memoir consistently sets its stories among family and extended kin who serve as networks of support. Family is also what is torn apart amidst the displacements from home or dispossessions of property. Presently, the Philippine state, unable to provide enough opportunities to absorb its labor force, instead facilitates the out-migration of Filipinos because the national economy relies upon the repatriation of capital from Filipinos abroad, sometimes as exploited or expendable labor. In a country where roughly 10 percent of its population in 2008 worked abroad and where labor is one of its top exports, it is not uncommon to have parents estranged from their children. Villamin's husband risks his safety working in a Vietnam at war in order to provide for his new wife and child. Without a job, housing, or a support network in the United States, Villamin and her husband make the difficult decision to leave their three-year-old daughter behind until they establish themselves in the U.S., a heartbreaking parting that Villamin describes well. The memoir's focus on Villamin's father in particular illustrates a complicated struggle with love, family, national identity, gender, and class. Her father betrays the love of her mother, yet is a heroic Hukbalahap fighter for land reform and for his nation.

Like so many of her anecdotes, the father's story ought to be read both as deeply personal narrative and as an allegory about reconciling the present with the past. The memoir concludes with a statement of its purpose: "I wrote this book for not only you, the new generation of Filipino-Americans like my daughters and the PCE members, but also for your parents, whose sacrifice and dedication need to be recorded." We are thus invited to understand the memoir as an

Nieves Catahan Villamin

attempt to breach the cultural and generational gap between first and second generation Filipino Americans. But by starting with the story of her father as well as with other life mentors in her homeland, the memoir also gestures toward a larger process of understanding the present through the past. Though the reflection back is often nostalgic, Villamin's memoir balances nostalgia against critical reflection and the longing for home against actively redefining what home means for a Filipina migrant.

GRACE I. YEH, PH.D.
Assistant Professor
Ethnic Studies Department
California Polytechnic State University
San Luis Obispo, CA 93407-0662

The Pilipino Cultural Exchange (PCE)

In 1996, the Los Angeles Times reported that Filipinos are the largest Asian population living in California. Also mentioned was that more than two out of five said they have integrated so well into mainstream culture that they have lost their identity as Filipinos. Filipino-American historian Fred Cordova had shared this phenomenon. "You ask a Chinese-American or Japanese-American who they are and they know. Not so with the Filipinos." I didn't have to look further than my own backyard to find clues. My two daughters are living proof of what Fred Cordova was talking about. They grew up as brown English-speaking and western-thinking women who could not relate to my culture and appreciated very little of anything Filipino. It wasn't their fault. I taught them naught about Filipino customs and traditions. Except for a few words, not a speck of my culture could be drawn from them.

History had accounted Pilipino footsteps trekking back as early as 1587, perhaps long before any other Asian group settled in the United States. In spite of us being one of the first, our march toward progress in most areas of endeavors had been slow as compared with other ethnic groups. Most historians attributed this to our history of colonization by Spain, Japan, and the United States. The diversity of genes that came from this mixed bag made us who we are, disagreeable and disunited in ideas and principles. Our academic achievements are above par from most ethnic groups, yet sadly, we do not have a strong voice on matters of Filipino-American issues because we are not united. Until the next generation Filipino-Americans think differently, our progress in the United States as a race will continue to be sluggish.

Nieves Catahan Villamin

There were several who had broken the mold and became well respected for their leadership abilities. As pioneer labor organizers they had fought and succeeded for their brother farmers' better wages and improved working conditions.

The historic Delano Grape Strike began on September 8, 1965, when Filipino-American farmworkers voted at the Filipino Community Hall in Delano, CA, to strike. The Agricultural Workers Organizing Committee (AWOC), AFL-CIO, led by veteran labor leaders Larry Itliong, Philip Villamin Vera Cruz, Pete Velasco and Benjamin Gines, initiated the strike. The AWOC was comprised of mostly Filipino-American farmworkers, who together – over 1,500 strong – initiated the historic strike when they walked off the farms of area table-grape growers, demanding wages equal to the federal minimum wage. One week after the strike began, on September 16, 1965, the predominantly Mexican-American National Farm Workers Association (NFWA) led by Cesar Chavez, Dolores Huerta and Richard Chavez, voted to join the strike at the Our Lady of Guadalupe Catholic Church in Delano, CA. Ultimately, the two groups merged, forming the United Farm Workers of America (UFW) in August 1966. The strike lasted more than five years.

MANONG LARRY ITLIONG — MANONG PHILIP VERA CRUZ — MANONG PETE VELASCO

Gene Viernes and Silme Domingo were children of immigrants who grew up in the U.S. and became engrossed with the problems of their

⚘ Bittermelons and Mimosas ⚘

the Legacy of Silme Domingo and Gene Viernes

parents' homeland during the Marcos regime. Viernes was the son of a migrant worker, who worked in the fields of Yakima Valley in Washington State, and in the canneries of Alaska. Domingo's father and brother were labor activists. He helped them organize cannery workers who were facing discrimination in the workplace. In the 1970s Domingo and Viernes' paths crossed. Like many children of immigrants who grew up in the U.S. who were outraged by the dictatorial regime in the Philippines, Domingo and Viernes became two among the thousands of U.S.-based Filipinos who fought the Marcos government. They were harassed and killed on June 1, 1981, by three assassins who were later arrested and convicted. The families and allies of Domingo and Viernes knew the dictatorship was behind the murders. On Wednesday, November 30, 2011, Domingo and Viernes were added to the roster of heroes and martyrs of the Bantayog ng Mga Bayani – the first Filipino-Americans to have their names included on the respected foundation's Wall of Remembrance honoring those who died fighting the regime of Ferdinand Marcos. Domingo and Viernes, both of whom died at the age of 29, joined the ranks of such respected figures as Ninoy Aquino, Jose Diokno, and Chino Roces.

When we first came in 1972, the competitive block for immigrants was still harder to penetrate even with the affirmative action law. In order to fit in and survive, we learned to bow our heads in silence, socialized a little, and concentrated on our jobs. Most of us immigrated to the United States to find the mighty dollar, not to impose our cultural and political convictions on anyone. We were so focused on being financially sound that teaching our children about our history and our past society was never given any importance. Our children followed our path. With our prodding, they studied hard, found a career, and started their own family. And so it seemed that history in the making would just be a continuation of what their parents had started.

In 1998, I became the advisor for the Pilipino Cultural Exchange (PCE), the on-campus association for Filipino-Americans at the California Polytechnic State University (Cal Poly), my employer for 14 years. During that time, a big change was sweeping the nation. Affirmative action was on its way out, and diversity was knocking in every college's door. Becoming aware of each ethnicity was just the beginning. The Filipino-American students' desire to know about their parents' origins was all the rage. Being a proud Filipino, I was very lucky to be there to lead the students to their quest for their roots. During club meetings students peppered me with questions about the Philippines, covering everything from politics to parenting. They were searching for answers, perhaps to justify their parents' values and decision-making that often played a major part in their adult lives. The best way for them to learn, I decided, would be for me to take them to their parents' homeland so they could experience first-hand the society, customs, landscape, and food, things they may have only heard about in passing from their parents.

Our first trip to the Philippines in December 1999 involved six students who returned home after two weeks, overwhelmed with cultural pride and eagerness to tell other Filipino-American students about the wonders they had discovered. The students' extraordinary experience spawned two more journeys, in 2001, and 2003. Three participants have written an account to share their experiences and how visits had made an impact on their lives as Filipino-Americans.

In 2003, the third batch of PCE members raised seed money and helped break the ground for a Health /Day Care Center in Sumacab. With smiles on their faces, they shoveled dirt and poured cement under the blistering heat of the midday sun. Dr. Barbara Andre, Assistant Director of Cal Poly International studies and an advocate of the study abroad programs, joined our group. Dr. Andre, the PCE students, and I witnessed the signing of an MOA for a three-year Student Exchange Program between Cal Poly and Mapua Institute of

Bittermelons and Mimosas

Technology. Mapua sent three students to Cal Poly the following year. For many years, TIP welcomed with open arms the many Cal Poly students and professors I took there for an exchange of knowledge and ideas. A Faculty Exchange MOA is currently in effect between Cal Poly and TIP. This agreement was the result of a collaborative effort amongst Dr. Taufik at Cal Poly, Dr. Elizabeth Lahoz of TIP, and me.

The award that TIP bestowed on me in 2002 in appreciation of my efforts as one of the very few alumni who didn't forget to look back was very nice. (Award or not, I would have done the same.) However, the invitation to be TIP's commencement guest speaker at the 2008 graduation ceremony was, I thought, cool, perfectly very cool! I had planned to take Naty and Ofelia (we heard Nora died in 2005) with me to hear me speak before the thousands of graduates on April 10, 2008. Regrettably, Naty died in January 2008. Ofelia is still alive, but not well.

To all my PCE friends and travel mates, wherever you are now: I am very proud of you all for having the courage to trace our roots. It was a great honor for me to know that I helped you find your identities. And ultimately embrace them and become proud of who you are. I wrote this book for not only you, the new generation of Filipino-Americans like my daughters and the PCE members, but also for your parents, whose sacrifice and dedication need to be recorded.

Students' Observations During Our Educational/Cultural Trips

It's Hard to Appreciate What One Does Not know

As a Filipino-American who was raised here, I always wondered what my life would have been had my parents not immigrated to the States. After a trip back to the homeland a month ago, I was able to find out. Traveling with five of my peers from our Pilipino club (Pilipino Cultural Exchange) at the California Polytechnic State University, San Luis Obispo, California, and our club advisor, Auntie Nieves Villamin, we arrived in Manila to be greeted by Dr. Lino Catahan. He welcomed us with much hospitality, which I thought was forced since he was Auntie Nieves' brother. Later, I learned that this is a very common characteristic of most Filipinos. Everywhere we went, we were treated like royalty. Whether it was a relative, friend, or stranger, no one ever made us feel like we weren't welcome. Even at ABS-CBN, the TV stars that we met treated us with warmth and respect.

Other places we visited were San Miguel Brewery, The Technological Institute of the Philippines, College of St. Benilde (De La Salle University), Araullo University, Nueva Ecija Science of Science and Technology, and City of College of Manila. Each of them entertained and fed us with more than enough food, which makes me wonder why there are so many starving Filipinos. Although we were always received with such friendliness, I was still saddened to

Bittermelons and Mimosas

see how many Filipinos suffer from poverty. I remember leaving a McDonalds to be followed by several children who begged for some of my ice cream. I wanted to give some but I didn't have enough for all of them. How can such a generous society consist of so many deprived people? I realized that this is the reason why thousands of others came to the states: to live a better life.

A wise man once said that he who cries because he has no shoes has yet to meet a man who has no feet. This trip demonstrated how true that is because very few young Filipino-Americans realize how fortunate they are. We take many things for granted such as warm water, running water, freeways, clean air, and even law enforcement. I hope that one day someone will make a difference in the lives of Filipinos and change that economy around. It's true that one of the main causes of the low economy is the overpopulation that has resulted since the Catholic religion doesn't condone birth control. But it's also true that the Catholic religion is against premarital sex. If the Philippines is one of the most well educated countries in the world with some of the brightest minds, perhaps the education system can inform the youth on abstinence before and after marriage. Perhaps the government can impose laws similar to those in China, enforcing a limit on childbirths per family. Perhaps law officers could be paid more so that they wouldn't accept bribes to ignore unlawful citizens. Perhaps instead of fleeing the country to avoid the chaos, more will try to make a difference in changing trends. Perhaps I don't even know what I'm talking about.

I learned a lot from this visit and I wish many of today's Filipino-American youth may experience this sometime in their life. Maybe Filipino-Americans can do something to help their brothers and sisters overseas.

MANUEL ZARATE
BS Aeronautics Engineering, Cal Poly
PCE 1999

Philippines 2001 Experiences and Lessons

When asked to write a few comments of my 2001 Philippines trip experiences, I looked back on all that I saw and took part in. Realizing now the extremity of our itinerary in such a short period and the planning involved, I appreciate even more the hard work that went on behind the scenes. For us six young Cal Poly college students, Chris, Melissa, Anna, Analyn, Eric, Edison and myself, Dilian, this trip would not have been possible with out Auntie Nieves and all that she had done for us. Her hope of bringing exposure and exploration of the Philippines to those that were interested was a success with my travel mates and me. For this, I deeply thank you Auntie Nieves.

Traveling to the Philippines during my college years was a great opportunity to see my parents' country of origis from a much older and mature perspective than when I visited there before as a child. It allowed me to have my own experiences, make my own judgments and interpretations, and appreciate what I have back at home in America. I could see many flaws in the Philippines, but I also was able to see several beauties and joys of the Philippines.

Disorder is a word that first comes to mind when thinking of Manila, our home base where most of our trips started off. This was most apparent from riding through the streets of Manila, a city I

Bittermelons and Mimosas

would not willingly drive through myself. Drivers run red lights, make right turns from the second lane over, and drive on the opposing side of the road to bypass traffic. Corruption is a part of it as well, seeing first hand a police officer being paid off in broad daylight with heavy traffic from a person pulled over for a traffic violation.

But amidst all this disorder, there actually was some order. Cars would honk to let others know where they were when cutting in or pulling off what would normally be considered in America as a gutsy and inconsiderate move. What was amazing was that cars would come extremely close to each other in what is normal driving there and somehow collisions were avoided.

Poverty was there and not hidden in anyway. Families with kids, even toddlers, have makeshift homes of cardboard and sheet metal built under bridges. Their stove is a fire pit dug in the ground. As we passed residential buildings our driver told us about squatters who take over apartments and do not pay rent. They are not evicted because of the overwhelming number of those that do this and the lack of enforcement.

Bridges that we drove over crossed what are known as "feces" rivers because of the blackness of them and their fill of garbage. The major streets themselves are full of pollution from thick smog in the air and the foul stench of sewage on the ground. And I remember passing through many underdeveloped areas throughout the countryside when going from one major area to another. Roads were often just bumpy dirt paths with no signs of maintenance.

Aside from the many setbacks seen, the Philippines have much to offer. Auntie Nieves was great at bringing us to fantastic locations throughout the countryside. We were in Tagatay where we rode boats on a huge lake created from a volcano crater. In the center of the lake was a volcano island. On the island we took donkey rides up to the island's peak. Everyone had his or her own donkey except for me who had a small passenger ride along with me, a little tour guide no more than 8 years old. At the top, the viewpoints were spectacular with the surrounding walls of the volcano hole.

Other locations included a trip to the cooler city of Baguio up in the mountains, starting with the lion's head to greet us. We enjoyed the horse ride through the streets, the viewing of cadets in formation marching at the Philippines Military Academy and walking through Fort Santiago and taking pictures with some local Igorots. We dined at Villa Escudero where delicious food was served in front of a waterfall and water flowed beneath our feet at the tables.

I also had the opportunity to visit Boracay, which was a tropical island paradise. It is unfortunate the resorts on the island are opened by foreign investors and that money made on the island does not stay within the Philippines. But regardless, Boracay remains a beauty of the Philippines. The identity in the Philippines is difficult to identify. One could say that the Philippines had lost its culture. There was the great influence from the Spaniards before the 1900s. But the Filipinos stood up for themselves and had begun to regain their independence. The people remember famous locations of marches and speeches, and national heroes such as Bonifacio to this day. Some of the spots were pointed out to us as we drove through Manila.

It was reassuring that the there is a sense of pride in their country. However with changing times, it was unfortunate the American influence was soon to follow, and the Japanese invasions of World War II. Driving through the countryside, dilapidated buildings still partially stand where they once were used as whorehouses and rape from the Japanese. Then leading up to this day there have been several struggles in power, guerrilla warfare, separatists, and corruption in politics all making it a struggle to maintain unity within the country.

Coming in to the Philippines, I had a pre-biased view that Filipinos wanted so much to be like the American culture. And this was true to some extent as seen with name-brand clothes that many strived for and the American music and television viewed by the younger generation. Of course a major blame would be the powerful marketing schemes from major American corporations. But with the love for pop music, there is much talent seen with the live band at the Hard Rock Café and the love for dancing, the Filipinos definitely know how to party. The love for America is also felt in tragedies.

The 9/11 attacks were tragic and very dramatic; it seemed almost

Bittermelons and Mimosas

unreal seeing it on television while in another country. But you could see that everyone was very drawn to the news feeling for those who had died. The compassion of the Philippine citizens was exemplified with a speech addressed to the U.S.A. from President Gloria Arroyo.

Looking beyond the pop culture and despite things having come about to the present day, the Philippines is rich with its own culture. Traditional dancing such as the Tinikling is still practiced and presented at festivals and special events. Even little kids practice the dance on the street at a small dance studio. Authentic Filipino dishes, often cooked from the hospitality of hosting families, were extremely delicious with a taste that is hard to match elsewhere.

One memorable night was a casual gathering of the neighbors and the neighbors' kids with everyone singing and dancing on the street. We even performed a ritual like dance using fake swords. Also, an adorable girl and little boy presented a courting dance that brought smiles to everyone's face. Finally breaking off from the group for a few days, I was able to visit relatives. Hanging out with them brings a reminder of how strong family values are in the Filipino culture.

We had a view of some of the education system in the Philippines. We donated a couple of computers to a small elementary and were shown a few classrooms. For most part the classes were well disciplined and energetic in greeting us with a Mabuhay! I was fortunate to see a high school during an activities day and see the students enjoying themselves with fun race games. Then we visited a few different universities, which was most interesting being also college students as well at the time. Observing the engineering department at one college and having an engineering background myself, I was a bit disheartened with the outdated equipment used in the labs.

But where the Philippines may not excel as being a technological influence in the world, it perhaps specializes in other areas. We had visited the agriculture department of another college where we saw extensive studies on rice, a major staple of the Philippines. At the time, research was done on finding natural pesticides for rice and also studies done on the flavors and aromas of different grains of rice. The presentation from Edison on Fiber Optics in front of students

Nieves Catahan Villamin

and city officials sums it up that there is the willingness and drive to learn. The questions asked showed the wanting to improve their city and way of life.

Seeing the Philippines has opened my eyes to other parts of the world and to views outside of America. There are many luxuries that are taken for granted here in the U.S. that I am now grateful for, but have come to appreciate and admire aspects of the Filipino lifestyle. Remembering my trip to the Philippines reminds me to travel more and keep an open mind to the rest of the world. Being a Filipino-American man, a trip to the Philippines is always a great chance to see my roots, where my parents are from and give place to the stories they have told, where traditions, customs, and values I practice today have started. Also, I am able to have a better understanding of what my parents had to go through with what they had to sacrifice to bring us to where I am today. So with all the hustle and bustle here, I would still like to return on occasion to the Philippines. There is so much to do there and it is a good way to help me stay grounded and take things from a worldwide perspective.

DILIAN REYES
BS Electrical Engineering, Cal Poly
2001 PCE member

The Constant Hypothetical Question

When someone asks me what my nationality is, I think to myself, "Well, I was born in California, so I guess that makes my nationality America." But I understand the true intention of their question. They are really interested in my ethnicity, which is Filipino. When asked this question, I typically answer, "I was born in America, but my parents are from the Philippines." Putting two and two together, they infer that I'm Filipino-American.

Growing up Filipino-American has been both a fruitful and yet sometimes confusing experience for me. I was taught Filipino values and traditions by my parents, but in an American society where they are not necessarily applicable and at times contradictory. For example, I was taught to treat elders with respect and consider them above you always. Filipinos are constantly seeking the approval and favor of their elders.

In America, elders are sometimes treated as nothing more than peers. The current generation would rather pursue their own passions and establish their own identity than "live up" to the previous generation's standards. But being brought up the "Filipino way" has also enriched me with a diversity of ideas and perspectives in life. Because of it, I appreciate things like family, education, and opportunity much more. I understand the meaning of sacrifice and why it's important in one's life. I try to never take anything for granted and constantly remind myself to be thankful for all the blessings I have. I've often wondered what my life would be like if my parents had not immigrated to the states. If my mom did not decide at the last minute to join my dad to go to California, I would have certainly been made in the Philippines.

As I was going through school in California, I would wonder what my life would be like had my mom chosen otherwise. I would ask myself, "What courses would I be taking? How would the quality of education compare? What would my dating life be like? What's university life like?" These questions were the primary reason I decided to take a student exchange trip to the Philippines during my college career that was sponsored by the Filipino club of Cal Poly, San Luis Obispo.

September 6, 2001, was the day we embarked from San Francisco for the Philippines. For some of us Filipino-American college students, it was our first time to visit the land of our parents. For others, it was the first time to return home since immigrating to the United States at a young age. And for our Filipino club advisor, Nieves Villamin, it was her second time escorting a group of her students. The plan was to visit historical sites, interact with students in college campuses, meet the locals, and of course, eat authentic Filipino food. In exchange, we would share our experiences as being young Filipinos growing up in America.

There were two places where we would have a chance to interact with Filipino college students: one was in the city of Cabanatuan in Nueva Ecija and the other was at the Technological Institute of the Philippines (TIP) in Manila. In Cabanatuan City, I was asked to make a technical presentation in front of locals and college students from different universities across Cabanatuan and Manila. Since my master's thesis was related to network communications, I decided to share my research in digital communications. I felt that this was an appropriate topic for a third world country that needed improvement in its communications infrastructure. The morning of the presentation, a respected lawyer in town, Attorney Ruperto Sampoleo, and his assistant escorted me. They gave me a brief tour of the city and even treated me to a haircut by a local barber. I was pleasantly surprised by their kind gestures of hospitality. I thought to myself that

Bittermelons and Mimosas

there was no way a foreign college student would be treated this way in the States.

As we reached our destination, I'll never forget the shock I felt when I saw the large banner posted outside the banquet hall that read, "Welcome Edison David, the computer expert." This really put pressure on me to have a successful presentation. But it was a testament to how Filipinos respected the American education system and how they look up to us for advice and new ideas.

After my presentation, I was asked inquisitive questions by professionals in the telecom industry, which showed that they had the desire to explore ways to improve their infrastructure. At the conclusion of the workshop, Ruperto unexpectedly presented me with an award and gifts to show his gratitude for my work. It surprised me a bit because in the States, I probably would have simply received a round of applause and maybe even some criticism. But in a way, I was not at all surprised because showing respect to visiting guests was a custom I've been taught by my parents.

We next visited the TIP in Manila. I remember entering the courtyard of the university and seeing a group of about thirty students gathered outside the door of the room we would use for our meeting. As we waited for the host, I felt tension between our group and their group because we both knew we were here for the same meeting, but neither knew how to introduce themselves.

Although we were ethnically the same, we didn't necessarily understand how to communicate with one another. No one in our group was comfortable speaking in Tagalog and for most Filipinos English is a second language. I never thought it would have been this challenging to interact with people whom we considered our own people. The host finally arrived and opened the door. This visit was a more casual setting than our previous visit. The purpose of the meeting was to simply get to know each other with us sharing our experiences of being Filipino-American students in America and them sharing their experiences of being Filipino students in the Philippines. To break the language barrier, we played one of the videos we used to attract first year students to join our Filipino club during orientation. It showed clips of what our club does throughout the year: spread Filipino cultural awareness across campus by performing cultural dances, songs, and skits. The TIP students reacted well to the video. I think they found it fascinating to see their culture exhibited in another country. I also think that just like us, they wonder what living in another country would be like and the video gave them a small glimpse of it.

After the video, we had a Q&A session where the TIP students asked the questions. The first person asked me if I could perform one of the dances they saw me doing in the video. Unprepared, I humbly declined. The next person asked each of us to recite at least once sentence in Tagalog. I was first in line and rather than making a fool of myself, I got the rest of our group together and convinced them to join me in singing the Tagalog nursery rhyme about a frog Analyn La Guardia had been singing the entire trip. I lip synced while the rest of the group sang. The students laughed at the lyrics and at our attempt of singing in Tagalog. The next question was a more serious question.

A female engineering student first asked if any of the females in our group were engineering majors and if so, what was it like at Cal Poly to be a female in a male-dominated discipline. Chris Miller, a mechanical engineering major in our group, responded by saying that it can be a challenge and at times intimidating, but for the most part, female engineers in California are respected and treated as equals. It seemed that most people in the room were shocked to hear Chris's answer since equality for female professionals of math and science in the Philippines was still far behind the States. This reminded me of my cousin in the Philippines who told my grandfather that she wanted to study computer science and my grandfather responded, "You can't because you're a girl." After our meeting, I asked the director of engineering why females are not encouraged to pursue technical disciplines and he simply said, "I guess it's just the culture."

Returning to the country of my roots as a college student gave me the chance to answer the constant hypothetical question of, "What would my life be like had I been born in the Philippines." I would probably be looking for ways to improve my country, like the telecom

Bittermelons and Mimosas

professionals in Cabanatuan City. Maybe I would be studying engineering at a technical institution like my father and grandfather did before me. I would probably have a strong passion for song and dance like the students at TIP. Maybe I would accept the inequalities of females in technical disciplines or maybe I would fight for my female cousin so that she can have the same opportunities as me. Or maybe I would immigrate to America in search of a better future like my parents did or like the students in the Philippines dream to do.

Either way, this student exchange trip taught me that besides the Philippines being a poor nation and the Unites States being a rich nation, the Filipino students I met were not so different from me. We both share a lot of the same values such as family, education, and career. We both have a passion for music, dance, and theater. And in the end, we're both proud to be Filipino.

EDISON DAVID
MS Electrical Engineering, Cal Poly
PCE 2002

1st Batch PCE Cultural/Educational Trip

L-R: Manny Zarate, Eugene Cooper, Irman Arcibal, Roger Delgadp, Walter Talens, and Irwi Bautista.

First group of PCE students being welcomed at the Manila City Hall.

❦ Bittermelons and Mimosas ❦

First group of PCE students with the St. Benilde De La Salle students.

First PCE group with TIP faculty and staff. Back row, R-L: Mario Herrera, Manny Zarate, Eugene cooper, me, President Teresita U. Quirino. The rest are TIP faculty. Front L-R: Irman Arcibal, Walter Talens and Irwin Bautista.

Nieves Catahan Villamin

First PCE group with the Araullo University Dance Troupe.

First PCE group with NEUST students.

~ Bittermelons and Mimosas ~
2ⁿᵈ Batch PCE Philippine Cultural/Educational Trip

L-R clockwise: Ana Aguila, Chris Miller, Dilian Reyes, Melissa Rillera, Eric Pangilinan, Analyn La Guardia, and Edison David.

At the Pantabangan Dam. L-R: A dam official, Ellen Serrano (President, CCA,USA), Dillian Reyes, Chris Miller, Eric Pangilinan, Ana Aguila, Edison David, Analyn La Guardia.

Nieves Catahan Villamin

Edison David (right) presented a workshop at the La Parilla Hotel in Cabanatuan City. Workshop was coordinated with Atty. Ruperto Sampoleo, Academic consultant of Colleges and Universitites in Cabanatuan City, and former Vice-President of Araullo University.

Third PCE group with faculty and staff and students from TIP.

3rd Batch PCE Philippine Cultural/Educational Trip

Third PCE group: Chandani Patel and May Dayao shoveling sand for the Sumacab Health Center groundbreaking.

Third PCE group: Analyn La Guardia and Chandani Patel with the Sumacab folks.

Nieves Catahan Villamin

Third PCE group: My turn to "entertain" TIP students.

Cal Poly State University Associate Director of International Studies'

Bittermelons and Mimosas

Dr. Barbara Andre and TIP Dean Dee Quirino, 111.

The building that the students helped break ground in 2003 is now a day care center.

⁓ Nieves Catahan Villamin ⁓

Cal Poly SLO's Dr. Taufik during his first TIP visit in Dec 2007.

Standing: Dr. Taufik and me. In the background are TIP student attendees of the three-day workshop.

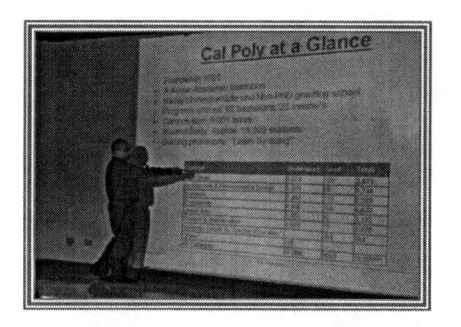

Dr. Taufik introducing Cal Poly to TIP students.

L-R: Angelo Lahoz, me, Dr. Taufik, TIP President Dr. Elizabeth Lahoz, and Atty. Ruperto Sampoleo.

Standing (L-R) Jemuel Castillo, Ariel Magat, Cecil Venal, Cynthia Llanes, Ferdinand Milan, Oliver Daitol, Severino Pader, Angelo Lahoz. Seated (L-R): Me, Dr. Taufik, and TIP President Dr. Elizabeth Lahoz.

Bittermelons and Mimosas

Cal Poly SLO's Dr. Taufik during his second TIP visit in Dec 2009.

Standing (L-R): Angelita Soliven, Reynaldo Chinjen, Cynthia Llanes. Seated (L-R): Severino Pader, Ma. Consuelo Flora, Gloria Salandanan, Dr. Teresita U. Quirino, Jemuel Castillo, Dr. Taufik, and Elizabeth Pader.

Nieves Catahan Villamin

PCE extended its cultural outreach by inviting the Karilagan Dance Society, a cultural organization from Edmonton, Canada, in 2000 and 2002. Founded in 1971, the dance society has been promoting the Filipino culture and traditions through story telling, folk dances and songs not only in Canada but also in other parts of the world. The leadership of Elmina Cochingco (Karilagan Dance Society President, Artistic Director & Choreographer), and the strict but loving guidance of the parents, had been instrumental in nurturing the children who grew up and became respectable members of the community. The association not only taught them their cultural heritage through story telling, songs, and dances, it also taught them how to pursue their lives with good moral values. As they got older and moved on, they made their families proud of what they had become: matured Filipino-Canadians who fully embrace their cultural heritage and who are also very proud of their Filipino ancestry.

Elmina Cochingco (Karilagan Dance Society President, Artistic Director & Choreographer).

Karilagan Dance Society's first U.S. visit in 2000.

꧁ Bittermelons and Mimosas ꧂

Karilagan Dance Society's second visit in 2002.

Current members from left: Julia Denisse Cochingco, Arzly Edrad, Aylah Angeles, Keoni Malbog-Tan (face hiding), Isabella Abuan and Sharon Calapre. The boys from left are: Rayden Hagglund, Rayjay Diego, Gearyn Born, Garrett Born, Bryan Panganiban and Radley Valdez.

Bibliography – Suggested Books and Reading Materials

1968. http://www.nyu.edu/library/bobst/collections/exhibits/arch/1968/Index.html

Constantino, Renato. *The Philippines: A Past Revisited, Vol. 1*

Death-of-the-President
jfklibrary.org/JFK/JFK-in-History/November-22-1963

Francisco, Josephine J. *Movement of Filipinos: Trends, Issues and Implications.* Philippines

Hukbalahap Rebellion
History.com – History Channel

Lanzona, Vina A. *Amazons of the Huk Rebellion: Gender, Sex, and Revolution in the Philippines.* Madison, WI. University of Wisconsin Press, 2009.

Pimentel, Benjamin. Why young Filipinos should know the tragic, inspiring story of Gene Viernes and Silme Domingo. *Philippine Daily Inquirer*, Tuesday, November 29, 2011

Pimentel, Benjamin. *U.G. An Underground Tale.* Anvil Pub, 2006.

Ocampo, Ambeth. Flooding and the Sto. Niño de Tondo
Philippine Daily Inquirer
First Posted 00:41:00 10/07/2009

Prytulak, Walter. On Pain Suffering: Reminiscences, Musings and Reflections. AuthorHouse, 2001, page 28

Pulido, Councilman Mark. The historic Delano Grape Strike. Cerritos, California.

Zaide, M. Sonia. *The Philippines: A Unique Nation.* Quezon City, Philippines. All Nations Publishing Co, Inc. 1994

About the Author

Nieves Catahan Villamin obtained her Bachelor's Degree in Accounting at the Technological Institute of the Philippines (TIP), Manila, Philippines. Fresh from graduation in 1967, she was hired as the school's accountant and taught Business Courses during the evenings. Married with one child, in 1970 she moved back to Cabanatuan City, her birthplace, and taught Business Courses at the Araullo University. A promotion to head the management of the university's Business Department ensued. But President Marcos' martial law declaration in September 1972 tempered the joys brought by the unexpected promotion and the anticipated arrival of a second baby. Eight months pregnant, she and her husband immigrated to the United States on October 13, 1972. They left a three-year-old daughter, but brought with them $75.00 as *baon*, and a letter of introduction to a newlywed couple who took them in until they could afford a place of their own.

Nieves brought her passion for the Pilipino culture and history to Cal Poly, San Luis Obispo, California, where she worked as an administrative analyst for almost fourteen years. During her tenure as advisor of the PILIPINO CUTURAL EXCHANGE (PCE), a Cal Poly Filipino-American student club (1998 to 2004), she brokered a student exchange program between Mapua Institute of Technology, Manila, Philippines, and Cal Poly, San Luis Obispo, California, and a faculty exchange between TIP and Cal Poly. In the years 1999, 2001, and 2003, she took several groups of students to the Philippines to have them experience the Philippine culture and history first hand. She retired in the summer of 2008 to concentrate on writing her memoir and to pursue other interests. Nieves is also the letter N of the Eden in Eden Canyon Vineyards, said to be the first Filipino-American owned and operated estate winery in the United States producing award-winning vintages.

For the past 25 years Nieves has been involved with many charitable organizations that give financial aid to disadvantaged kids mostly in the Philippines. In recognition of her philanthropic deeds and cultural endeavors she was awarded the TIP Outstanding Alumni Award in 2002, the Outstanding Woman of the Year award from Cal Poly in 2003, and the Outstanding Daughter of Cabanatuan City, Philippines, in 2004.

CPSIA information can be obtained at www.ICGtesting.com
Printed in the USA
LVOW100347140213
319996LV00003B/5/P

9 781592 996025